THE DIVINE HELMSMAN

Studies on God's Control of Human Events,
Presented to Lou H. Silberman

THE DIVINE HELMSMAN

Studies on God's Control of Human Events,
Presented to Lou H. Silberman

Edited by
JAMES L. CRENSHAW and SAMUEL SANDMEL†

KTAV PUBLISHING HOUSE, INC.
NEW YORK

© 1980 Vanderbilt University Divinity School

Library of Congress Cataloging in Publication Data

Main entry under title:

The divine helmsman.

  Bibliography: p.
  Includes index.
  CONTENTS: Works by Lou H. Silberman.—Crenshaw, J. L.
The birth of skepticism in ancient Israel.—Harrelson, W.
Ezra among the wicked in 2 Esdras 3-10.—Keck, L. E.
[etc.]
    1. Providence and government of God (Judaism)—
Addresses, essays, lectures. 2. Bible—Criticism,
interpretation, etc.—Addresses, essays, lectures.
3. Silberman, Lou H.—Addresses, essays, lectures.
1. Silberman, Lou H. II. Crenshaw, James L.
III. Sandmel, Samuel.
BM645.P7D58   296.3'11   79-29644
ISBN 0-87068-700-X

Manufactured in the United States of America

DEDICATORY PREFACE

LOU Hackett Silberman was born on June 23, 1914 to Lou Harry and Myrtle Mueller Silberman. His higher education took him from the University of California, Berkeley (B.A., 1934; graduate study in philosophy) to Hebrew Union College, Cincinnati, from which institution he was awarded three degrees (Bachelors, Masters, and Doctorate in Hebrew Letters, 1939, 1941, 1943) and was ordained to the rabbinate (1941). In addition, he journeyed to the University of Basel, where he heard lectures by Karl Barth, to name only the most eminent of the professors there. Lou Silberman's teachers included, among others, Jacob Lauterbach, Julian Morgenstern, Jacob Mann, Samuel S. Cohon, and Edward Strong. On June 14, 1942 Lou married Helen Epstein; to them were born two daughters, Syrl and Deborah.

In 1943 Lou became assistant rabbi at Temple Emmanuel, Dallas, Texas, later moving to Temple Israel, Omaha, Nebraska as rabbi in 1945 and serving there until 1952. At that time he came to Vanderbilt University as Associate Professor of Religion, replacing Samuel Sandmel, who had moved to Hebrew Union College, Cincinnati. Promoted to Professor in 1955, Lou Silberman served as Acting Chairman of the Graduate Department of Religion from 1960-61 and chaired the Department of Religious Studies from 1970-76. For distinguished service in the councils and government of the university, he was chosen for the Thomas Jefferson Award in 1979. In those twenty seven years at Vanderbilt he has been visiting professor at several distinguished institutions: the University of Vienna, Judaistik Institut (1965-66), Carleton College (winter, 1972); John Carroll University (winter, 1973); Emory University (spring, 1973); the University of Chicago Divinity School (winter-spring, 1978). In addition he was visiting scholar at the Oxford Centre for Postgraduate Hebrew Studies (summer, 1978), and has given a number of noted lectures (for example, he was the Albert Schweitzer Centenary Lecturer at Candler School of Theology in 1975).

The range of Professor Silberman's intellectual interests is far-reaching; in that respect he resembles the vanishing "renaissance scholar." A glance at the accompanying list of publications will reveal the scope of his mind: folklore, history of American Jewry, Qumran, biblical texts and midrashic exegesis, theology, and much more. Regardless of the subject matter, he brings a disciplined, informed critical capacity to bear on the topic which has seized his imagination. His influence has been felt in many circles, perhaps most prominently in Qumran studies and in Jewish theology. Whoever studies the Habakkuk Pesher, Manual of Discipline, Copper Scroll, Hodayot, and 4 Q Florilegium stands in Lou Silberman's debt. Similarly, no one who endeavors to understand contemporary Jewish theology can escape his overpowering presence, both as constructive critic and as imaginative theologian. His surveys of current theological literature in *Judaism* kept theology before readers who might otherwise have forgotten that the Jewish tradition does, after all, have convictions about God that speak to contemporary religious seekers with unforgettable power.

In a sense Professor Silberman's greatest impact has come at yet another place. For more than a quarter of a century students have sat in awe of this teacher who represented for many of them their first real contact with Judaism. "Lou the Jew" became for them an expression of deepest respect, and a significant body of legends sprang up around this eloquent advocate of a way of life that had nurtured the one to whom they owed primary allegiance. His classes were an experience in rigorous thinking and articulate expression. The memory of those rare occasions when he preached in Benton Chapel lingers in the minds and hearts of countless students who heard through him the voice of God. That message was frequently tinged with apocalypticism, but a ray of hope invariably forced itself into view. His colleagues will remember, among other things, the lively conversations at lunch when he brought to bear upon every topic limitless illustrative material from world literature, art, music, philosophy, and folklore. They will also recall with gratitude the many ways in which he enriched the intellectual atmosphere within which they worked, the unselfish manner in which he gave his energies to the university at large, and the courage with which he stood for justice in society during difficult times.

Lou Silberman was a rabbi before he became a professor, and that vocation continues to this day. His contribution to the Central Conference of American Rabbis is immense, as his varied publications reveal. Still, he found time to enrich the religious life of the Temple in Nashville, where he regularly worshipped. That labor of love did not go unnoticed; by underwriting the expenses of this volume, many of his friends have found a tangible means of expressing their appreciation to him and Helen. By allowing the following names to appear in this dedicatory preface, the editors wish to express their appreciation to those whose generosity made this volume possible.

Mrs. Frank Block
Mr. & Mrs. Sidney E. Cohn
Mr. & Mrs. Robert D. Eisenstein
Mrs. Herbert Eskind
Dr. & Mrs. Irwin Eskind
Mr. & Mrs. Richard Eskind
Rabbi & Mrs. Randall Falk
Mr. & Mrs. Gilbert Fox, Jr.
Mr. & Mrs. Abe Freeman
Dr. & Mrs. Fred Goldner
Mr. & Mrs. Carl Goldstein
Mr. & Mrs. Ira Katz
Mr. & Mrs. Joe Kraft
Mr. & Mrs. Stewart Kresge
Mr. & Mrs. Jack W. Kuhn
Mr. & Mrs. Howard Levy
Mr. & Mrs. Noah Liff
Mrs. Henry Loewenstein
Mr. & Mrs. Mitchell Magid
Mr. & Mrs. Dan May
Mr. & Mrs. Jack May
Mr. & Mrs. Bernard R. Schweid
Mrs. David Steine
Mr. & Mrs. Bernie Steiner
Mrs. Albert Weinstein
Mr. & Mrs. Albert Werthan
Mr. & Mrs. Bernard Werthan, Sr.
Mr. & Mrs. Harry Zimmerman
Mr. & Mrs. Raymond Zimmerman

Those who know Lou Silberman best have gained fresh insight into some reasons that may have prompted the author of Proverbs 31 to describe the virtuous wife in such glowing terms. In every way Helen has been a worthy equal, widening Lou's horizons and summoning him to ever-new dimensions of living. She has shared his interests in art, sculpture, architecture, literature, and religion. Together they have clung to a quality of life that most others can only aspire to. They will therefore understand when we, the editors of this volume, borrow and adapt a Yiddish proverb. Helen and Lou Silberman have taste and flavor, that is, style. They acquired that *style* from the Divine Helmsman.

James L. Crenshaw and Samuel Sandmel†

†After this preface was written, the deaths of Helen Silberman and Samuel Sandmel occurred.

CONTENTS

A BIBLIOGRAPHY OF LOU H. SILBERMAN'S WRITINGS

BOOKS

Silberman, Lou H., ed., *Rabbinic Essays* by Jacob Z. Lauterbach (Cincinnati: HUC), 1951.

ARTICLES

1942

"Lag Beomer," *Universal Jewish Encyclopedia* 6, 508-509.
"Original Sin," *Universal Jewish Encyclopedia* 8, 323-324.

1943

"The Minority Problem: From the Inside Looking Out: A Frank Discussion of Negro Anti-Semitism and Jewish Jim Crowism," *HUC Monthly*, April, 6, 21-22.

1944

"A Case of Damages," *The Jewish Layman* 18, no. 6 (March), 3-5.

1949

"The Sefirah Season: A Study in Folklore," *HUCA* 22, 221-237.

1953

"The Recent History of Reform Philosophy," *Yearbook of Central Conference of American Rabbis*, 63, 282-289.

1955

"The Two 'Messiahs' of the Manual of Discipline," *VT* 5, 77-82.

1956

"Language and Structure in the Hodayot (1QH3)," *JBL* 75, 96-106.
"Survey of Current Theological Literature," *Judaism* 5, 357-364.
Review of *A Jewish Understanding of the New Testament* by Samuel Sandmel, *The Observer* (Nashville), May 4.

1957

"Survey of Current Theological Literature," *Judaism* 6, 70-76.

"Survey of Current Theological Literature," *ibid.*, 171-180.
"Survey of Current Theological Literature," *ibid.*, 267-271.
"Survey of Current Theological Literature," *ibid.*, 353-358.
"Jewish Communities in the Changing South," *Assembly Papers,* Council of Jewish Federations and Welfare Funds, New York, 1-8.

1958

Prophets and Philosophers: The Scandal of Prophecy, The Goldenson Lecture for 1958 (Cincinnati: HUC).
Review of *History of the Old Testament; Theology of the Old Testament: Christ in Prophecy,* by Paul Heimsch, translated by W. G. Heidt, 1956, *Jewish Social Studies,* 20, 124-125.

1959

"The Search for Relevance," *A People and Its Faith: Essays on Jews and Reform Judaism in a Changing Canada* (Toronto: University of Toronto).
Review of *The Dead Sea Scriptures in English Translation with Introduction and Notes* by Theodor Gaster, *JNES* 18, 87-89.
"The Philosophy of Abraham Heschel," *Jewish Heritage* 2 (no. 1), 23-26, 54.

1960

"A Note on the Copper Scroll," *VT* 10, 77-79.

1961

"Milton Steinberg's Anatomy of Faith," *Judaism* 10, 86-90.
"Unriddling the Riddle: A Study in the Structure and Language of the Habakkuk Pesher (IQpHab.)," *RdQ 11,* 323-364.
"Jewish Leadership in Southern Communities," *Assembly Papers,* Council of Jewish Federations and Welfare Funds, New York.

1962

"Survey of Current Theological Literature: Karl Barth: Liberal Prostestantism," *Judaism* 11, 169-174.
"The Paradoxes of Freedom and Authority," *The Hibbert Journal* 60, 297-304.
"Survey of Current Theological Literature: The New Quest for the Historical Jesus," *Judaism* 11, 160-167.
"Survey of Current Theological Literature: Jews, Christians, Germans," *ibid.*, 357-363.
"Esrabücher, nichtkanonische," *Biblisch-Historisches Handwörterbuch,* 1 (Göttingen), 442-443, and "Fastenrolle," *ibid.*, 466.

1963

"Problems and Trends in Biblical Scholarship," *Judaism* 12, 92-97.

"Conversations in Theology—The Return of History," *ibid.*, 203-205.

"Rome's New Frontier," *ibid.*, 344-350.

"Guttmann's *Die Philosophie des Judentums,*" *ibid.*, 469-474.

"Farewell to O AMHN," *JBL* 82, 213-215.

"A Presentation Poem and a Bibliographical Note," *Studies in Bibliography and Booklore,* 6, 101-102.

"Atonement, Day of, "Essenes," "Hasmonean Dynasty," "Passover," "Pharisees," "Sadducees," "Septuagint," "Synagogue," "Torah," *Encyclopedia International.*

"The Jewish Image of God: The Meaning of Faith for the Modern Jew," *Tradition as Idea and Contemporary Experience* (Washington, D. C.: B'nai Brith Hillel Foundations), 37-47.

1964

"La Actualidad Literaria en Materia Teologica: Die Philosophie des Judentums de Guttmann," *Davar: Revista Literaria,* 102 Buenos Aires, 32-41 (Translation of "Guttmann's *Die Philosophie des Judentums,*" 1963).

"Do We Live in A Post-Christian Age? Questioning the Question," *RL* 33, 180-184.

"Honig" *Biblisch-Historisches Handwörterbuch* 2, 747.

"Jubilees, Book of" *Encyclopedia Britannica* (14th ed., revised), 13, 100-101.

American Impact: Judaism in the United States in the Early Nineteenth Century, The B. G. Rudolph Lectures in Judaic Studies, Syracuse University.

Review of W. D. Davies, *The Setting of the Sermon on the Mount, Judaism* 13, 506-510.

1965

Review of *Tradition and Transmission in Early Christianity* by Birger Gerhardsson, *JBL* 84, 459-60.

1966

"Religion and Freedom of the Artist," *RL* 35, 132-139.

"Religious Education and Style," *Religious Education* 61, 102-103.

"Farewell to Confirmation," *Central Conference of American Rabbis Journal* 13, 31-34.

"The Union Prayer Book: A Study in Liturgical Development," *Retrospect and Prospect: Essays in Commemoration of the Seventy-fifth*

Anniversary of the Founding of the Central Conference of American Rabbis, 1889-1964, Bertram W. Korn, editor (New York: Central Conference of American Rabbis) 3, 48-60.

"The Task of Jewish Theology," *Rediscovering Judaism: Reflections on a New Theology,* Arnold J. Wolf, editor (Chicago: Quadrangle Books, Inc.), 15-28.

"Ha-herem b'natzrut" (Excommunication in Christianity), *Encyclopedia Hebraica,* 17, 56-57.

1967

Review of *Israel's Sacred Songs* by Harvey H. Guthrie, Jr., *RL* 36, 299-301.

1968

"Prolegomenon," *The Synoptic Gospels* (reprint) by Claude G. Montefiore (New York: KTAV), 1-18.

"Reprobation, Prohibition, Invalidity: An Examination of the Halakhic Development Concerning Intermarriage," *Central Conference of American Rabbis Journal* 15, 2-15, 43.

Review of *Kingship of God* by Martin Buber (third edition) (translated by Richard Schiemann), *RL* 37, 305-306.

1969

"Concerning Jewish Theology in North America: Some Notes on a Decade," *American Jewish Year Book,* Milton Himmelfarb, editor (Philadelphia: Jewish Publication Society), 37-58.

"Death in the Hebrew Bible and Apocalyptic Literature," *Perspectives on Death,* Liston O. Mills, editor (Nashville and New York: Abingdon), 13-32.

"Prophets, and Philosophers: The Scandal of Prophecy," *Interpreting the Prophetic Tradition* (Cincinnati and New York: HUC and KTAV) Reprint of the Goldenson Lecture of 1959, 81-100.

"The American Jewish Community and its Values," *Relationships Between Jewish Tradition and Contemporary Social Issues* (New York: Wurtzweiler School of Social Work, Yeshiva University), 31-38.

"The Interreligious Situation: A Not Entirely Bleak View," *Twenty-five Years—An Appraising Look Back—An Explanatory Look Ahead* (New York: National Jewish Community Relations Advisory Council).

"Is There a Tomorrow?" *Proceedings, 1968 Biennial Convention National Women's League of the United Synagogue of America,* New York, 34-40.

1970

"The Universities and Jewish Studies," *The Teaching of Judaica in American Universities*, Leon A. Jick, editor (New York: KTAV), 7-16.

"Between God and Man: The Meaning of Revelation for the Contemporary Jew," *Tradition and Contemporary Experience*, Alfred Jospe, editor (New York: Schocken Books), 91-111.

"Reprobation, Prohibition, Invalidity: An Examination of the Halakhic Development Concerning Intermarriage," (reprint from CCAR Journal of April 1968), *Judaism and Ethics*, Daniel J. Silver, editor (New York: KTAV), 177-198.

"Prophets and Philosophers: The Scandal of Prophecy," (reprint of the Goldenson Lecture of 1958), in *Arguments and Doctrines*, Arthur A. Cohen, editor (New York: Harper and Row), 158-173.

"Teologia Yehudit baasor haaharon," *Tfuztot Yisrael* 8, no. 3 (May-June), 16-35. Hebrew translation of "Concerning Jewish Theology in North America" (1969).

1971

"The Making of the Old Testament Canon," *The Interpreter's One-Volume Commentary on the Bible*, Charles M. Laymon, editor (New York: Abingdon), 1209-1215.

"A Midrash on Midrash" (Mimeographed paper, privately circulated at the meeting of Studiorum Novi Testamentum Societas, Amsterdam, 1971).

"Abraham Joshua Heschel: Rebbe for Our Day," *Jewish Heritage*, 13, 39-43.

1972

"Chosen People," *Encyclopedia Judaica* 5 (Jerusalem: Macmillan) columns 498-502.

"Compassion," *ibid.*, columns 855-856.

"Joy," *ibid.*, 10, columns 319-321.

"Justice and Mercy of God," *ibid.*, 7, columns 669-670.

"Schoeps, Hans Joachim," *ibid.*, 14, column 991.

1973

"Social Ethics and/or Social Action: A Problematic Situation," *Centennial Papers: Social Ethics, the Moral Role of the Jew in Contemporary Society* (New York: Union of American Hebrew Congregations), 1-18.

"Manus Velatae: The significance of IQS vii, 13-14, 15," *The Gaster Festschrift, JANES* 5, 383-388.

"The Theologian's Task," *Reform Judaism: A Historical Perspective*, edited by Joseph Blau (New York: KTAV) 152-165. Reprint of an essay that appeared originally in the *Yearbook* of *The Central Conference of American Rabbis*, 73, 1963, 173-182.

"Judaism" *Encyclopedia Britannica* (15th ed.) Macropaedia 10, 284-302.

Review of *The Song at the Sea, being a Commentary on a Commentary in Two Parts* by Judah Goldin, *JNES* 32, 499-500.

"The Sources of Obligation in Judaism," and "The Historical Situation and the Specificity of Jewish Ethics," 2 taped lectures, *Religious Ethics: Four Views* (Canfield, Ohio: Alba House Communications).

1974

"The Human Deed in a Time of Despair: The Ethics of Apocalyptic," *Essays in Old Testament Ethics (J. Philip Hyatt in Memoriam)* ed. J. L. Crenshaw & J. T. Willis. New York: KTAV, 191-202.

"Judaism and the Bible," *Instruction and Supplementary Materials*, Ewing P. Shahan, editor (Nashville: Department of Religious Studies) section 6, 1-14.

"Jewish Reactions to Liberalism and Marxism," *ibid.*, section 8, 1-8.

"The Queen of Sheba in Judaic Tradition," chapter in *Solomon and Sheba*, J. B. Pritchard, editor (London: Phaidon), 65-84.

1975

———. "Ha-pe'ullah ha-anoshit ba-'ittot ye'ush: ha-etikah shel apoklip-tiyah," Hebrew translation of "The Human Deed in a Time of Despair," Mimeographed. School of Education, University of Haifa, Israel.

1976

Review of *A History of Judaism* by Daniel J. Silver and Bernard Martin (Basic Books, 1974), *CCAR Journal*, 75-77.

"Theology and Philosophy: Some Tentative Remarks," *Hebrew Union College-Jewish Institute of Religion at One Hundred Years*, ed. by Samuel E. Karff (Cincinnati: HUC), 383-430.

"Response to Louis Marin, 'A Parable of Pascal,' " *Semiology and Parables* (Pittsburgh Theological Monograph Series, Number 9), edited by Daniel Patte (Pittsburgh: Pickwick), 236-241.

"Apocalyptic Revisited: Reflection on the Thought of Albert Schweitzer," *JAAR* 44, 489-501.

"Views Concerning Halakhah from Various 'Reform' Perspectives," *Encyclopaedia Judaica Yearbook, 1975-76.*

"The Art of Personal Prayer," *Sh'ma: A Journal of Jewish Responsibility, 6/105 (January 9), 36-38.*

1977

"Between Chaos and Creation: A Survival Myth," *Journal of the Central Conference of American Rabbis*, 24, no. 98, 107-119.

Review of *Between God and Man: An Interpretation of Judaism from the Writings of Abraham J. Heschel*, by Fritz A. Rothschild (The Free Press, 1976), *Judaism* 26, 501-502.

1978

"Anent the Use of Rabbinic Material," *NTS* 24, 415-417.

" 'Habent Sua Fata Libelli': The Role of Wandering Themes in Some Hellenistic Jewish and Rabbinic Literature," *The Relationships Among the Gospels: An Interdisciplinary Dialogue*, ed. Wm. O. Walker, Jr., (San Antonio: Trinity University), 195-218.

"A Note on Ruaḥ Ha-Kodesh in Rabbinic Thought," 4 pp. mimeographed. Privately circulated for the Meeting of the American Theological Society, New York City, March 31-April 1.

Review of *The Emergence of Contemporary Judaism. Volume Two: Survey of Judaism from the 7th to the 17th Centuries*, by Philip Sigal. *JAAR*, 46, 390-91.

SERMONS, MISCELLANEA

1937

"Dialogue" (a poem), *HUC Monthly*, 24, 18.

1942

"The Teaching of the Sage is a Fountain of Life: Jacob Zallel Lauterbach, January 6, 1873-March 21, 1942," in *HUC Monthly*, 29, 4 (April), 7, 18.

1949-50

"Fulfillment" in *A Set of Holiday Sermons*, Commission on Information About Judaism, Union of American Hebrew Congregations, Central Conference of American Rabbis.

1958

"The Birthright and the Bomb," *Assembly Papers*, Council of Jewish Federations and Welfare Funds, New York, 1-8.

1963

"Stranger or Friend," *The Revolution of Our Time*, Council of Jewish Federations and Welfare Funds, New York.

"John Fitzgerald Kennedy—In Memoriam," *The Observer* (Nashville), November 29.

1964

"Proclaim Liberty," *The Observer* (Nashville), July 10.

1967

"The Unconstrained God," *Rockefeller Chapel Sermons of Recent Years,* Donovan E. Smucker, editor (Chicago: University of Chicago), 86-91.

THE BIRTH OF SKEPTICISM IN ANCIENT ISRAEL

JAMES L. CRENSHAW
VANDERBILT DIVINITY SCHOOL, NASHVILLE, TN 37240

" "THE deepest, the only theme of human history, compared to which all others are of subordinate importance, is the conflict of skepticism with faith."[1] The author of this astonishing observation, the poet Wolfgang von Goethe, described that antipathy between doubt and a vision of a transformed society with extraordinary power in Faust's final surge of humanitarianism which elicited the fateful request, "Stay, thou art so fair," signaling the loss of his wager with Mephistopheles and, by a curious non sequitur, the ultimate triumph of virtue. I wish in this essay to examine that conflict between faith and doubt in ancient Israel; my desire to do so arises from a conviction that Lou Silberman's unflinching honesty has often forced him to look religious doubt squarely in the face, while his sustained vision has made him an eloquent witness to transcendence.

The Skeptic's Vision

To begin with, we must distinguish between skepticism, pessimism, and cynicism. In my view, skepticism includes both a denial and an affirmation. The negative side of a skeptic's mental outlook consists of the doubting thought, whereas the positive affirmation of a hidden reality indicates that it is altogether inappropriate to accuse skeptics of unbelief.[2] This powerful vision of a better world inherent within skepticism prompted Blaise Pascal to write that "there never has been a real complete skeptic."[3] The matrix formed by the disparity between the actual state of affairs and a vision of what should be both sharpened critical powers and heightened religious fervor. Doubt, it follows, is grounded in profound faith.[4]

Once skeptics lose all hope of achieving the desired transformation, pessimism sets in, spawning sheer indifference to cherished convictions. Pessimists believe chaos has the upper hand and will retain control

1

forever; they lack both a surge for transcendence and faith in human potential. Since they own no vision which acts as a corrective to the status quo, pessimists can muster no base upon which to stand and from which to criticize God and the world. The inevitable result is a sense of being overwhelmed by an oppressive reality.[5]

Cynics go a step further; by their disdain for creaturely comforts and sensual pleasure they show contempt for everything life has to offer. No vision moves them to reject an imperfect present reality while awaiting a more perfect one which God and humans bring into being, and no feeling of helplessness makes them throw up their hands in despair. Instead, they demonstrate an amazing capacity for survival despite outward circumstances to which they are inwardly indifferent.[6]

Skeptics freely raise their voices within the Hebrew Scriptures, and pessimists occasionally add their cry; but we listen in vain for cynics' sighs. The reason is easily perceived: the presupposition of cynicism, contempt for the material world, is wholly alien to Hebrew thinking. In what follows, I shall concentrate on skepticism, though rare expressions of pessimism will be permitted to surface as well.

Now doubt may be what Jean Jacques Rousseau called "reverent doubt" and skepticism, "unwilling skepticism."[7] That is why Tennyson was on target when observing that there is more faith in honest doubt than in half the creeds. For some reason not yet fathomed by flesh and blood, certain eras lend themselves to wholesale skepticism, eliciting the painful admisson that "We of this generation are not destined to eat and be satisfied as our fathers were; we must be content to go hungry."[8] Such deprivation resulting from a complete breakdown in cultural values offers a unique opportunity for fresh breakthroughs[9] which rejuvenate human society. Once dogma freezes, traditions become lifeless fetters, and can only be thrown off by a resurging vital faith that dares to challenge the most sacred belief in the name of a higher truth.[10]

It has been said that skepticism without religion is impossible, and religion without skepticism is intolerable.[11] To be sure, the skeptic's faith does not necessarily name God as its object. For example, the French Enlightenment was a great age of skepticism in which faith sought new outlets—first nature and after that, men and women. Unwilling to sanction the tyranny of the church any longer, these skeptics found a new and wondrous object of trust in nature, particularly when epochmaking geological discoveries cast serious doubt on established views about divine providence and the date of creation. Furthermore, the complexity of human beings approached the mystery formerly relegated to God as the individual emerged into the limelight and fresh knowledge of previously unknown cultures stirred the imagination. Long before corrupt ecclesiastical officials aroused strong resolve to crush the infamous thing, Israelites, too, chafed under an oppressive yoke. The name of Job suffices to remind readers that religion can easily become an instrument of cruelty unless it is tempered with a skeptic's honesty.

By assisting religion in its endless struggle to prevent belief from becoming hollow testimony to a reality belonging only to the past, skepticism functions as religion's handmaid. Many of Israel's noblest insights resulted from the interplay between faith and doubt. Confronted with the void, her skeptics fought to sustain their vision of an eternal order where justice prevails. Here and there we hear a triumphant shout when skeptics affirm their faith while walking in utter darkness. Perhaps the most moving such expression of confidence occurs in the unparalleled seventy-third psalm, where the poet ultimately feels the touch of a father's hand and knows that God is present to one who has honestly faced doubt.[12]

Skepticism's indispensability may be seen in the fact that the great ideologies correspond to three syntactic moods.[13] Theology affirms the declarative, humanism informs the imperative, and skepticism supplies the interrogative. The prominence of narrative in the Hebrew Bible derives from the basic truth that theology is essentially affirmation. Once that declarative statement imposes strong demands upon men and women, humanism intrudes to maintain the dignity of persons upon whom the divine imperative has fallen. Skepticism dares to penetrate beneath the statement and consequent demand; it inquires about the ultimate basis for the declaration and presses toward determining motivation for obedience. Self-knowledge emerges largely through interrogation; for example, the question, "Why am I suffering?," early became a means of dealing with guilt, and eventually revolutionized Israel's understanding of reality itself.[14]

Ironically, this Joban onslaught fought against a world view which resulted directly from the first decisive breakthrough in our intellectual history.[15] I refer to the principle of universality—the ideal of rationality according to which no individual possessed the truth, the universe was orderly, and human beings were spectators of a powerful drama which God directed toward a distant goal. The assumption of order precipitated crises in Mesopotamia, Egypt, and Israel, as is well documented in the relevant literature.[16] One need not envision mass distribution of these texts in Israel and elsewhere[17] to recognize the revolutionary impact of such thinking, for the doubting thought surfaced throughout recorded memory.

Dominant Hypotheses

From this observation it follows that I cannot subscribe to the theory that the decisive breakthrough in Israel coincided with the Solomonic empire and constituted a complete break with sacral thinking.[18] Skepticism within the canon can hardly be restricted to an understanding of the manner in which God governs history. Failure to recognize this important fact has seriously distorted analyses of the extent and complexity of Israelite skepticism.[19] This narrow understanding of skepticism has produced three significant half-truths which have dominated most discussions of intellectual development in ancient Israel: (1) skepticism signifies a worn-out culture;[20] (2) such rejection of established views is an elitist phenomenon;[21] and (3) skepticism arose as a consequence of historical crises.[22]

1. Skepticism signifies a burnt-out culture

To be sure, centuries of affirmation precede significant doubt. Society's givens accumulate slowly; in the beginning sanctions are consciously formulated, and later their acceptance becomes almost as natural as breathing. In this way a world view takes shape,[23] and legitimations reinforce it from every side. Cherished beliefs are promulgated consciously and unconsciously, and daily experience seems to support such values. Only after sanctions for life have evolved and demonstrated their dependability can doubt about their legitimacy arise. Ancient rabbis perceived this fact and applied it to their paragon of wisdom. According to them, Solomon wrote Song of Songs in his youthful days when desire surges, Proverbs during mature years, and Qoheleth when senility had settled in for good. Like individuals, civilizations grow old and cast off their youthful garments in order to don funeral shrouds.

The denigration of post-exilic Israel as a burnt-out culture may have coincided with prevailing interpretations of late Judaism, to use a term that is itself pejorative, but such a reading of Israelite history belongs inherently to certain streams of canonical tradition. The Deuteronomistic understanding of events as one great failure on Israel's part, with rare exceptions, and the apocalyptic notion of successive ages whose very names imply gradual decay must surely be responsible for the widespread belief that Israelite skepticism arose in the midnight hour of canonical history.

2. Skepticism is an elitist phenomenon

The claim that skepticism is a malaise suffered only by the well-to-do builds upon an assumption about the leisure class as guardians of Israel's intellectual tradition.[24] Acceptance of this plausible hypothesis about the authors of the sapiential corpus may permit one to make significant observations concerning Job and Qoheleth, but the skeptical voice reaches far beyond these dissenting cries. Parallels with neighboring cultures, particularly the Egyptian, are informative, but Israel's sages functioned in an entirely different context from that represented by Egyptian counsellors to the Pharaoh.[25]

3. Skepticism resulted from historical crises

The third misconception, that political catastrophe generates skepticism, possesses an element of truth, as a cursory reading in prophetic literature confirms. Still, various answers to the problem occasioned by defeat on the battlefield readily present themselves and secure faith intact: Israel has sinned; God is testing his people; foreign powers function as God's agents; external events do not accurately reflect true reality.[26] The amazing resiliency of faith enables men and women to survive events that had the capacity to shatter fondest dreams. Even Josiah's dark fate precipitated no discernible religious revolt against providence.[27]

Opposing Claims

Having acknowledged the partial truth in each of the three statements, I wish to formulate opposing assertions: (1) skepticism belongs to Israel's thought from early times; (2) it extends far beyond the intelligentsia; and (3) it springs from two fundamentally different sources, which we may call theological and epistemological. In short, skepticism is intrinsic to biblical thinking rather than an intruder that took Israel by surprise; this rich heritage of doubt often took up willing residence among the ordinary people in Judah and Ephraim; and skeptics turned their attention toward human ability to know anything as well as toward theories about God's works.

1. Skepticism arose early

Occasional texts confirm the relative antiquity of skeptical outbursts.[28] For instance, Isaiah pronounces a woe upon those who say:

Let him make haste, let him speed his work that we may see it; let the purpose of the Holy One of Israel draw near, and let it come, that we may know it (Isa 5:19).

Similarly, Zephaniah accuses his contemporaries of thinking that God will not do good, nor will he do ill'' (Zeph 1:12). Furthermore, an old account of Gideon's encounter with a heavenly visitor bristles with skepticism and describes Gideon as nearly laughing in the angel's face (Jdg 6:11-13). When tested in the crucible of experience, the people's miserable circumstances hardly accorded with religious convictions that God actively worked to sustain Israel.

Pray, sir, if the Lord is with us, why then has all this befallen us? And where are all his wonderful deeds which our fathers recounted to us . . . ? (Jdg 6:13)

In this case the interrogative mood threatened to swallow up the declarative, and youthful rebellion placed paternal teaching under a dark cloud. A full-fledged pragmatist, Gideon insisted on incontrovertible proof for theological statements. Naturally, such an one refused to surrender before the divine imperative until convincing demonstration of faith's assertions lay within his grasp. As Jer 44:15-19 shows, such empirical tests cut two ways: here the Jewish refugees residing in Egypt inform Jeremiah that they had prospered so long as they worshiped the queen of heaven, but fell victim to destructive forces when they abandoned their goddess. In their eyes, as in Gideon's too, devotion to Yahweh did not pay sufficient dividends.

Even without this evidence that skeptics came upon the stage long before Job and Qoheleth were written, we could reasonably conjecture that certain features of Yahwism made such doubt extremely probable. To begin with, Israel's understanding of God as one who withholds his name at the very moment of self-revelation openly invites skepticism.[29] Mystery clothes the one who freely makes himself known, whether to Moses as "I am who I am" (Exod 3:14) or to Manoah as "wonderful" (Jdg 13:18).[30] In the last resort, Israel's sovereign refuses to bow before human manipulation, and thus retains his freedom in all circumstances. As a result, this God gains a reputation as one who comes to assist oppressed peoples, although an occasional suspicion that he is demonic also lingers in the hearts of those who encounter stark mystery.[31] Inherent within such conviction is the belief that God dwells afar off (Jer 23:23), so that we can know only what he allows us to perceive. Like Adam long ago, we merely observe the surgeon's finished work. Even the celebrated "mighty acts of God" which generation after generation recited in sacred assembly and in the family circle were inferences drawn from footprints in the Judean hills, for no eyes ever penetrated the veil shielding God from frail creatures.

Naturally, such theology gives rise to emphasis upon creaturely finitude. Between humans and God stretches a vast chasm, and no bridge spans the abyss. The defiant post-deluvian generation was not the only one that dreamed of linking heaven and earth. A favored two, Enoch and Elijah, were thought to have walked hand in hand with God into the sunset or to have ridden a heavenly chariot upon the clouds, but for most mortals access to God was completely circumscribed. It consisted of the divine image which included, among other things, verbal communication; by this means imagistic links occurred—poetic inspiration, prophetic visions, and the sage's intuition. The walls of God's heavenly castle were so steep that even "thoughts slipped below," to quote Goethe once again, and the entire enterprise which aimed at uniting the two realms crashed to the ground like the ill-fated plans to build the tower of Babel. Those who live on borrowed breath can hardly boast about their strength, especially when events overwhelm human victims and crush them indiscriminately.

The earliest sages also knew that their knowledge came up against limits beyond which it could not go.[32] Careful plans could always clash with God's secret intentions, and in such cases man proposed but God disposed. When the deity's glory consists in hiding things, the stage is already set for anxiety in the face of apparent injustice. That worry intensifies the moment true wisdom is placed outside human reach, for men and women inevitably ask why God retains her for his private possession.

Given these two extraordinary facts, a God who hides and creatures who are dependent, skepticism's appearance in Israel was no great surprise. Some texts seem almost to encourage expostulation with the deity as if he longed to have probing questions directed his way. For example, the narrative concerning the Lord's destruction of Sodom and Gomorrah pictures the deity standing before Abraham in open invitation to discuss the moral implications of the decision to demolish entire cities. Obviously, God is not the only one who has qualms about wholesale slaughter, for the author of the prose tale allows Abraham to utter his own weighty objections. A single question gathers together the entire moral dilemma into which God has placed himself: "Shall not the Judge of the whole earth do justice?" The skeptic's criticism appeals to a vision of right conduct to which even God's deeds are subject.

2. Skepticism enjoyed popular support

This intrinsic nature of skepticism means that it refused to become the exclusive property of an intellectually elite group of people. Admittedly, breakdowns often fail to achieve decisive breakthroughs for lack of popular support. Such aristocratic revolutions always abort because they do not succeed in capturing the imagination of common people. The mere presence of potentially revolutionary thoughts cannot alter the human situation unless the idea seizes the minds of those who alone can implement lasting change.

Of course, revolutions can be attempted without popular support, but the outcome is predictably disappointing. Akenaton's remarkable break with the past achieved no permanence, despite the powerful sanctions accompanying the reform, and Egypt soon reverted to pre-Amarna thinking. Similarly, the French experiment in recent times collapsed for lack of enthusiasm among the masses.[33] For these people religious belief survived the devastating attack upon faith launched by the intelligentsia. Even widespread clerical corruption failed to convince ordinary church goers that the reality to which they prayed did not deserve their supreme devotion.

Perhaps the most astonishing failure in this regard occurred in ancient Babylonia, where the revolutionary idea of linearity surfaced but became a victim of a more powerful belief in divine caprice. Lacking faith in God's control of human events so as to bring them to a distant goal envisioned by the deity, Babylonian religion failed to achieve the idea of *telos* which shines with such dazzling splendor in the Hebrew Scriptures. No vision of the *eschaton* transformed Babylonian cultic dominance, and no linear purposive progression put an end to circular thinking. Divine caprice turned these people into what has been called the most pessimistic civilization in history.[34]

For several reasons, the hypothesis that Israel's skepticism was elitist misses the mark. Such a restriction of the doubting thought to the perimeters of wisdom ignores the widespread phenomenon of skepticism throughout Israelite society. I have elsewhere discussed numerous instances of skeptical defiance which confronted canonical prophets and prompted intemperate language and considerable soul-searching.[35] To be sure, not all of these antagonists challenged prophetic utterances on the basis of enduring visions of transcendence,[36] but it can hardly be denied that many of them protested against bogus promises and insisted upon complete honesty in assessing the theological situation.

In this respect compilers of canonical Psalms displayed considerably more appreciation for those who uttered the perennial interrogative: "How long, O Lord?" In these expressions of lament and praise occurs a mighty crescendo of expostulation with the deity concerning justice above all. It seems that the most devout worshiper cannot decide whether to acknowledge God's justice in the face of evidence to the contrary or to concede divine blindness, nay indifference, as irrefutable fact. Even when the psalmist cites such low opinions of God and attributes them to fools, the very articulation of skeptical views satisfies a need for honesty on the part of the worshiping community.

Within the wisdom corpus itself certain bits of evidence suggest that the skeptical mood threatened to overwhelm the entire sapiential enterprise. The sheer bulk of the skeptical literature, including Job and Qoheleth, must surely have suggested to many that the proper scholarly pursuit comprised the study of comparable texts. More importantly, Ben Sira feels constrained to enter into lively dialogue with a group of skeptics[37] who offered his own students a viable alternative to the confessional theology he had lately interpolated into wisdom's repertoire. In attempting to refute their arguments, he borrowed an old debate form and used it freely. One element of that literary device, the actual quotation of an opponent's argument, permitted skeptical views wide audience, particularly when Ben Sira's teachings became part of the canon. Even though the doubting thought is dismissed for one reason or another, it continues to sink deeply into the minds of all who read Sirach. Perhaps an awareness of this persuasive whisper moved the author of Wisdom of Solomon to register the opinion that doubt's mere presence renders one incapable of receiving divine revelation (1:2). Such warning can only mean that skepticism posed a real threat in the eyes of this sage, and that makes the hypothesis of minimal impact by skeptical literary works wholly unacceptable.

3. Skepticism flowed from two separate streams

My third assertion, that skepticism arose in two distinct contexts, requires considerable elaboration. On the one hand, skepticism addresses itself to a specific theological situation; in short, it signifies a crisis of faith in God. On the other hand, the skeptic also isolates a wholly different kind of bankruptcy—the loss of faith in human beings. It will not do to label one stream Yahwism and the other wisdom, although the inclination to do so arises from a valid intuition. Nevertheless, the two streams converge at decisive locations, and in the end both tributaries flow into the same reservoir.

The starting point for an analysis of these streams must surely be the conviction that the cosmos was essentially orderly, which we have earlier called the first decisive breakthrough in our spiritual history. Without a firm sense of predictability, Israel could never have developed certain legitimations that undergirded society. The declaration that the universe could be relied upon (Gen 9:8-17) bursts upon the scene precisely when the deluge seemed to render life utterly perilous; its formulation constitutes a mighty expression of confidence in God's goodness despite the memory of raging waters. In time that optimism yielded further affirmations, especially the claim that virtue bore rich fruit, just as vice produced its own unwanted harvest. To be sure, minor fissures occurred here and there, but skillful hands nearly always filled those cracks with reliable cement.[38]

Alongside this belief in a calculable universe stood an equally compelling conviction that Israel was a covenant people who enjoyed God's favor. No task was too great, no enemy too powerful, to frustrate this desire on God's part to bestow life upon Israel at any cost. Other nations fell like flies before this covenant God, and not even sin by the favored people could thwart God's purposes. Having established the covenant relationship in the first place, Israel's sovereign was not about to let anything frustrate his designs for her.

The principal arena in which God carried out his hopes for Israel was political, and the decisive medium, the Davidic monarchy. To a large degree, the prophetic witness coincided with the period of the monarchy, a fact that has not been sufficiently appreciated in critical research. Both corporate and individual existence achieved significance in the course of history, upon which the divine word worked with matchless success. Israel's enemies fled when the Lord lifted his mighty arm, and God's people marched joyously from bondage into liberty. Valiant soldiers wasted away when the death angel spread its wings and flew into the midst of God's enemies. So ran the embellished account of Israel's history,[39] a story so far from the truth that it sowed seeds of skepticism at almost every telling. The disparity between present reality and grandiose confessions of God's mighty deeds in the past demanded an adequate explanation lest wholesale abandoning of the Lord take place.

The response to this need succeeded in reducing divine sanctions of society to a book, that is, Deuteronomy. This single event paved the way for crystallized dogma and precipitated a sharp attack on a closed cosmos, an offensive that eventuated in outright skepticism. In Deuteronomy life stands over against death, and individuals are exhorted to choose which of the two they wish to embrace. Any intermediary position has vanished from sight, and the earlier dynamic juxtaposition of the one and the many has likewise disappeared altogether. In the process a decisive shift in ethos occurs. By ethos I mean the belief system, values, world view, aspirations and givens of ancient Israelite society. Slowly the family loses its hold over allegiances,[40] and individuality surfaces in a way that was hitherto unknown. Ownership of disposable property, urban concentration of the population, religious syncretism, political violence and the like both brought this change about and shaped new attitudes that soon became widespread through conscious and unconscious dissemination.

The Deuteronomistic theory of exact retribution encouraged the rapid growth of skepticism by emphasizing human corruption, a theme that permeates the Yahwistic primeval history. Paradoxically, the canonical prophets also stimulated a sense of moral defeatism by repeated denunciations of the people as a *massa damnationis*. Perhaps to a certain extent such indictments became self-fulfilling, and moral impotence resulted since all self-esteem had been stripped away by well intentioned prophets. Precisely where such thinking leads can be seen in 2 Esdras' lament that it would have been better not to have been born.

Blind bards, like the unknown author of Psalm 37, who had never seen the righteous forsaken or his descendants begging bread, tried desperately to withstand the tide of skepticism within the populace, and others wrote and rewrote actual history to remove the discrepancy between celebrated story and real fact. In the process the Deuteronomistic national focus vanished in favor of rigid emphasis upon retribution at the individual level.[41] Long before the Chronicler engaged in his effort to formulate an adequate account of earlier history, individual choice played a prominent role in determining destiny. Indeed, in the Yahwist's view, the original sin introduced an alien force which even God could not eradicate. Its effect upon the human will was so irresistible that no righteous person existed throughout the land. Subsequent thinkers like Jeremiah and Qoheleth agreed wholeheartedly with this low estimate of human beings. Lacking both the will and the power to achieve virtue, individuals have no choice but to rely upon God's mercy. Accordingly, they praise God for accomplishing what men and women cannot do. As human potential decreases, divine power increases; nothing exists outside God's sovereignty. Of course, the appropriate human attitude is submission before the Almighty.

The ultimate step is to deny knowledge to humans. Thus we come to the second aspect of my assertion that skepticism has two distinct sources. Theological claims about God that conflict with reality and about humans that degrade them are matched by an epistemological view which encourages skeptical thoughts. The knowledge which humans acquire concerns terrestrial affairs, for Wisdom dwells with God, and none born of woman can approach her house. Once reason surrenders its throne to an alien power, the best the human intellect can do is to teach men and women "to bear in an understanding silence what must be borne." In such a situation, Agur's opening lament functions as a suitable motto: "There is no God at all, and I am powerless."[42]

Since the discussion of theological sources for skepticism has addressed issues as they arose in Yahwism generally, this analysis of the epistemological crisis will concentrate on Israelite wisdom. The earliest collection in Proverbs requires an acknowledgment that the terms theological and epistemological are inadequate, for the sages' subsequent admission concerning a bankruptcy of knowledge rests ultimately upon convictions about God which surface in the very beginning. For example, human preparations for warfare may abort, since the battle belongs to the Lord. All efforts to master the universe labor under a single unknown factor—God's freedom. Thus an element of surprise hovered over every attempt to control fate, and no means of fathoming that secret ingredient presented itself. Still, the sages saw no great threat in that unknown quantity so long as they believed in God's goodness.

A decisive shift occurs in the Book of Job, which wrestles with an awareness that God sometimes becomes an enemy to the one who faithfully trusts him. Job complains that God cannot be found, for he is unfathomable and so remote that sin does not affect him in the least. The same note is sounded with greater velocity by Job's three friends and by the youthful intruder, Elihu. In their view, humans are unclean, as are heavenly beings, and God alone possesses innocence. On this fact everyone is agreed except Job, who would prove God guilty to demonstrate his own purity. Job's predicament forces him to abandon the rational principle, although his argument presupposes the truth of exact retribution for good and evil. The divine speeches remind Job of fixed limits which have been imposed upon human knowledge and power.

Qoheleth advances in yet 'another direction; in his opinion, God is wholly indifferent to human beings, a thesis that picks up one aspect of Job's friends' theology. In addition, knowledge is limited to earthly things, and even there it does not amount to anything permanent. The reason, of course, is that death cancels everything,[43] rendering all human striving a chasing after wind and utterly meaningless. A twisted world mocks all human effort, since none can straighten what God has made crooked; mystery clothes the beautiful creation and prevents men and women from making use of God's gift implanted in their hearts.[44] Moral impotence naturally flows from such a thoroughly pessimistic view.[45]

Sirach internalizes the burden which weighs heavily upon one and all; anxiety functions as a powerful means of equalizing things which otherwise appear to refute any belief in justice. Confronted by divine control over the inner life as well as outward events, men and women rely more and more upon God's mercy. Accordingly, Ben Sira seems never to tire of praising the Lord for compassionate dealings with sinful creatures who repent of their deeds. Earlier sages had remained silent on this theme, for they believed sufficient knowledge and power belonged to them to secure life.[46]

By far the most extreme statement of pessimism comes from Agur, who boldly rejects the theistic hypothesis and concedes that the consequence is devastating.[47] That confession stands at the polar position from earlier optimism; its simplicity and brevity electrify. In a word, "I cannot." Nevertheless, this foreign sage stopped short of the *ennui* which grips the author of the Babylonian "Dialogue of Scepticism." In his chaotic world nothing commends itself sufficiently to stave off a desire to terminate life. Agur, on the other hand, resorts to rhetorical questions which underscore human frailty and ignorance.

> Who has ascended to heaven and come down?
> Who has gathered the wind in his fists?
> Who has wrapped up the waters in a garment?
> Who has established all the ends of the earth?
> What is his name, and what is his son's name:
> Surely you know. (Prov 30:4)

Such cognitive dissonance[48] brings about a wholly new situation with regard to persuasive discourse. The impossible question, saying, and task rapidly come to the forefront in wisdom literature.[49]

> Can a man carry fire in his bosom and his clothes
>   not be burned?
> Or can one walk upon hot coals and his feet not be
>   scorched? (Prov 6:27-28)
> Can papyrus grow where there is no marsh?
> Can reeds flourish where there is no water? (Job 8:11)

Here the sages argue from what is universally acknowledged to be true; ironically, they focus upon human inability. In these instances rhetorical questions function as strong assertions: no one can carry fire in his clothes without suffering the consequences of stupidity. The choice of such rhetorical questions as the appropriate language for God when he finally addresses Job springs from the authority pervading this type of speech. No stronger statement can be imagined, particularly since the questions place Job in the unpleasant role of a student who has stirred up the teacher's ire.

Concomitant with an increasing awareness of human frailty runs the growing use of such impossible questions, especially in Qoheleth and 2 Esdras.

> How many dwellings are in the heart of the sea,
> or how many streams are at the source of the deep,
> or which are the exits of hell,
> or which are the entrances of paradise? (2 Esd 4:7)
> Consider the work of God;
> who can make straight what he has made crooked . . . ? (Qoh 7:13)
> That which is, is far off, and deep, very deep,
> who can find it out? (Qoh 7:24)

Similarly, impossible tasks isolate vast areas in which human strength and ingenuity fail miserably.

> Go, weigh for me the weight of fire,
> or measure for me a measure of wind,
> or call back for me the day that is past. (2 Esd 4:5)
> Count up for me those who have not yet come,
> and gather for me the scattered raindrops,
> and make the withered flowers bloom again for me;
> open for me the closed chambers,
> and bring forth for me the winds shut up in them,
> or show me the picture of a voice. (2 Esd 5:36-37)

Occasionally, it seems that a numerical proverb has been altered to conform to this linguistic usage.

The sand of the sea, the drops of rain, and the days of eternity—who can count them? The height of heaven, the breadth of the earth, the abyss, and wisdom—who can search them out? (Sir 1:2-3)

Impossible sayings function in the same way that related questions and tasks do.

> But a stupid man will get understanding,
> when a wild ass's colt is born a man. (Job 11:10)
> My son, if the waters should stand up without earth,

and the sparrow fly without wings,
and the raven become white as snow,
and the bitter become sweet as honey,
then may the fool become wise. (Ahikar 2:62)

Such texts could easily be multiplied, but these suffice to demonstrate their power to render a negative judgment on all human striving. Impossible questions, sayings, and tasks went a long way toward impressing upon ancient Israelites the futility of trying to steer their course on the high seas once the divine helmsman had relinquished his post.

Conclusion

To sum up, Israel's skeptics severed a vital nerve at two distinct junctures. They denied God's goodness if not his very existence, and they portrayed men and women as powerless to acquire essential truth.

Then I saw all the work of God, that man cannot find out the work that is done under the sun. However much man may toil in seeking, he will not find it out; even though a wise man claims to know, he cannot find it out. But all this I laid to heart, examining it all, how the righteous and the wise and their deeds are in the hand of God; whether it is love or hate man does not know. Everything before them is vanity. . . . (Qoh 8:17-9:1)

Faced with this formidable onslaught, God's defenders removed him from the human scene altogether, or placed sufficient emphasis upon divine mercy to eclipse "the human deed in a time of despair."[50]

What, then, did these skeptics accomplish? Precisely this: they inscribed a huge question mark over that first great revolution in human thinking, and they turned the spotlight upon the cognitive act. That is, they refused to take confessional statements concerning divine control of human events at face value, and they insisted that boasts about human ingenuity also be taken *cum grano salis*. Pressing the interrogative mood thus placed linearity in jeopardy, as the quotation from Qoheleth in the preceding paragraph demonstrates with crushing finality, but it also showed the inadequacy of the critical tool by which divine purpose was discarded.*

NOTES

[1]Quoted by Franklin L. Baumer, *Religion and the Rise of Scepticism* (New York: Harcourt, Brace & World, Inc., 1960) 3. If this claim approaches the truth, as I think it does, the silence of contemporary Old Testament theologies with regard to religious doubt represents a serious oversight, for we have not taken the dialogue with doubt half as seriously as Israel's thinkers did.

[2]Baumer, *Religion and the Rise of Scepticism*, 11.

[3]*Ibid.*

[4]Robert Davidson, "Some Aspects of the Theological Significance of Doubt in the Old Testament," *ASTI* 7 (1970) 41-52, takes a significant step toward clarifying the contribution skeptics made to the Hebrew Scriptures. Concerning the Psalms, Davidson writes: "The confession of confidence again and again springs out of a situation where life has called such confidence into question, and where a man or a community has had to walk in a darkness which has all but overwhelmed faith . . . Is there, for example, no evidence that the very challenge to faith is a creative element in the development of faith?" 44.

[5]Two canonical texts, the teachings of Agur and Qoheleth, belong to the category of pessimism. From this observation it follows that I concur in John Priest's judgment that "The skepticism of Koheleth ends, however much some commentators cry to the contrary, as pessimism pure and simple" ("Humanism, Skepticism, and Pessimism in Israel," *JAAR* 36 [1968] 323-24).

[6]Johannes Pedersen, "Scepticisme israélite, *RHPhR* 10 (1930) 360-61 contrasts Qoheleth's exhortation to fear God with world renunciation, and rightly interprets this submission as wholly devoid of love.

[7]Baumer, *Religion and the Rise of Scepticism*, 65.

[8]*Ibid.*, 139-40 (The quotation comes from Olive Schreiner, *Story of an African Farm*, 1883, 151).

[9]Eric Weil, "What is a Breakthrough in History?" *Daedalus* (Spring, 1975) 21-36. The title of this volume is *Wisdom, Revelation and Doubt: Perspectives on the First Millennium B.C.*

[10]See the author's essay entitled "The Human Dilemma and Literature of Dissent," in *Tradition and Theology in the Old Testament*, ed. Douglas A. Knight (Philadelphia: Fortress, 1977) 235-58.

[11]Priest, "Humanism, Skepticism, and Pessimism in Israel," 326.

[12]Martin Buber, "The Heart Determines," in *On the Bible* (New York: Schocken Books, 1968) 199-210.

[13]Priest, "Humanism, Skepticism, and Pessimism in Israel," 326.

[14]Paul Ricoeur, *The Symbolism of Evil* (Boston: Beacon Press, 1969) sheds fresh light on this significant issue.

[15]Weil, "What is a Breakthrough in History?" 22-24.

[16]Hans Heinrich Schmid, *Wesen und Geschichte der Weisheit* (BZAW 101; Berlin: Walter de Gruyter, 1966).

[17]Contra Gerhard von Rad, *Wisdom in Israel* (London: SCM, 1972) 237-39.

[18]Although the hypothesis pervades von Rad's literary corpus, it was first expressed in "The Form Critical Problem of the Hexateuch," *The Problem of the Hexateuch and other Essays* (Edinburgh & London: Oliver & Boyd, 1966). German edition, 1938.

[19]In addition to the aforementioned essays by Pedersen, Priest, and von Rad, one may also consult Martin A. Klopfenstein, "Die Skepsis des Qohelet," *ThZ* 28 (1972) 97-109; Robert H. Pfeiffer, "The Peculiar Skepticism of Ecclesiastes," *JBL* 53 (1934) 100-09; Charles Forman, "The Pessimism of Ecclesiastes," *JSS* 3 (1958) 336-43; and Hartmut Gese, "Die Krisis der Weisheit bei Kohelet," *Les sagesses du Proche-Orient ancien* (Paris: Presses Universitaires de France, 1963) 139-51.

[20]Pedersen, "Scepticisme israélite," 331.

[21]von Rad, *Wisdom in Israel,* 237-39.

[22]Pedersen, "Scepticisme israélite," 347; von Rad, *Old Testament Theology,* vol. 1 (Edinburgh and London: Oliver & Boyd, 1962) 453-59.

[23]See the author's recent book entitled *Gerhard von Rad* (Waco, Texas: Word, 1978) 138-60, but above all Brian W. Kovacs' unpublished Ph.D. Dissertation from Vanderbilt University entitled "Sociological-Structural Constraints upon Wisdom: The Spatial and Temporal Matrix of Proverbs 15:28-22:16," 1978.

[24]von Rad, *Wisdom in Israel,* 15-23; R. N. Whybray, *The Intellectual Tradition in the Old Testament* (BZAW 135; Berlin and New York: Walter de Gruyter, 1974); Robert Gordis, "The Social Background of Wisdom Literature," *HUCA* 18 (1943/44) 77-118.

[25]W. Lee Humphreys, "The Motif of the Wise Courtier in the Book of Proverbs," in *Israelite Wisdom: Theological and Literary Essays in Honor of Samuel Terrien,* eds. John G. Gammie, Walter A. Brueggemann, W. Lee Humphreys, and James M. Ward (Missoula: Scholars Press, 1978) 177-90.

[26]For discussion and bibliography, see the author's "Theodicy" in *The Interpreters' Dictionary of the Bible, Supplementary Volume* (Nashville: Abingdon, 1976) 895-96.

[27]Stanley B. Frost, "The Death of Josiah: A Conspiracy of Silence," *JBL* 87 (1968) 369-82.

[28]von Rad, *Old Testament Theology,* I, 453 concedes that skepticism crops up now and again as early as the eighth century; in his view, the historiography which produced the Joseph narrative and the succession document removed God from daily events so as to conceal his manipulation of the strings that governed human destiny. Von Rad writes that "the thought of God's eternity [in Ps 90] was so overwhelming that it swept the imagination away to even greater distances, back to creation and beyond it" (453). But the powerful skepticism in Qoheleth is seen as a marginal note on the farthest frontier of Yahwism approaching the tragic dimension (455-59).

[29]Davidson, "Some Aspects of the Theological Significance of Doubt in the Old Testament," 50.

[30]See my *Samson: A Secret Betrayed, A Vow Ignored* (Atlanta: John Knox, 1978) 71-77.

[31]This idea is developed in *Prophetic Conflict* (BZAW 124; Berlin: Walter de Gruyter, 1971).

[32]von Rad, *Wisdom in Israel*, 97-110.

[33]Baumer, *Religion and the Rise of Scepticism*, 42.

[34]Besides Weil's essay, "What is a Breakthrough in History?," see in the same volume Benjamin I. Scwarz, "The Age of Transcendence," 1-8; A. Leo Oppenheim, "The Position of the Intellectual in Mesopotamian Society," 37-46; and Paul Garelli, "The Changing Facets of Conservative Mesopotamian Thought," 47-56.

[35]*Prophetic Conflict*, 23-38.

[36]Baumer, *Religion and the Rise of Scepticism*, 33 distinguishes various moods in skeptics. He writes that in some "righteous indignation predominates, in others triumphant doubt and a sense of emancipation, and in still others sheer indifference or else the reverse, a longing for a religious faith which seems intellectually unattainable." Similarly, Davidson observes that Old Testament thinkers recognized that some skepticism was inappropriate, for example, the fool in Ps 14:1 who denies God's existence ("Some Aspects of the Theological Significance of Doubt in the Old Testament," 51).

[37]I have examined this confrontation in some detail in an essay entitled "The Problem of Theodicy in Sirach: On Human Bondage," *JBL* 94 (1975) 47-64.

[38]Jerry Gladson, "Retributive Paradoxes in Proverbs 10-29," Vanderbilt University Ph.D. Dissertation, 1978.

[39]One need only mention the controversy surrounding von Rad's emphasis upon salvation history to see how modern interpreters have also stumbled over the disparity between Israel's celebrated story and actual history. On this problem, see D. G. Spriggs, *Two Old Testament Theologies* (SBTh 30; Naperville, Illinois: Alec R. Allenson, 1974), and Martin Honecker, "Zum Verständnis der Geschichte in Gerhard von Rads Theologie des Alten Testament," *EvTh* 23 (1963) 143-68.

[40]Pedersen, "Scepticisme israélite," 357.

[41]Both Ezekiel's atomistic thinking and Ben Sira's claim that a single act determined one's destiny carried such individualism to an intolerable extreme, despite good intentions on their part.

[42]I follow R. B. Y. Scott, *The Way of Wisdom in the Old Testament* (New York: Macmillan, 1971) 166 in interpreting Agur's enigmatic opening words ("I have no God") but depart from his reading of the sequel ("but I can [face this or survive]").

[43]James L. Crenshaw, "The Shadow of Death in Qoheleth," in *Israelite Wisdom: Theological and Literary Essays in Honor of Samuel Terrien*, 205-16; and Priest, "Humanism, Skepticism, and Pessimism in Israel," 324 ("The real crux of his pessimism [is] the immutable fact of death which brings an end to all human aspiration, striving, and realization").

[44]See my article, "The Eternal Gospel (Eccl 3:11)," in *Essays in Old Testament Ethics: J. Philip Hyatt in Memoriam*, eds. J. L. Crenshaw and John T. Willis (New York: Ktav, 1974) 23-55.

[45]Pedersen, "Scepticisme israélite," 347-49. Many Psalms emphasize human frailty (e.g. 14;39;44;49;103).

[46]J. Coert Rylaarsdam, *Revelation in Jewish Wisdom Literature* (Chicago: University Press, 1946).

[47]E. J. Dillon, *The Sceptics of the Old Testament* (London: Isbister & Company Limited, 1895) 155, writes that negations in mataphysics were compensated for amply in Job, Qoheleth and Agur *by ethics*. I find no such compensation in Agur and Qoheleth.

[48]Although I do not wish to pursue Festinger's categories in this connection, the idea of cognitive dissonance seems to apply nicely to Israel's skepticism. R. P. Carroll, *When Prophecy Failed: Reactions and Responses to Failure in the Old Testament Prophetic Traditions* (London: SCM, 1979) has demonstrated the usefulness of Festinger's concepts in understanding biblical prophecy.

[49]I have examined these extraordinary forms in two essays ("Impossible Questions, Sayings, and Tasks in the Old Testament," in *Gnomic Wisdom*, ed. J. Dominic Crossan [Missoula: Scholars Press, in press], and "Questions, dictons, et épreuves impossibles," in *La Sagesse de l'Ancien Testament* (Bibliotheca Ephemeridum Theologicarum Lovaniensium, 51; ed. Maurice Gilbert [Gambloux: Duculot, 1979], 96-111).

[50]This sentence alludes to Lou Silberman's contribution to *Essays in Old Testament Ethics* under the title "The Human Deed in a Time of Despair: The Ethics of Apocalyptic," 191-202.

*Samuel Terrien, "The Sceptics in the Old Testament and in the Literatures of the Ancient Near East," Th.D. Dissertation, Union Theological Seminary, New York, 1941 was not available to the author.

EZRA AMONG THE WICKED IN 2 ESDRAS 3—10

WALTER HARRELSON

VANDERBILT DIVINITY SCHOOL, NASHVILLE, TN 37240

THE apocalyptic writing called 2 Esdras or 4 Ezra deals in a special and distinctive way with the theme of the present volume dedicated to our friend and colleague Lou Silberman. For some years I have been struck with the way in which the author of chapters 3-10 underscores the fact that Ezra will not permit himself to be counted among the righteous few whom God will spare in the day of judgment to come. Despite all that the angel Uriel can do or say, Ezra insistently places himself with the many who must be destroyed.

The recent dissertation by Alden L. Thompson[1] has made a good deal of this theme, relating it to a scheme intended to show the literary and structural unity of chapters 3—14, with the first three visions in 3—9 (3:1—9:25) and the last three in 11—12, 13, and 14 enveloping the fourth vision, which portrays the heavenly Jerusalem (9:26—10:59). I am not persuaded that the Thompson exposition gives proper or sufficient weight to this theme. Indeed, I think it more probable that chapters 3—10 form a distinct entity, with the fourth vision as the crowning one. Chapter 14 may be from the same author, dealing with the issue of the authoritativeness of Scripture in relation to the perhaps contemporary debates at Jamnia (Javneh). But the visions of 11—12 and 13 are, I am convinced, the product of other hands, brought together here as the Ezra tradition yields to a more traditional apocalyptic solution.[2]

Chapters 3—10, in my view, constitute a unity in which the basic theme is how God can permit the bulk of the human race to go to perdition. The author is concerned with Israel's election, but that concern is prompted at least in part by the larger one. How God will use Israel to overcome this vast destruction awaiting evildoers—that is how our writer underscores Israel's election and God's historical dealings with Israel. The apocalyptic vision of 9:26—10:59 is the solution received by the seer. It is a real answer, I believe—one more potent and more in line with prophetic eschatology than interpreters normally have found it to be. In the following pages, dedicated to my longtime friend and faculty colleague, I hope to show this to be the case.

I. Outline and Structure of 2 Esdras 3—10

In such a work as this, much depends on our dividing the materials correctly. The seven visions do clearly constitute a loose unity, a set of revelations that deal with the consummation of the history of the nations and the triumph of God's purposes for the nations and for Israel. But the apocalyptic Eagle Vision of chapters 11—12 and that of the Man from the Sea in chapter 13 are so different from chapters 3—10 that they must be from a different hand and tradition. They reflect traditional apocalyptic imagery that is strikingly unlike anything found in chapters 3—10. Chapter 14 is directly connected with Ezra and the Ezra tradition. It is possible, indeed, that a five-fold visionary structure once obtained in the Ezra apocalypse, with the fifth vision (chapter 14) dealing in more matter-of-fact ways with how God provided for the needs of humankind by giving the Torah afresh and offering to the wise such revelations as inquiring minds require. But as one reads chapter 14 directly after concluding the reading and study of chapters 3—10, one can hardly fail to come to the conclusion that in chapter 14 too one has entered an entirely different world.

I outline the four visions in chapters 3—10 as follows:

I. Vision I: 3:1—5:20
   A. Introduction, 3:1-3
   B. Ezra's lament and question, 3:4-36:
       Israel is in exile for her sins, but is Babylon more righteous than she?
   C. Dialogue between Uriel and Ezra, 4:1—5:13:
       1. Uriel offers unanswerable questions to Erza, driving Ezra to doubt that life is worthwhile, given the impossibility of understanding the meaning of things, 4:1-13.
       2. The fable of the trees and the sea in warfare against one another, 4:14-21, presented by the angel, requires Ezra to grant that both were foolish.
       3. Ezra's basic question: why has God abandoned the people whom he loves? 4:22-25.
       4. Uriel gives the apocalyptic answer: God will come to sweep away wickedness, and the righteous will have their reward, 4:26-32.

5. How long will it be before the End? The angel answers Ezra that it will not be long at all, 4:33-37.
6. Is the End perhaps delayed because of the sins of us who are alive on earth; do we prevent the righteous from receiving their reward? No, says the angel; nothing can delay the coming day, just as a pregnant woman must give birth when her time comes, 4:38-43.
7. Are we more than halfway to the End? Much more than halfway, says the angel. The vision of flame, cloud, and rain, with what remains when they pass by, shows how close the End is, 4:44-50.
8. Will Ezra live to see the End? The angel cannot say, 4:51-52.
9. Signs of the End are presented: terror, confusion, the spread of evil; the presently ruling kingdom will be overthrown; an unexpected ruler will exercise rule; anomalies will occur on earth; wickedness will increase to such an extent that it will dominate all of history, 5:1-13.

D. Ezra now awakes, is comforted by the angel, 5:14-15.
E. Phaltiel comes from the Jewish exiles to inquire about Ezra. He reminds Ezra that the exiles depend upon him as their shepherd. Ezra sends him away for another seven days, and begins preparation for another vision by fasting and mourning. 5:16-20.

II. Vision II: 5:21—6:34
A. Introduction, 5:21-22.
B. Ezra's lament and question, 5:23-30: from the many God has selected one people, given them the law, but now has abandoned them into the hands of their enemies—why? Why did God not, at the least, punish them himself for their sins?
C. Dialogue between Uriel and Ezra, 5:31-6:34:
1. Uriel asks Ezra if he thinks that he, Ezra, loves Israel more than God does. Ezra replies that he does not think so, but that he is suffering agonies trying to understand Israel's fate, 5:31-34.
2. It is impossible to understand, says the angel. Why, then, was Ezra born?, 5:35.
3. Ezra is told to perform a list of impossible tasks. Since he cannot do them, he cannot expect to understand God's ways, says the angel, 5:36-40.
4. What is to happen to the generations not alive on the day of

judgment—those who died beforehand and any who are to come thereafter? The angel answers that God's judgment is like a circle: there is no before it or after it, 5:41-42.

5. Could the whole of creation not better have been called into being at once? No, says the angel; the world would not have been able to contain all at once, 5:43-44.

6. But if the world one day will hold all who are brought to life, why cannot it hold all persons now? The angel answers that the earth produces its creatures as does a woman—one after another, not all at once, 5:45-49.

7. Is our mother the earth still young or has she grown old? The angel answers that she has grown old, as can be seen from the fact that persons born today are smaller of stature and weaker than were those born in former times, 5:50-55.

8. Through whom will God visit the earth? Just as God brought forth the whole of creation and was himself before all things that he made, so also will God bring the consummation himself, and not through any other being, says the angel, 5:56-6:6.

9. What is the point that divides historical time from the End? The division between the present age and the coming one is like that between Abraham and Isaac. That is, there is no interval; the consummation follows directly on the heels of present time, just as Jacob held to the heel of Esau, 6:7-10.

10. What further signs of the End can be disclosed? Ezra stands, hears a great voice like the sound of many waters. He is told of days to come that will be marked by a great reversal of all ordinary realities, with matters first becoming worse and then becoming altogether good, with evil blotted out and truth disclosed, 6:11-28.

11. Ezra feels the earth shaking. The angel tells him that because of Ezra's uprightness and purity God has permitted him to see all of these things. Ezra is to believe and not to be afraid; he is not to think vain or hasty thoughts, 6:29-34.

III. Vision III: 6:35—9:25
    A. Introduction, 6:35-37.
    B. Ezra's lament and question, 6:38-59:
       Ezra gives an account of God's creation in the form of a prayer or meditation. God the creator called forth all of the creation on

six successive days. He formed Adam, and from Adam he brought Israel and the other nations to birth. The world was created for us Israelites, whom God loves, says Ezra. But why, then, are we handed over to the nations?

C. Dialogue between Uriel and Ezra, 7:1—9:25 :

1. The angel begins with a parable of the broad sea with a narrow entrance, and of a large and broad city with a narrow gate. The way into the fulfillment of God's promise is narrow. The earth was made for Israel's sake, says the angel, but then Adam sinned, and the path that leads to life and good was narrowed. Israel now suffers, must pass through difficult times. But think, says the angel, about the good that is to come, 7:1-16.

2. The righteous alone will have this time of fulfillment, says Ezra. For the wicked there is no hope—is that not right? 7:17-18.

3. The angel warns Ezra not to think of himself as wiser than God. Let the many now living perish rather than have God's law ignored. And in any event, says the angel, God gave the law to the wicked so that they are without excuse, 7:19-24.

4. For the righteous, however, blessing awaits, as the Messiah appears, rules for 400 years, dies, and the earth returns to primeval silence. Then, says the angel, the last judgment will come, with the wicked handed over to death while the righteous enter into eternal life. 7:25-(45).

5. Ezra asks again about the sinners. Who has not sinned? Will not the number handed over to eternal punishment include almost all of humankind? 7:(46-48).

6. The angel replies that it is for this reason that God made not one world but two. The righteous belong to the righteous world to come. It will not do, moreover, to mix lead and clay with precious stones, will it? The earth has much less gold than it has of metals of lesser value, does it not? Rare things are always more precious for being rare. So it is with the righteous. God will rejoice over the few saved, who have honored his name, given him glory in the world. God will not grieve over the many who perish; they are like a mist, insubstantial, not to be lingered over. 7:(49-61).

7. Ezra points out that dust has produced minds who know their evil fate. It would have been better had the dust of

earth not done so. Beasts, in fact, are better off than human beings, for the latter know their inevitable end. 7:(62-69).

8. The angel replies that the wicked had their opportunity; they had understanding of the judgment that would befall evil-doers, but still they sinned, and thus they are without excuse. 7:(70-74).

9. Ezra asks when the torment is to begin—at the time of physical death or at the last judgment? The angel says that he will answer the question, but first he points out to Ezra that Ezra is not to count himself among the wicked. Ezra has a treasure of works laid up; he has nothing to fear. 7:(75-77).

10. On death, the angel replies that evil ones die and their spirits wander over the earth in grief and terror before the coming last judgment. The good spirits, however, will have rest immediately upon physical death. They will be guarded by angels and will be prepared to behold God's face at the time when the judgment is unfolded. 7:(78-99).

11. Will the souls have time to see what is to happen to them, after they are separated from the body and before their destiny begins to be fulfilled? Yes, says the angel; they will have seven days. 7:(100-101).

12. Will the righteous be able to intercede for the wicked, for their relatives or friends among the wicked? No; no one shall ever pray for another on that day. But why, asks Ezra, was it otherwise with Abraham, Moses, Joshua, Samuel, David, Solomon, Elijah, and Hezekiah? This world, says the angel, is entirely different from the coming world where judgments and rewards will be meted out. 7:(102—115). (Older versification takes up at 106=36).

13. Ezra exclaims that it would have been better if the earth had not produced Adam, then; or if it was to produce him, restrain him from sinning. What have you done, Adam, says Ezra. All of the promised goods and glories count for nought, for we have sinned and must perish. The angel replies that this is the case unless human beings fight against evil and prevail, just as Moses said. We are to rejoice over those saved, not grieve over those who are doomed. 7:(116-131).

14. (We now go back to regular versification). In a commentary

on Exodus 34:6-7, Ezra praises God for his mercy and long-suffering. Were God not so merciful, only the tiniest fragment of humankind would be left alive. The angel responds that this world in fact was made for the many, but the world to come for the few. Many have been created, but few shall be saved. 7:62(132-)-8:3.

15. Ezra now meditates and prays. He points out the extraordinary care extended to human beings by God, in the womb already, in the nurture the mother is able to provide the child, in the instruction given by God through the family and community, along with reproofs, and often throughout a long lifetime. Why should God exercise such care for the life of human beings if in fact the life of most of them is doomed to meaninglessness and destruction? 8:4-14.

And leaving aside humankind as a whole, what about Israel? There follows a long and beautiful prayer for Israel. God is implored to consider not the faithless ones but the faithful; at least God could show tolerance for the wicked while returning the love of the faithful. Indeed, says Ezra, none is faithful; all have sinned. We have no store of righteousness and must depend upon God's forgiveness, God's mercy to sinners in their sin. 8:4-36.

16. The angel replies that Ezra's words contain some well-said thoughts and some not so well spoken. But of the whole prayer, the angel picks up only the word about being concerned for the righteous, and overstating Ezra's point to have it mean that Ezra was ready to see God have no concern for the wicked. 8:37-40.

17. The angel goes on to say that just as the farmer sows many seeds and not all come up or survive after coming up, so it is with people. But Ezra points out that human beings are not seeds, are not to depend for their survival on whether sufficient rain falls on them, and not too much, as in the case of seeds. 8:41-45.

18. The angel insists that Ezra cannot love the creation more than God does. And in any event, Ezra must not continue to place himself among the wicked! It is praiseworthy that Ezra is humble enough to call himself a sinner, to avoid the temptation to pride. But actually, for Ezra and those like him God has marvelous things in store: paradise, rest, good

things, complete separation from all that is evil or hurtful. Thus, Ezra is to give up all thought of the wicked. They had their freedom, their full opportunity to share in the coming blessedness. They chose to show contempt for God and for the righteous among humankind. God did not intend their destruction, but their misdeeds led inevitably to their doom. Not everyone knows this; only a few like Ezra have been told. 8:46-62.

19. Ezra then asks to know when the End will come. The angel mentions signs that will precede the End, providing sufficient warning. But the angel stresses once again that those faithful by their deeds of righteousness and those who believe in God will be spared. Ezra is not to show curiosity about how God will torment the sinners but rather is to fix his attention on how God will deal with the saved. 8:63—9:13.

20. Ezra repeats his observation that the number of those to perish is incalculably greater than the number to be saved. On that point he will not be silenced. The angel tells how at the time of creation, when none existed but God alone, God created all humankind, lavished his care upon them, but they corrupted their ways. The very creation itself had become corrupt. What could God do? He saved a few, like one grape from a cluster, one shoot from a forest, and labored to protect and deliver these few. Let the multitude that lived in vanity now perish, while the grape and the plant are saved. 9:14-22.

21. The angel concludes the vision by promising yet more conversation with Ezra. He is to go into a field of flowers, an uninhabited land, and there eat only flowers—eating no meat or drinking no wine—and is to pray, preparing for the coming vision. 9:23-25.

IV. Vision IV: 9:26—10:59
  A. Introduction, 9:26-28 (see 9:23-25).
  B. Ezra's lament, 9:29-37:
  Ezra laments before God that while the law had been sown in the hearts of God's people, beginning in the wilderness, the people had not kept the law. They had, accordingly, perished. The law, God's own creation, had not of course perished. Why, Ezra implies, might God not have arranged for the hearts of the

ones who did not keep the law to be spared so that they might try once again to be faithful? When the ground receives seed, or the sea a ship, or a dish receives food or drink, if the content is destroyed the container is not. Why should it be otherwise with God's faithless people? Could God not give them another chance?

C. Ezra sees a woman in terrible grief, weeping, with her clothes torn and ashes on her head. He breaks off his own meditation in order to talk with her, inquiring what brought on such grief. The woman tells how for thirty years she and her husband had no children, though praying night and day to God for them. Finally, God gave them a son. The son grew up, a wife was found for him, he married, and as he was going into the bridal chamber he fell down dead. The mother then fled the city, and will now fast and mourn until she dies, for the tragedy is unbearable. 9:38—10:4.

Ezra rebukes the woman for weeping over the loss of one son when Zion, the mother of us all, is in such grief over the loss of her children. Then Ezra deals with mother earth, rather than mother Zion, pointing out the enormous loss mother earth suffers as most of her children go inevitably to perdition. Just as you lost the fruit of your body, he says to the woman, so the earth returns to God (who made earth itself) the fruit of her body, in the host of human beings marked for destruction, almost all that mother earth bears. The woman should keep her sorrow to herself, bear her troubles bravely. Ezra says to her, "If you acknowledge the decree of God to be just, you will receive your son back in due time, and will be praised among women." Ezra tells her to return to her husband in the city. But the woman refuses; she will stick to her plan and will die. 10:5-18. Ezra then turns to Jerusalem, showing the woman how Zion's troubles should help her to put into perspective her own loss. The sanctuary is laid waste, the altar destroyed, the holy things profaned, the people and their leaders dead or in captivity or sold as slaves or sexually abused. Zion has lost the seal of her glory which has been handed over to her enemies. The woman, then, should cease her personal grief and await God's mercy. 10:19-24.

D. Now, suddenly, the woman is transfigured, her face agleam. She cries out in an unearthly voice, disappears, and in her place appears an established city, with massive foundations, and with vast extent. Ezra is overwhelmed, cries out for Uriel, is prostrate and undone before the vision. 10:25-28.

E. The angel appears, raises him up, gives him an explanation of the vision (in fact, a rather labored interpretation), and tells him that he may enter the city for a short while and see what his eyes are able to see. 10:29-57.

F. Verses 58-59 promise additional dream visions to come and are to be considered an editorial addition, connecting the other dream visions with these initial four, in our view.

The structure of the four visions is quite uniform:

1. Introductory statement, giving the setting.
2. Lament by the seer, with a particular question often summing up the lament, in each case the subject matter of the lament being the condition of humankind or of Israel in God's world.
3. A series of exchanges between the seer and the angel, where often the latter speaks directly, oracularly, in God's name. Sometimes the exchanges are brief. Sometimes extended stories, or parables, or fables, or riddles are used by the angel. Occasionally, Ezra prays or meditates or comments upon Scripture, but he always gets around to his actual theme.
4. Conclusion of the dialogue, and preparation for the next vision.

In the fourth vision, the seer does not get to put his direct question, for he is interrupted by the appearance of the weeping woman. Even so, the question is implicit, as noted in our summary above.

Regarding the character of these dream-visions, it is of course impossible to know whether the author actually experienced visions and later recorded their contents, or whether the visions are to be understood as no more than a literary convention. I believe that the author lived in the vicinity of Jerusalem and frequently made his way to the site of the destroyed town, before the city was rebuilt in the days of Hadrian. There the seer probably meditated on his theme. Visions may have come on many such occasions, in connection with the thought that took shape and found its way into chapters 3—10 of the book.

It is difficult also to know just how to understand the relation between the figure of Ezra and that of the interpreting angel. Gunkel[3] eloquently presents the view that the two represent the torn thought and feelings of the seer himself, that Ezra is addressing God in the form of the Ezra speeches and is hearing God's reply in the form of the Uriel responses, while in fact both speeches are a part of Ezra's own dream-visions. He plays both parts, because in fact our apocalyptist, according to Gunkel, is convinced of the truth of what the angel, or the Lord, gives back as replies to the questions, but has the greatest difficulty accepting that truth and being content with it. Not until the later apocalyptic visions, the fifth and sixth especially, does the apocalyptist come to some sense of renewed faith and trust in God, according to Gunkel.

That kind of psychological interpretation of the first three visions seems to me improbable. I rather prefer to see the dialogue as a running meditation on the part of the author with the theological traditions of his own community. He has the angel give these traditional responses, but the author himself is not thereby accepting the answers. But on the other hand he is not flatly rejecting them or permitting them to have no weight whatever. His refusal to be content with the answers is much like the refusal of Job to be content with the answers that come from the friends.

But do the speeches of the dialogue belong to an actual series of dream visions? I am quite confident that the author understood them to have arisen in such a series of visions, although it is highly probable that, as in the case of the prophetic visions, actual experiences are told later and retold frequently, only finally assuming a fixed and written form. Since our author is certainly a writer, he may have stylized the actual dream-visions more self-consciously than prophets normally did.

II.   Ezra Among the Wicked

The opening question of the work is quite traditional: it is explicit in the book of Habakkuk and it echoes in individual and communal laments of the Psalter and in the book of Job.[4] The seer does not deny the sin of Israel. In this respect he does differ from the outlook of some of the laments of the Psalter. What he does deny is any satisfactory relation between the sin committed and the punishment for sin that is meted out. God surely loves his people, even though they have sinned. Can God not at the least punish them himself? This theme is reflected in the old story of David's census of the people and the punishment that was required to fall upon him for doing so (see 2 Samuel 24). Why should God treat his people with such contempt as to let their enemies, and God's own enemies, exercise the divine punishment against his own elect people? Psalm 44 says the same: God sold his people for a trifling sum; for God's own sake they are killed all day long, counted as sheep to be slaughtered.

The striking new point begins to emerge in 4:38-43, as the seer wonders whether our sin is delaying the time of reward for the righteous. This passage is of course ambiguous. The author may be saying that we sinners (he clearly includes himself among the sinners) are a stumbling block to the righteous who otherwise would not have so long to wait for their pain to be eased. But he may also be raising the question (hoping the answer to be yes) whether God does not delay the End until something can be done to reduce the number of the wicked. Our thinker's overall theme suggests the latter alternative. Ezra wants the angel to say something about how the sin of the wicked appears in the sight of the Most High: does God not possibly have more in mind than the mechanical completion of the number of the elect (4:34-37)? Might God not be moved by the vast number of the wicked? Could not this fact cause God to restrain his wrath?

No, not according to Uriel. Just as a pregnant woman must give birth on the appointed day, so God must bring on the day of consummation in accordance with a fixed number. We are familiar with this kind of thinking from New Testament apocalyptic texts.[5] Ezra's first challenge of it is rejected by Uriel.

The next effort in behalf of the wicked comes in the second vision (in 5:43-49). Ezra asks why the whole of creation could not have been brought into being at once so that the story, the dreary story of human apostasy, might look differently. Hearing that God does his deeds in the manner of a mother's bearing children, that is, one after the other, Ezra notes that if one day all will be together for the judgment, why could not all be together before the judgment? Apparently, the author wants to show by implication that the vast majority of human beings will not be on hand for the Last Day, since God has decreed that most of them will pass into perdition, their souls wandering on the earth in torment. And that is his concern from first to last: what God intends really to do with a sinful Israel and a sinful humankind. The seer, we can see, thus puts the question why God could not have called into existence all humankind at once and dealt with all equally in order to underscore the dreadful reality of the ages-long production of the human race which will be followed by a day of judgment in which most of those who have lived will not in fact be on hand to reap the benefits of a transformed cosmos at the Last Day.

In 6:23-34, the angel stresses Ezra's uprightness and purity, saying that because Ezra is worthy in God's sight he is permitted to have the visions that are being disclosed to him. The irony of such a revelation to Ezra is evident. Ezra sees himself all the more without hope as he discovers more details about God's handing over almost all of humankind to desolation.

Even if he should have some merit in God's eyes, and be enabled to have the visions being revealed, Ezra is sure that in fact he belongs among the wicked who are marked for eternal destruction.

In the third vision the seer gives his most explicit picture of the fate of the wicked and the hard path of the righteous that finally leads to blessing for the few. The author begins with a beautiful, even though conventional, exegesis of Genesis 1, portraying God's works of creation on each of the first six days. The creation culminated in the placing of Adam over all works of God as their ruler. But Adam and all the nations descended from Adam—what is to happen to them? The initial question posed is, to be sure, the familiar one about the fate of Israel. Israel the first-born, the one for whom the world was created, is being devoured by the nations, by those said by God to be no more than a drop from a bucket in his eyes. But implicit is the seer's showing the incredible lack of concern on God's part for the *human* community created to take charge of all God's carefully-contrived and arranged creation. The argument implied is that if God lets his special treasure Israel suffer at the hands of foreign nations, that is bad enough. But God also apparently intends the destruction of all, or virtually all, that was so carefully brought forth in the act of divine creation. The world over which Israel was to rule she has had stripped from her. But the nations too—they are for the most part also marked for destruction. Is this the end God intends for a creation brought into being on the first six days?

As the angel replies we are able to see that the whole point is not that Israel has to suffer and be tested among the nations and thereby be refined and purified. The point is that humankind is being trimmed down to a mere trickle of its initial size as the refining process is carried forward. The law has been provided not alone to Israel but also to all born on earth (7:21). The vast majority, however, has spurned God's law and are therefore doomed to perish. In the whole of the often lyrically beautiful picture of God's transcendent glory (7:39-42) that follows, this is the refrain. God's day of deliverance that is so firmly fixed and sure is a day when only a very small number have any hope of actual deliverance. The messianic interlude that our author presents does not in any way affect that fact (7:27-31); the corruptible shall perish, while the lot of the faithful few will be rest and the paradise of delight.

Small wonder, then, that Ezra pronounces blessing on the righteous (7:45) but cries out that those for whom he has prayed are by no means blessed or comforted by what the angel has disclosed. The world to come will bring delight to few, but torments to many (7:47). And we are among those, says Ezra, who are brought into corruption by the evil heart that has grown up in us. The angel will have Ezra recognize that the few are all the more precious to God because they are few; Ezra should not grieve over the many who perish, just as the Lord does not grieve. The perishing are like a mist, lacking any kind of substantive reality. Ezra should rather rejoice over the faithful few, precious in God's sight and therefore to be precious in the eyes of Ezra as well.

Ezra cannot accept this counsel. He argues that it would have been better that there be no creation at all than that this result of creation should have to ensue. The mind cannot stop knowing that most human beings are doomed; how can the mind bear such knowledge? "We perish and know it!" (7:64). Beasts are much better off.

The angel gives the usual rejoinder: God is entirely just and fair in his judgment, for all those who perish do so because they sinned. They had understanding, had the law, knew the way that led to life, but they sinned, of their own volition.

But more important to the angel is Ezra's unwillingness to see that all of this talk of the wicked of earth applies not to Ezra but to others. Ezra has a treasure of works laid up (7:76-77) and is entirely secure in God's hands.

Later on in the vision Ezra puts the question whether the righteous may intercede for the wicked on the day of judgment. He is told that such a thing is not possible; each soul bears its own righteousness or unrighteousness. The prayers of intercession offered by Israelites of old were effective because they belonged to this present age; on the day when definitive judgment is pronounced it will be too late for any such interventions.

Again Ezra declares that it would have been better had there been no human race, if such an outcome as this is the only possible one. Adam sinned and fell, but so also do all who follow after, or almost all. We gain no benefit from mere possibilities if in fact we do not seize those possibilities. We were promised an eternal age, but we do deeds that bring death; promised an everlasting hope, we crush it and death is our lot; promised a secure home, we have lived in wickedness and lost that home; promised protection from God, we know that only the pure have such protection, and we are not pure; promised paradise itself, we know we are unworthy of it and will not see it; promised faces that gleam on the day when the righteous receive their rewards, we who are righteous know that our faces will be blacker than darkness. We have lived out our lives and have sinned, and even though we did not sin with full awareness of the consequences of that sin, we have to grant that we are without excuse. Now eternal darkness awaits us.

The angel simply says in response that people were told to choose the right way. If they did not do so, as Moses had told them to do, it is too bad. No grief at their destruction is called for but simply joy at the salvation of the righteous.

Now there follows a remarkable exegetical treatment of Exodus 34:6-7, with comments on why God has been designated as merciful, gracious, patient, bountiful, compassionate, giver, and judge, all intended to underscore the extraordinary mercy of God for sinners. The exegesis is intended to encourage God to be true to his own nature, and therefore find a way to show mercy to the wicked on the day of judgment. If God were not unbelievably merciful, where would human beings be now? This is the character of God—to be merciful. Surely, therefore, God must intend mercy for sinners.

This point is carried forward in Ezra's two great prayers, 8:6-19 and 8:20-36. The first prayer is a plea for God to enter into the history of human beings as he does in the processes of their birth, enter to such an extent that he keeps them from such apostasy as would doom them. These tenderly-cared for beings surely are not to be handed over to eternal death. If God will not save human beings as such, let him at the least save sinful Israel whom he loves in a special way. Is that asking too much?

The second prayer, which has been preserved in the Mozarabic liturgy under the designation *oratio Esrae*, opens with an apostrophe of praise to God the creator and Lord of all things. It then presents Ezra's plea that God not look on sinners but on the faithful; that God not judge humankind on the basis of the faithless but with an eye to those who have kept the faith. We indeed have sinned and our forebears before us have sinned; we are marked for death. But look, Lord, says the seer, at the saints! Look at those who have kept the commandments. Deal with us as though we had! To be merciful to those who have no good works to offer—that would be to display your righteousness and goodness in a way appropriate to such a God as you are.

The angel now takes a look back at the series of Ezra's observations, laments, and questions and notes that within them are some that are entirely right and good. Others, however, are not so good. The point about being concerned for the wicked is ruled out. Ezra's entire effort to underscore the need of the sinners for the mercy of God is therefore flatly rejected. Ezra should know that when seeds are sown, by no means do all germinate and grow up to form plants. Ezra seeks to make the point that people are not to be compared with seeds; surely God must recognize the inadequacy of such an analogy.

The rejoinder is an almost intemperate insistence by the angel (8:47-49) that Ezra should not keep placing himself with the wicked. He does not belong with them; why cannot he see and acknowledge that fact? Ezra has no reason at all to keep asking questions regarding the wicked.

In the closing section of the third vision the seer asks about when the End will come, but shortly thereafter the subject again shifts to the fate of the multitude of evildoers. Ezra must not continue to be curious about the fate of the wicked (9:13), says the angel, apparently trying to shame Ezra into submission. At no point has Ezra exercised a morbid curiosity about how God will punish the wicked; it is the massiveness of the loss of human life that has driven Ezra to near despair. But the angel insists that Ezra must fix his eye upon the future awaiting the righteous.

Ezra's closing rejoinder is that he holds fast to his view that the number of those destroyed is incomparably larger than the number to be saved (9:14-16). The angel does not deny the point but says that with much labor God has perfected the few that are to be saved, has saved something from the general ruin.

The fourth vision is the author's answer, if not solution, to the whole concern and preoccupation of the apocalypse, I believe. It registers first a powerful rhetorical point by showing Ezra's grief over Zion, over the ruined land and people, in face of which the personal losses and tragedies of life pale into insignificance. The grieving woman must set aside her grief, must see that the loss suffered by God's people, and the loss of most of human life as such, make it possible for her to put her own grief into perspective.

The irony of this comfort given to the grieving woman by Ezra has often been overlooked or underestimated by interpreters.[6] How is it possible to believe that the author's own personal counsel to his readers is contained in 10:15-17? To tell the woman to go home, control her grief, acknowledge that God's decree is just, and have faith that God will restore her son in due season—is that to console himself? Can our apocalyptist really be content with such counsel? Is Ezra, after all that he has said and all that he has been unwilling to accept, now able to say that one must acknowledge God's decree to be just, and patiently to wait for a return of the fortunes of Zion?

I find it impossible to accept such a view. These verses are an ironic answer to the woman, an answer that Ezra cannot accept for himself. And it is the woman herself who gives the lie to this answer. She is in a twinkling transformed into the Zion of the future, a Zion the limits of which are beyond human capacity to conceive. Who is in that city? Only the faithful Israelites who scrupulously kept God's law? Only those who acknowledged that God's decree was just, a decree dooming most of humankind to eternal death? Or rather a vast multitude of humankind who at Zion learn the meaning of Torah and find peace and life and wholeness from this center, this navel of all the earth?

This is a vision of the sort we have in several passages of the Hebrew Bible and in the New Testament, a vision that is always concerned with the fulfillment of God's purposes not alone for Israel but for the nations as well. Isaiah 2:2-4 and Micah 4:1-4 are the most famous parallels, but there are many others as well. Often the ambiguity is maintained: Zion glorified at the expense of the foreign nations versus Zion glorified in behalf of the whole of humankind. This ambiguity is present in Revelation 21-22 as well, and in our passage. But the weight of emphasis falls on how the transformation of the woman into a vast city with massive foundations testifies to God's coming fulfillment of his purposes for wicked and suffering humankind, and for destroyed and ravaged Zion, in such a way as to be glorious beyond belief. Here is no narrowness of vision in which the maintenance of God's justice requires that most of those who have lived, and who have affronted God's justice, be disposed of.

The narrow logic of sin and punishment is expanded and transfigured. The fulfillment of Zion's glory is a work of God accomplished in a twinkling. It takes no account of the question of numbers of faithful or faithless. But it also offers no picture of a suffering servant on the strength of whose faithfulness to death God has been reconciled to sinners in their sin. Ezra is overwhelmed, bewildered, unable to cope with the glory of this vision. But one thing is unmistakable: Zion has become the sign of the triumph of glory over despair, of love over mere flat justice.

The angel's explanation of the vision, though flat and allegorizing to some extent, does preserve the mystery, and it concludes with the angel's invitation to Ezra to enter the city and see what splendors are there, hear what glories God has in store. There the original visions of Ezra break off, I believe. The possibility does exist that they might once have been followed with a story of Ezra's translation into the heavens (see 14:48, Syriac).

The answer to the fate of the multitude of sinners, then, is found to be much akin to Paul's answer in Romans,[7] a New Testament book with which our apocalypse has many affinities. God's love for the sinners in their sin, for the whole world (see John 3:1-21), is so deep that God, like Ezra, will not be content finally to apply the traditional logic on the day of judgment. More important than the day of judgment is the miracle of God that awaits, when in a trice, with no mediation, not a single act of preparation, Zion bursts forth in its splendor, its extent beyond fathoming, its citizenry not in any census of human devising.

Indeed, we might well ask whether the ambiguity does not apply to the name of the city itself. Is this Zion, heavenly Zion, or is this the earth itself, transformed under the sign of a city? In the vision itself the city is not named. The identification by the angel is contained in a prosaic and allegorizing interpretation that may well not belong to the original vision.

The apostle Paul argues that God has come in the fullness of time to bring redemption to his people and to all humankind through the one who died for sinners, who shared their life and their lot, who in his faithfulness to God and his love for fellow human beings was God's instrument to bring to death both sin and death. God's love for sinners while sinners knew no bounds; he sent his own Son in the likeness of sinful flesh and for sin, to do sin to death.[8] Our apocalyptist is as deeply concerned about a world laden with sin, unable to lift or to cast off its burden of guilt and sin, as was the apostle. Ezra's solution is to press directly back into the hands of God this plight of humankind and of Israel and not to permit any escape for God. And God's response, a visionary one rather than one tied to a concrete event of history, to a person and the person's human fate, is that God weeps over his world with such a lamentation that the woman can only join in, and Ezra can only join in. But not as though the grief will never end. The promise of God given through Israel's prophets is yet fixed and firm. The city will appear, not made with human hands. Glory awaits, in the mysterious purpose of God. God will sweep away the sin, the pain, the doubt, the tears, and the new community will be planted firmly on new foundations. See also Revelation 21-22.

Our apocalyptist, then, ends his central vision with a picture of the city transformed, of earth itself renewed and re-created, a community delivered from its sin by mysterious consummating action of God. Does it thereby encourage fatalism or quietism? Not if the impulse to this vision has rightly been identified as prophetic. For the coming Day of prophetic eschatology is one that shatters all complacency, just as it rejects all self-pitying notions about the cruelties and injustices of life. The city will arise in this world, as the consummation of all God's works, on new and massive foundations erected by God's miraculous act. It comes, however, as people refuse to be seduced by particularisms or narrow logic or small-minded notions of God's love for them alone. It comes as God's own mercy engenders mercy in his creatures, making them unable to acquiesce in the cruelties of time and history, fighting and struggling and praying and hoping for the Day of Consummation. And those who risk all on the truth of the Consummation also share in it, before the transformation has quite occurred.[9]

Ezra refused from beginning to end to let the angel place him among the righteous. It is this seriousness of moral commitment that makes his apocalypse so special among the apocalyptic literature. Nowhere else in the literature of this genre is there such a single-minded concentration upon the issue of how God will deal with sinners who cannot themselves extricate themselves from their sin. This is a worthy and indeed glorious apocalypse, a testimony to the utter dependence of the human community upon the mercy of God, but without any resort to the mediation that is the center and the glory of Christian faith. It is therefore a Jewish answer to the problem of sin in the world, an answer closely akin to the Christian one, and one that is in the tradition of Israel's prophets though found in the midst of an apocalyptic vision of the End. If our writing had not suffered the fate of drawing to it other eschatological visions of a quite different sort, its great strength and rigor of faith would have stood out all the more clearly. It would not then have been necessary for Hermann Gunkel and C. G. Montefiore,[10] the two scholars who most clearly in recent times have seen the power of this apocalypse, to have come to the conclusion that the author after all remained captive of the view presented by the angel. Not at all; Ezra wins the day, and much in the way that Job wins the day. Our vision of the transformed city/earth is much akin to the vision found in Job 42:1-6. Here too, as in Job, the visionary finally sees so deeply into the mystery of what God has in store, that repentance in dust and ashes merges into an entering into the blessedness of the Lord.

NOTES

[1]A. L. Thompson, *Responsibility for Evil in the Theodicy of IV Ezra. A Study Illustrating the Significance of Form and Structure for the Meaning of the Book* (SBLDS 29; Missoula: Scholars Press, 1977). See especially 218-235; 257-290.

[2]The treatment by G. H. Box, *The Ezra-Apocalypse* (London: Pitman, 1912), Introduction, which also appears in abbreviated form in R. H. Charles (ed.), APOT, II 549-553, goes too far in source-separation. Even so, the problems to which Box and others before him had called attention are not adequately addressed by the solution that traditional materials have been collected and given a structural or thematic unity. More literary-critical attention is called for than is provided by Hermann Gunkel in his often magnificent treatment of the apocalypse (E. Kautzsch, ed., *Die Apokryphen und Pseudepigraphen des Alten Testaments* [2 vols.; Tübingen: Mohr, 1900]), II 350-352. The same applies to Thompson (*Responsibility for Evil* 121-148) and to the treatment by J. M. Myers, *I and II Esdras. Introduction, Translation and Commentary* (AB 42; Garden City, N.Y.: Doubleday, 1974) 119-121.

[3]Gunkel, APAT, II, 342-343.

[4]Hab 1:2—2:4; Pss 73 and 44.

[5]Rev 14:1-5; Rom 11:25; Mark 13:27, etc.

[6]This is the great weakness of Thompson's study, in my judgment. See *Responsibility for Evil* 219-220; 229-232.

[7]Rom 11:25-36.

[8]Rom 5:6—6:14; 7:7-25.

[9]See my treatment of prophetic eschatology in "Famine in the Perspective of Biblical Judgments and Promises," in George R. Lucas, Jr. and Thomas W. Ogletree (eds.), *Lifeboat Ethics: The Moral Dilemmas of World Hunger* (New York: Harper and Row, 1976) 84–99. I have also dealt with the subject at more length in an unpublished paper titled "Christian Misreadings of Basic Themes in the Hebrew Scriptures."

[10]Gunkel in Kautzsch, II 338-339; C. G. Montefiore, *IV Ezra: A Study in the Development of Universalism* (London: George Allen & Unwin, 1929) 12-16.

THE LAW AND "THE LAW OF SIN AND DEATH" (ROM 8:1-4): REFLECTIONS ON THE SPIRIT AND ETHICS IN PAUL

LEANDER E. KECK

YALE DIVINITY SCHOOL, NEW HAVEN, CONNECTICUT 06510

ROM 8:1-4 is foundational for Paul's ethics, no less than for his theology. True, strictly speaking, Paul does not write "ethics" any more than he writes "theology" in the technical sense. What he says with regard to the particulars of human behavior, such as marriage or civil authority, is exhortation and counsel. The relevance of Rom 8:1-4 for ethics is not immediately clear, for no particular behavior is called for or prohibited. Nonetheless, the passage is literally "foundational," for what Paul says here belongs to the foundations on which his "ethics" rest.

At the same time, and perhaps for the same reasons, it embodies major issues in the interpretation of Paul. Not only are key terms mentioned—law, Spirit, flesh, sin, death—but the passage uses them in somewhat unusual ways. Besides, because it occurs at a transition in the Letter, how one interprets Paul here will affect the interpretation of what precedes and what follows. A full discussion of all these matters would exceed the possibilities of an essay. Nonetheless, by attending to major elements here, we will illumine important aspects of Paul's thought which affect his ethics.

I

(1) So there is now no condemnation for those in Jesus Christ.

(2) For the law of the Spirit of life in Christ Jesus has set me[1] free from the law of sin and death.

(3) For what the law was not able to do, in that it was weakened through the flesh—God, in sending his own Son in the likeness of sinful flesh[2]

   and to deal with sin[3]

condemned sin in the flesh[4]

41

(4) so that "the just requirement of the law" [RSV] might be actualized in us who live, not according to the flesh, but according to the Spirit.

It is quite possible that v. 1 (together with 7:25b) is an interpolation or gloss.[5] Advocates of this possibility rightly point out that if v. 2 were to follow 7:25a, the flow of thought would be improved:

7:24b	I am a miserable man! Who will rescue me?
25a	Thanks be to God, through Jesus Christ our Lord!
25b	So therefore I myself serve the law of God with my mind
25c	but with my flesh [I serve] the law of sin.
8:1	So there is now no condemnation. . . .
2	For the law of the Spirit of life has set me free. . . .

7:25bc clearly mars the flow of thought. That 8:1 also disturbs it is not quite so clear. Since *katekrinen* appears in v. 3 and *katakrima* in v. 1, one might infer that the motif of condemnation frames the unit. However, the words appear to be used in somewhat different senses: in 8:3 *katekrinen* refers to God's action vis-a-vis sin, whereas in v. 1 *katakrima* refers to the divine Judge's definitive, negative verdict on human life, especially as it has been portrayed in the preceding verses. Moreover, and more important, conceptually v. 1 stands like Melchizedek—without antecedent or successor (despite the *gar* at the beginning). One suspects that once 7:25bc was inserted, a sensitive copiest realized that a transition from 7:25c to 8:2 was impossible (because of the *gar* in v. 2), and so introduced v. 1, with an eye on *katekrinen* in v. 3, and perhaps on *katakrima* in 5:18 as well. In any case, the difficulties of the transitions from one clause to another are so great that one should not base the interpretation of vv. 2-4 on the present connection with v. 1. Michel's proposal that v. 1 originally followed v. 2 simply underlines the difficulty without solving it.[6]

Whereas the beginning of our paragraph is somewhat uncertain, the end is clearly seen in v. 11. Not only does v. 12 begin afresh with "so therefore" *(ara oun),* but vv. 5-11 develop the theme of the concluding phrase of v. 4. Moreover, vv. 10-11 give an eschatological outlook to Christian existence, so that vv. 2-11 are a kind of resumé of Pauline theology, as is Rom 5:1-11. It will be clear that our study of vv. 2-4 cannot ignore the rest of the paragraph.

Nor can we ignore what Paul had just written, for there are several links between our passage and chap. 7.[7] (a) Commentators point out that the liberation mentioned in v. 2 appears to pick up the theme of 7:1-6—the somewhat awkward analogy of the woman who, on the death of the husband, is "free from the law" (*eleuthera estin apo tou nomou* 7:3; cf. *ēleutherōsen me apo tou nomou tes hamartias kai tou thanatou* 8:2). Because of this connection, 7:7-25 is sometimes called an excursus.[8] Were 7:7-25 a true excursus, however, one would scarcely expect links between it and our passage; yet *ho nomos tēs hamartias kai thanatou* clearly picks up *nomos hamartias* of 7:23.[9] (b) Moreover, 8:7 speaks of the "law of God" as does 7:22, and the motif of "inhabiting" appears in 8:9-11 (*oikein, enoikein* resp.) and in 7:18,20 (*enoiken, oikein,* resp.). (c) Similarly, the question, "Who will rescue me?" (7:24) is answered in 8:2. The liberation theme of 8:2 was already announced in 6:18, 20-22, where Paul writes rhetorically about being liberated from sin, enslaved to righteousness. (d) The phrase "in Christ Jesus" (8:2), whether it is adjectival or adverbial,[10] takes up a theme which first appeared in 6:11.[11] Indeed, the whole of chap. 6 is an exposition of what it means to be "in Christ Jesus" through participation in his death. Assuming that 8:1 is a gloss, after 6:23 "in Christ Jesus" does not appear again until 8:2. One might even say that had Paul not first expounded this theme in chap. 6, the phrase might well have been only partly intelligible to the Roman readers, whom Paul had not taught personally, when they came to 8:2.

In sum, Rom 8:2-4 gathers up various themes and connects them with motifs in adjacent chapters.

II

It is apparent that the sentence which begins at v. 3 is extremely awkward. We expect Paul, having written "for what the law was unable to do . . ." to continue with something like "God did by sending his own Son . . . through whom he condemned sin. . . ." Instead, the sentence appears to begin all over, thus turning the initial clause into an anacolouthon in the nominative (or accusative) absolute.

On closer inspection, it appears that one reason for this awkwardness is that Paul incorporates a traditional phrase, which Schweizer classified as one of the "Sendungsformeln"—early Christian sentences which formulate a christology in terms of God's sending of his Son (pre-existence being assumed).[12] The exact wording of the traditional material is difficult to recover.

It is instructive, however, to compare our passage with Galatians 4.

Galatians	*Romans*
when the fulness of time came	what the law was unable to do . . .
God sent out his Son	God having sent his Son
born of woman	in the likeness of sinful flesh
born under the law	and to deal with sin
	condemned sin in the flesh
in order that he might redeem	in order that the right
	requirement of the law
those under the law	might be fulfilled in us, etc.

It appears that we have a pattern of thought: God sent his Son in order that . . . might be achieved for the human situation. "In the likeness of sinful flesh" in Rom 8:4 has its functional equivalent in "born of woman," etc. in Gal 4:4. That is, in both cases, the qualifying phrases interpret the "sending" in terms that link it specifically with the immediate conceptual context.[13] (Moreover, *en homoiōmati sarkos hamartias* in Rom 8:3 should be compared with *en homoiōmati anthrōpōn genomenos* in Phil 2:7; in Romans Paul uses "flesh of sin" because this is the theme of the context, whereas the hymn in Philippians was concerned with the movement from equality with God to humanness.) The pattern is linked to its context also by the introductory phrases. Accordingly, in Galatians Paul wrote of "the fulness of time" because the context concerned the maturation of the heir *(eph' hoson chronon . . . to plērōma tou chronou),* and in Romans he emphasized the incapacity of the law to deal with sin and flesh, the theme of the previous chapter.

I have deliberately written of a "pattern" instead of a tradition (apart from a possible "sending-formulation") because I doubt whether a fixed tradition can be recovered here. Paulsen, however, has suggested that Paul used a tradition which itself had been expanded before it reached him. That is, first came the "sending-formula," then the addition of the purpose clause.[14] There is simply not enough firm evidence to warrant such a conclusion. Indeed, precisely the evidence he cites—namely Dahl's compilation of phrases which suggest a "teleological scheme" characterized by a christological statement + a soteriological purpose clause[15]—suggests a pattern more than a two-stage pre-Pauline tradition. It is better, therefore, to regard the purpose clause here as Paul's own, though it is quite possible that he followed a pattern of early Christian preaching in formulating such a clause. A pattern which is traditional is not yet a tradition—a more or less fixed formulation.

In fact, Paul appears to be following a more extended pattern, as the parallel sequence of motifs in Romans 8 and Galatians 4 suggests:

Galatians 4	*Romans* 8
the sending of God's Son	the sending of God's Son
soteriological result	soteriological result
	life by the Spirit
sons of God	sons of God
Abba	Abba
heirs	heirs, fellow-heirs with Christ

Only in these passages does Paul refer to "Abba." It is likely that he is reusing his own pattern of thought, rather than following one common to Hellenistic Jewish Christianity. What Paul has done in Romans 8, then, is to appropriate a traditional way of speaking about God's Son, as well as to rework his own pattern of thought.

Whereas Matt 5:17 has Jesus say that he did not come to abolish the law but to fulfill it, Paul says that God's Son was sent so that Christians might fulfill its *dikaiōma*. Paul never says that Jesus fulfilled the law or its *dikaiōma*, as Markus Barth clearly implies.[16]

III

When we begin to analyze the argument of our passage, we note first that it consists of two sentences, each of which makes its own point, so that either of them could stand alone. On the surface, the logic of neither requires the other. Yet they arc linked; the *gar* in v. 3 clearly implies that what is said in v. 2 is the result of what is said in v. 3. In other words, the liberation "from the law of sin and death" follows from God's condemnation of "sin in the flesh." Understanding the argument requires us to grasp the relationship between the act of God in Christ *(katekrinen)* and the act of the Spirit in persons *(eleutherōsen)*. At first glance, a connecting link in the argument appears to be missing. Moreover, the second sentence contains its own stated result of God's action—the fulfillment of *to dikaiōma tou nomou* in those who live by the Spirit. This suggests that being emancipated by the Spirit and living by the Spirit are intimately linked. To live by the Spirit is to be freed from the law of sin and death. This is clear enough. The "missing link" is a phrase that would connect the sending of the Son (to condemn sin) and the sending of the Spirit. Paul evidently assumed that this did not need to be stated explicitly. The third thing, however, is more problematic: How is the "fulfillment" of *to dikaiōma tou nomou* related to the emancipation from "the law of sin and death?", and how, in turn, is this related to "what the law could not do"?

A. Our passage initiates a discussion of the Spirit, which includes the subsequent paragraph (vv. 12-17). Moreover, the end of the first paragraph (v. 11) mentions the "vivification" of the mortal body through the Spirit; the next (vv. 12-17) also ends with the same theme, now expressed as "glorification." The next paragraph (vv. 18-30) develops this motif by linking the glorification of the Christian with the liberation of all creation; the paragraph begins and ends with the note of *doxa* (also the last word in v. 17; see v. 18, 19, 30; also 21). The peroration (vv. 31-39) follows. In other words v. 3 initiates the discussion of Christian existence, carefully constructed by linking terms. This suggests that v. 2 functions as a topic sentence, and that vv. 3-30 are its exposition. If this is the case, then v. 2 states the whole theme in a nutshell. Therefore clarity with regard to v. 2 is crucial.

The heart of the matter lies in Paul's uses of the term *nomos* in our passage (and in v. 7):

v. 2a *ho nomos tou pneuma tēs zōēs en Christō Iēsou*
    2b *ho nomos tēs hamartias kai tou thanatou*
    3   *ho nomos*
    4   *to dikaiōma tou nomou*
    7   *ho nomos tou theou*

Vv. 3 and 7 clearly refer to the revelation of God in Scripture, the Torah, and v. 4 also has this in view, though with a particular nuance. The crucial question is whether v. 2a also refers to the Torah.

Recently, Lohse[17] has insisted that this is the case. He admits that in 7:21 Paul uses *nomos* in a general sense, "I find it to be a law that when I will the good, evil is present to me." Nonetheless, he argues that in chap. 7 Paul repeatedly writes of *nomos* because he is presenting the human situation under law, be it that of the Jews under the Torah or that of the gentiles under their own "law." Not even Paul's reference to "another law" in one's members refers to a law other than the Torah, but to the same law. "It contains the will of God and is therefore *nomos theou;* but because there has developed a destructive relation between sin and law, the law is always *nomos hamartias* for the unredeemed person." Therefore *ho nomos tēs hamartias kai tou thanatou* in 8:2 expresses not what the law in itself is, but what it has become for the unredeemed self. However, where the Spirit creates life, there the law is "the law of the Spirit of life." Correct as Lohse may be in saying that "Paul the Christian has by no means become indifferent to the law," and that Paul believes his understanding of the law restores it to its true original meaning as witness to justification by faith (p. 287, 283, resp.), one must dissent from

Lohse's interpretation of Rom 8:2. In fact, Lohse's intent is better served by a different interpretation of this verse.

Even more drastic are the assertions of von der Osten-Sacken.[18] He not only identifies "the law of sin and death" with the Torah, but also argues that the "other law" in 7:23 which fights against the law which the self affirms is really the same law—the Torah. This is because, he claims, the willing of the good (Torah) itself does evil, because the Ego covets while willing not to covet. Fundamental to this position is the view that Paul never speaks of the law as such but only in relation to the self, so that the law changes as the self decides for or against the gospel. This manifests existentialism's penchant for refusing to speak of anything save in relation to the deciding self.

Nor is Käsemann's interpretation (see *An die Römer, ad loc.*) finally satisfying; even though he rightly sees that *nomos* in v. 2 is used in an extended sense, he still insists that one is supposed to think of the Torah at the same time. True, Paul does not yet think of the famed *tertius usus legis;* true also is the observation that "the law of the Spirit" is "the Spirit itself, understood according to its ruler-function in the domain of Christ." Not true is that the Spirit separates one "from the irreparably perverted law of Moses," a conviction in which Paul is said to agree with the enthusiasts. Where does Paul ever speak of something bad that has befallen the Torah in such a way as to pervert it? Both Lohse's and Käsemann's interpretations come too close to answering Paul's question, "Did the good [the law] become death for me?" with a Yes! Paul, however, answered *mē genoito!* (7:13). In commenting on this verse, Käsemann correctly writes, "Paul was no antinomian. . . . The law in its truth does not belong together with sin and death. Nonetheless it has been misused by the power of sin, which always perverts the good, and now achieves the opposite of what is intended."

In fact, when we look at the verbs which state the human plight, we find that their subject is never the law but always sin. Law is involved, but always as a rather passive instrument, as something that, as a counterweight to sin, has been neutralized—or as 8:3 says, "it has been weakened" and so is ineffective. Note the following:

7:7   Is the law sin? By no means! For I would not have known sin except through the law *(dia nomou)*.

7:8   Sin, taking opportunity, through the commandment *(dia tēs entoles)* wrought . . . all coveting.

7:11 Sin, taking opportunity through the commandment *(dia tēs entolēs)* deceived me and through it *(di' autēs)* killed me.

7:13 Sin, through the good *(dia tou agathou,* vis., law) wrought death for me so that sin might be surpassingly sinful through the commandment *(dia tēs entolēs)*.

The law is, and remains, the law of God—holy; and the commandment is just, holy and good (7:13). Rom 7:7-25 implies that Paul's gospel is not accurately characterized by the slogan "freedom from the law." It is freedom from sin and death that is at the center. What is finally unsatisfying about Käsemann's interpretation is that it does not appear to represent adequately Paul's passion to indict sin by vindicating the law itself.

Paul achieves this by speaking of sin as a power; it is almost "personified." Sin is not something that one does, a transgression; rather, sin is something that does something to the doer. The coming of the commandment stimulated sin, until then inert ("dead," 7:8), so that it came to life and the self "died"—became subject to death. This is how the commandment, designed for life, was discovered to lead instead to death (7:7). How is it possible for things to turn out this way? Why cannot a law which is holy (7:13) and spiritual (7:14), or a commandment which is just, holy and good, produce the life it is designed to produce?

Rom 7:14 gives two answers, each interpreting the other: "I am fleshly" and "I am sold under sin." Vv. 15-23 explicate this startling assertion. Sin is domiciled in the self *(he oikousa en emoi hamartia,* 7:17,20). What resides in the self is not the good, but this tyrannical power.[19] If the good were inherent (even if, like sin, it were at first "dead"), hearing the law would activate it, so that one could achieve the life-giving good which the law intends. The law would then be an activator of the good, and self-actualization would be salvific. But the good does not reside in the self: what resides there is sin. It does not reside in the mind or the will, but in the flesh. Paul does not equate flesh and sin (though 8:3 comes close to it); rather, sin as a power resides in flesh, a domain, a field of force operating through one's body and its impulses. To be "fleshly" *(sarkinos)* is to have one's life controlled by the impulses, the power structure of the phenomenal which, by Paul's definition, stands over against the spiritual as a competing field of force. In short, for Paul the self never hears the law at ground zero, so to speak, as a neutral, free to achieve what is required. Only persons already involved with sin hear the law. For Paul sin is more powerful than even the holy law of God because sin resides in the self; it is already there when the law appears, so that it is in a position to pervert and thwart even the good which one intends. So consistent is this that Paul can write of "another law" in one's organs, one which is not only at war with the law of the mind but which actually wins ("making me captive to the law of sin which is in my members," 7:23). As a result, the self is victimized, so that the intended good is perverted into the unintended evil (6:19). It is not to evade responsibility that Paul writes, "so it is no longer I that achieves it [evil] but the sin domiciled in me that does" (7:20), but to emphasize as relentlessly as possible the compulsory power of sin. Vis-a-vis this situation, no law, not even God's holy law, is able to extricate the self. It is not the law of Moses which is "irreparably perverted" but doing. So powerful is sin operating through the flesh that it has vitiated the power of the law (8:3).

Having explored the human situation as Paul portrays it, we can now return to our point of departure—8:2. "The law of sin and death" is not the law of God in its relation to the unredeemed self, but "the law of sin" in the members (7:23) which opposes the law of God. "The law of sin" is a structure of power, which one inevitably obeys. It is not really a matter of "the bondage of the will" but of the bondage of the self which is free enough to will but not free enough to achieve what is willed.

Over against this structure of enslaving power, liberation has occurred by means of a superior power—the Spirit. To make clear that the resolution coincides precisely with the portrayed dilemma, Paul coins the phrase "the law of the Spirit of life in Christ Jesus." It is not really correct to say that he could have omitted "law" in both clauses in v. 2, as Friedrich suggested,[20] for that would not make explicit that the Spirit too is a "law"—a structure of reality, of power, which governs life because one "obeys" it. Even more misleading is it to call this law "religion"[21] for it is not a matter of one religion over against another. When Paul writes of the law of the Spirit liberating from the law of sin and death, it is clear that he assumes that there is no such thing as an autonomous self, but only a self in obedience to a structure of reality, of power. This is why he can go on to write of "existing" *(ontes)* or "living" *(peripatousin)* according to flesh or according to Spirit (8:4, developed in vv. 5-8).

B. In probing the argument of v. 2, we have already dealt with 3a—the flesh's weakening of the law. We have also laid the basis for understanding the divine action as stated here—condemnation of sin in the flesh. It is the sin domiciled in the flesh (see Note 4) that is condemned. In order to make that possible, the Son was sent "in the likeness of sinful flesh"—*en homoiōmati sarkos hamartias,* clearly meaning identification with the human condition, not mere similarity. Had the Son been only "like" flesh, he could not have condemned the sin "in the flesh," precisely where Paul had located the problem. Had the Son not participated in this kind of flesh, the "condemnation" would not have been liberating; it could only have exposed even more powerfully the human dilemma, so that the net result of knowing about such a Son would, like hearing the law, have only made one conscious of sin (3:20). This formulation of the radical identification of the Son with the full depths of the human condition is similar to that of 2 Cor 5:21—"him who knew no sin he made sin for our sakes. . . ." Christian theology, and especially Christian piety, has found it exceedingly difficult to follow Paul here because of the doctrine of Jesus' sinlessness. Whatever one may think about Jesus' sinlessness, Paul's formulations move on a different plane. They do not have in view the question of whether Jesus committed sins but whether the Son participated in the human condition sufficiently to achieve that which the human dilemma required.

At least equally important is Paul's understanding of the "condemnation." Büchsel is doubtless right in saying that here verdict and execution coincide because it is God's action, and that Paul has in view the Son-event as a whole rather than a particular item in it.[22] Schlier correctly observes that Paul does not explain *how* sin was condemned by this event.[23] Still, we can infer the logic from what he says in this whole section. The power of the flesh was broken by the arrival in the flesh of the pre-existent, and hence divine, Son, and tacitly by his resurrection from the dead as well. What Paul assumes is that the Spirit is the power of the risen Christ imparted to those who are baptized. Therefore the Son's liberation from sinful flesh and death is simultaneously the basis of the believer's liberation in the present and the prototype of the future consummation of liberation. This is what Paul actually says in v. 11: the Spirit of God who resurrected Jesus from the dead dwells now in the believer (just as sin had dwelt there before); therefore he who raised Jesus from the dead will vivify also the believer's death-bound body through the Spirit which now dwells in it. Because the Spirit now resides where sin had resided, Paul can say that "the law of the Spirit of life in Christ Jesus has liberated me from the law of sin and death."

It must be emphasized that Paul does not simply say that the Spirit liberates from sin and death. For him, it is the "Spirit of life in Christ Jesus." Apparently it never occurred to him to ask whether the Spirit did or does ever do this apart from the Son-event. This is because Paul's theology is ex post facto theology—it is reasoning after the fact. In other words, it was the experience of the Spirit, which could be had only by those who believed the gospel of the Son and his cross-resurrection, that led to this understanding of things. As E. P. Sanders has shown,[24] Paul's thought did not run from dilemma to solution but the reverse. It was the experience of being in Christ by faith in what the gospel proclaimed that induced him to understand the human dilemma and its resolution as he did. Paul does not portray accurately Judaism's understanding of the human condition vis-a-vis the law any more than he represents accurately a Hellenistic gentile's attitude toward the Torah—nor does he intend to. For him, *this* emancipating power of the Spirit would not have been possible apart from the Son-event. Paul does not argue from a general understanding of the innate capacity of Spirit over flesh or sin any more than he relies on a general consideration of the innate limitations of law, any law. He assumes that divine Spirit is a more powerful field of force than flesh, sin or law because he regards the gift of the Spirit as an eschatological event.

C. The precise meaning of the purpose clause (*hina to dikaiōma tou nomou plērōthē en hēmin tois mē kata sarka peripatousin, alla kata pneuma*) is difficult to determine. Interpreters sometimes refer to Rom 13:8,10 ("he who loves the neighbor has fulfilled the law," and "love is the fulfillment of the law") and conclude that also here Paul has in mind the obligation to love as the "just requirement of the law" (RSV). Käsemann, however, warns us that Paul does not actually speak of love here. One must scrupulously avoid interpreting the clause in such a way as virtually to rewrite it.

Paul did not write *hina hēmas plēroun* (or, *prassein*) *ton nomon* ("so that we might fulfill [or do], the law", as Ridderbos implies: "the work of the Spirit consists precisely in the working out of the law in the life of believers (Rom 8:4)."[25] Nor did Paul write about *ta dikaiōmata tou nomou* ("the ordinances, or commandments, of the law"), as JB and TEV suggest ("the law's just demands" or "the commandments of the law," resp.). There is also insufficient basis for Murray to translate it as "the ordinance of the law"[26] just as it is improper for the NEB to render it "the commandment of the law," for when the LXX has this meaning in view it regularly uses the plural. Nor did the Apostle write that the *dikaiōma tou nomou* would be fulfilled *by* not living according to the flesh but by living according to the Spirit, as if the latter were a means to the former. The *mē kata sarka ktl.* phrase does not set conditions but characterizes those in whom the fulfillment occurs. In fact, Paul did not write about its fulfillment through us (*di' hēmas* either, but rather "in us." Even though Paul abandons the 1st pers. pl. in v. 4 for the 2d pers. pl. in the verses that follow, *en humin* appears too often not to color the meaning of *en hēmin* in v. 1 (see *en humin* in v. 9,10,11 [*bis*]). Moreover, the repeated use of *en emoi* and related expressions in 7:15-23 suggests that the resolution of the dilemma described there also occurs *in* us, not by or through us.[27] These considerations too point away from Rom 13:8,10, for these verses have in view something to be done, not something done in us. In other words, the passive *plerōthē* must be taken seriously—something is accomplished in us.

That which is accomplished is *to dikaiōma tou nomou*. The word *dikaiōma* has a wide range of meanings. H. W. M. van de Sandt has reported the results of his investigation of the term.[28] (a) In Greek literature, *dikaiōma* was regularly used of legal matters, but with a range of meanings. Common among them was "legal claim" or right. In the papyri it appears mostly in the plural, usually referring to legal documentations. (b) In LXX the sg. is relatively infrequent, and the plural is used often for *ḥoq(ah)*, commandment, ordinance, statute—a meaning scarcely found in the papyri. Philo and the Apostolic Fathers follow LXX usage. Van de Sandt renders Rom 8:4 as "the legal claim of the law," and thinks it refers to the obligation to love. In a subsequent article,[29] he suggests that Paul's unusual phrase reflects a rabbinic tradition of summarizing the whole law, and he appeals to the phrase *(me)qayyem kol hattorah kulah*. Paul is said to have assumed that *plēroun* was the equivalent of *kol . . . kulah*, so that "performing the whole law" was turned into "totally performing the law." This is hardly persuasive.

Paul's own usage of *dikaiōma* is uneven. It is generally acknowledged that rhetorical considerations led Paul to write *dikaiōma* instead of *dikaiōsis* or *dikaiosunē* in Rom 5:16 (the surrounding terms all end in . . . *ma*). The same considerations evidently induced him to speak of the *dikaiōma* of the one man (Christ) over against the *paraptōma* of Adam in 5:18. The RSV therefore translates *dikaiōma* in v. 16 as "justification," and as "act of righteousness" in v. 18. In 2:16 Paul writes about the gentiles observing *ta dikaiōmata tou theou*, a phrase consistent with LXX usage. In 1:32 he writes of *to dikaiōma* which gentiles know. Here the RSV and NEB render it as "decree," JB as "verdict" and Barrett (*op.cit.*) as "God's righteous ordinance." The phrase *to dikaiōma tou nomou*, however, is found only here.

So we are thrown back on the context of 8:4. What has happened "in us"? The power of sin and death, which operated in the flesh, has been displaced by the power of the Spirit. One power structure has replaced another. Now one is no longer captive of the law of sin in one's members but is subject to a new order, that of the Spirit. Now willing the good is no longer thwarted by the "other law," for one has been emancipated from it. The mindset of those in the Spirit, or those in whom the Spirit resides, leads to life (8:5-9). In short, what the Spirit accomplishes is the *dikaiōma tou nomou*, the rightness, the right intent of the law—life. Paul expresses the achievement of the Spirit in this difficult phrase about *law* because so much of his foregoing discussion was concerned with the incapacity of the law to make good in the situation of the self without the Spirit.[30]

At the same time, Paul does not speak simply of fulfilling the law, for that would obscure the qualitative difference which he sees between the old situation and the new. Nor does he speak of fulfilling the "law of Christ" (Gal 6:2), for that might imply that Christ's law has replaced that of Moses, as if one body of precepts displaced another.[31]

The fulfillment of the intent of the law is not the goal of Christian doing but its basis. This is not because the law has been internalized (Jer 31:31 is not in the background) but because the Spirit has been internalized. It now resides where sin had settled in. That is where the problem lay. For Paul, the Spirit achieves what the spiritual law is really all about. The Spirit achieves this in those whose relation to God is made right by faith, apart from obedience to the law—that is, whose relation to God is not the result of successful law-observance. Those who believe are baptized into Christ, and so belong to him[32] because they now exist in his domain, and hence become recipients of the Spirit through which the risen Christ exerts his power on earth.

Because the right intent of the law is fulfilled, on the one hand, and because the consummation of what was inaugurated by the sending of God's Son is not yet consummated, on the other, Paul summons his readers to live by the Spirit. For Paul, one always lives "according to . . . *(kata)*" something, expressed in chap. 8 as the alternative of "Spirit" or "flesh." To live "according to" something is to heed it, to be determined by it and hence to obey it, to live within its jurisdiction. Persons dominated by sin and flesh simply cannot live "according to the Spirit" nor can they attain what the spiritual law intends. Because the law is spiritual, the life of Spirit-determined persons accords with the real intent of the law. It is not enhanced and perfected Christian doing that brings about the fulfillment of the *dikaiōma tou nomou* but the Spirit. Because the law is spiritual, being determined by the Spirit necessarily coincides with the fulfillment of the *dikaiōma tou nomou*.

Paul's exposition of the Spirit and the law, like his earlier discussion of faith and the law, could have ended with the same phrase: "we uphold the law" *(nomon histanomen* 3:31).

IV

In this context, the import of our passage for Paul's ethics must be left implicit, save for three brief comments.

First, Paul's understanding of the Spirit and the law clearly suggests that he did not regard the Spirit as a factor which enabled Christian persons to be more moral than non-Christian Jews. He himself had written that as a Pharisee he was "blameless" with regard to the righteousness of the law (Phil 3:6). The function of the Spirit was not to make people morally "better" but to emancipate them from the tyranny of sin which resided in the self. As noted, he discovered this about the self only as a result of being in the Spirit.

Second, the ongoing struggle between Spirit and flesh is precisely not what the NEB makes it—a tension between one's higher and lower nature (see the translation of Rom 8:5-8). Rather, it is the struggle between the power of the New Age and that of the Old, which continues until the End.

Third, what makes our passage foundational for Paul's ethics is what it reveals about his understanding of the doer, the moral agent. Getting his readers to reconsider that theme may well be Paul's perennial contribution to ethical reflection.

NOTES

[1]Although *se* (A BG 1739 it sy^p Tert Ambrst Ephr *et. al.*) is the more difficult reading, *me* (as the majority of witnesses reads) is probably to be preferred. *hēmas (Ps Marcion Or* Sy^{palbo}) clearly anticipates the *en hēmin* of v. 4. However, it is more likely that *me* in v. 1 resumes the *me* of 7:24 than that Paul should have switched to *se* for no clear reason. The observation that with "you" Paul moves to proclamation is not a reason, as Fuchs claims, but a necessary consequence of accepting this reading. Ernst Fuchs, *Die Freiheit des Glaubens* (BEvTh 14; Munich: Kaiser, 1949) 84. Fuchs is followed by Käsemann, *An die Römer* (Tübingen: J. C. B. Mohr [Paul Siebeck] 1973) and Heinrich Schlier, *Der Römerbrief* (Freiburg-Basel-Wien: Herder, 1977), 237-8. Cranfield sees that the appearance of *me* is quite unexpected, but having chosen it, concludes that Paul wanted to make sure that each reader applied the point to himself personally. This is scarcely satisfactory. C. E. B. Cranfield, *The Epistle to the Romans* (ICC; Edinburgh: T.&T. Clark, 1975) I 376-7. Barrett follows Origen in leaving it out altogether, thus turning the statement into a gnomic aorist: "Spirit liberates. . . ." *The Epistle to the Romans* (New York: Harper and Row, 1957) 153 n. 1. This is the least convincing solution. Curiously, Peter von der Osten-Sacken sees the sufficient reason for reading *me*—unity between 8:2 and chap 7—but still cannot decide the matter. *Römer 8 als Beispiel paulinischer Soteriologie* (FRLANT 112; Göttingen: Vandenhoeck & Ruprecht, 1975) 146 n. 11.

[2]Literally, "flesh of sin" *(sarkos hamartias),* analogous to "flesh of evil" in 1QS 11:9.

[3]The omission of this phrase by a few mss. is probably accidental, a case of homoioteleuton. More important is whether *peri hamartias* is an allusion to Christ as "sin offering" because the phrase is so used in the LXX (e.g., Lev. 9:2; 14:31; Ps. 39:7; Isa. 53:10). The NEB ("and as a sacrifice for sin") represents this interpretation, which goes back to Origen; so also, e.g., ASV and Käsemann. It seems better, however, to take the phrase more loosely as "to deal with sin," as do RSV and Cranfield, for instance.

[4]Instead of taking *en sarki* with *katekrinen,* as Cranfield does for instance, it is better to take it with *hamartian*; i.e., not "in the flesh condemned sin" but "condemned sin the flesh."

[5]So Rudolf Bultmann, "Glossen im Römerbrief," in *Exegetica,* Erich Dinkler ed. (Tübingen: J. C. B. Mohr [Paul Siebeck], 1967) 278-9 (orig. published *ThLZ* 72 [1947] 197-202). Bultmann is followed by Käsemann, *ad loc.* but rejected by Cranfield.

[6]Otto Michel, *Der Brief an die Römer* (KEK; Göttingen: Vandenhoeck & Ruprecht, 1955), *ad loc.*

[7]This was seen also by H. W. M. van de Sandt, "Research into Rom. 8,4a: The Legal Claim of the Law," *Bijdragen. Tijdschrift voor Filosofie en Theologie* 37 (1976), 253.

[8]Barrett, 154, calls 7:7-25 an excursus, as does Schlier, 237.

[9]The recurrence of the same phrase in 7:25b drops out of consideration if it is a gloss, as has been judged here.

[10]Schlier proposed a third possibility—that it modifies the whole phrase that precedes it.

[11]Perhaps the first occurence of the motif "in Christ" is Rom 5:10 (sōthēsometha en tē zōe autou); what the subsequent paragraph emphasizes is what occurred through (dia) Christ, not in (en) him.

[12]"Zum religionsgeschichtlichen Hintergrund der 'Sendungsformel' Gal 4:4f.; Rm 8:3f.; I Joh 4:9," ZNW 57 (1966) 199-210, esp. 207. The possibility that "sent his Son" was a more or less fixed formula was discussed already in 1903 in the pioneering study by Alfred Seeberg, Der Katechismus der Urchristenheit. This is now reprinted in ThB 26 (Munich: Kaiser, 1966); see 58-62.

[13]This observation carries out the suggestion by Henning Paulsen, Überlieferung und Auslegung in Römer 8 (WMANT 43; Neukirchen: Neukirchener Verlag, 1974) 41.

[14]Op. cit., 43-44.

[15]Nils A. Dahl, "Formgeschichtliche Beobachtungen zur Christusverkündigung in der Gemeindepredigt" in Neutestamentliche Studien für Rudolf Bultmann (BZNW 21; Berlin: de Gruyter, 1954) 7. Werner Kramer used Dahl to speak of a "splinter" of a pempein formula which appears more fully in John. Christos Kyrios Gottessohn (Zurich: Zwingli Verlag, 1963) 111-12. For relying on John, he was criticized by Klaus Wengst, Christologische Formeln und Lieder des Urchristentums (SNT 7; Gütersloh: Gerd Mohn, 1973²) 59 n. 22. (Kramer, it should be noted, regards the purpose clause as Pauline.)

[16]Jesus the Jew (Atlanta: John Knox Press, 1978), 19-20.

[17]Eduard Lohse, "ho nomos tou pneumatos tēs zōes. Exegetische Anmerkungen zu Röm 8,2" in Neues Testament und christliche Existenz (H. Braun Festschrift). H. D. Betz and L. Schottroff, eds. (Tübingen: J. C. B. Mohr [Paul Siebeck] 1973) 279-88. So also Kurt Niederwimmer, Der Begriff der Freiheit im Neuen Testament (Berlin: Töpelmann, 1966) 172,192.

[18]Op. cit., 210-11, 226-8.

[19]One can scarcely insist too vigorously that Paul did not write what common English translations (AV, RV, RSV, NEB, ASV) make him write—"nothing good dwells in me." Paul is not answering the question, How much good is in me? but rather, Does the good reside in the self? The consequences of this persistent mistranslation have been enormous.

[20]Gerhard Friedrich, "Das Gesetz des Glaubens. Röm 3,27," ThLZ 10 (1954), 407. Friedrich's conclusion is all the more remarkable because he has seen clearly that Paul deliberately takes up the phrasing of 7:23.

[21]So Barrett, op. cit, 155. Unavoidably, he must then regard "the law of sin and death" as the law of Moses, a religion, a way of life (his phrases) which has been replaced by another religion.

[22]Friedrich Büchsel, katakrinō, Kittel, ThWB III 593.

[23]Op. cit, ad loc.

[24]E. P. Sanders, *Paul and Palestinian Judaism* (Philadelphia: Fortress Press, 1977), 474-5, passim.

[25]Herman Ridderbos, *Paul* (Grand Rapids: Eerdmans, 1977; Dutch orig. 1966), 283. So also Andrea van Dülmen, *Die Theologie des Gesetzes bei Paulus* (SBM 5; Stuttgart: Verlag Katholischer Bibelwerk, 1968) 81 n. 38, 122, *passim*. She appears to see the tension between this view and the implication of *plērōthē* when she says that the passive suggests that the fulfillment depends not so much on one's own effort as on the life in the Spirit, 123.

[26]John Murray, *The Epistle to the Romans* (New Int. Comm.; Grand Rapids: Eerdmans, 1959; 1 vol. ed., 1977), *ad loc*. So also J. A. Ziesler, *The Meaning of Righteousness in Paul* (SNTSMS 20; Cambridge: Cambridge University Press, 1972) 204.

[27]Egon Brandenburger has called attention to the importance of "spatial" language in Paul, especially in Rom 5—8. *Fleisch und Geist* (WMANT 29; Neukirchen: Neukirchener Verlag, 1968), 54-57, 197-216. Brandenburger is concerned primarily with the relation of Paul's concepts to that of dualistic Wisdom in Philo.

[28]*Op. cit.* Essentially the same conclusions were reached by Schrenk, Kittel, *ThWB* II 223-7.

[29]"An Explanation of Rom. 8.4a." *Bijdragen. Tijdschrift voor Filosofie en Theologie* 37 (1976) 361-78.

[30]It is doubtful whether Paul means that the "new order" of the Spirit had previously revealed itself in the inner self's desire to do the will of God but was unfulfilled, as van Dülmen claims. *Op. cit.*, 119-20.

[31]This was seen also by C. H. Dodd, *"ENNOMOS CHRISTOY"* in *Studia Paulina* (de Zwaan Festschrift) (Haarlem: Bohn, 1953), 102-3.

[32]Niederwimmer expressed it aptly: *"Im* Herrn sein heisst *des* Herrn sein" ("To be *in* the Lord is to *belong* to the Lord"). *Op. cit*, 189.

ROMANS 10:4 AND THE "END" OF THE LAW

PAUL W. MEYER

PRINCETON THEOLOGICAL SEMINARY, PRINCETON, NEW JERSEY 08540

I

Paul defined the relationship of Christianity with Judaism and in this way gave it a structure which was never subsequently modified in spite of Marcion's attempts to do so, and so far as can be seen could never be called in question without shaking the very foundations of Christianity.

MAURICE Goguel used these words a third of a century ago to comment on the historical significance of the apostle Paul for Christian origins.[1] One will of course not hear them today quite as Goguel wrote them. He described the cause for which Paul struggled as "Christian universalism freed from all ritualism." When he varied this terminology to say that Paul "cut the gospel free from the chains with which Judaism was in danger of strangling it,"[2] he was skirting close to that equation of Judaism with "ritualism" which has become unacceptable today on grounds both historical and theological. And what he meant by "universalism" seems to have been a capacity on the part of the early Christian movement to adapt to its future in Greek culture rather than any fruition of its legacy from its Jewish past. Today one will be more inclined to argue that it was Paul's view of the relation of Israel to the Gentiles that gave to his doctrine of justification its characteristic structure and shape.[3] Or, as I would prefer, one might argue a similar case with respect to Paul's Christology: that he so defined the meaning of Jesus as the Christ for the new movement as to clarify for it at the same time its relation to the Judaism from which it emerged and so contributed to its identity; or that it was Paul's definition of the relation of Christianity to Judaism that gave his peculiar signature to his exposition of the meaning of Christ for the church. But all these are but variations that confirm the truth of Goguel's remark, not as an axiom settled for all time but as a heuristic proposition to be tested as one continues to explore the absolutely fundamental place

59

occupied in Paul's letters by the matter of Christianity's relation to Judaism. Goguel rightly saw that in one way or another this theme, and the problem of the right interpretation of it, lies at "the very foundations of Christianity."

Nowhere are these themes more incontestably intertwined than in Romans 9-11, which is at the same time the one place in Paul's letters where the historical horizons of his theology become most apparent, where he grapples most directly with the question whether God's purposes and judgments are sustained in the history of his people or whether that history shows God's word instead to have failed (9:6). Here we come, in other words, as close as Paul himself will allow us, to the question of God's control over the course of human events or lack thereof, in appearance and in reality. Yet, just because of the presence of those other themes that run through the rest of Romans—justification and the righteousness of God, the meaning of Christ, and the relation of Jew and Greek, of Israel and the church—these chapters do not yield to being isolated from their epistolary and historical context and treated as if they constituted an independent treatise upon "salvation history" or were the composition of a "theology of history."[4] Their most adequate interpretation is likely to continue to be located in full-length interpretations of the letter, i.e. in commentaries on Romans.[5] For in these the interpreter will remain to some extent accountable, if not in practice then at least in principle, to the combinations and conjunctions, the ordering and disposition, the arrangements and sequences of thought that were Paul's own at the time of his writing. This will not preclude the selection of some discrete aspect, even some minute detail, for separate discussion. But it will serve as a reminder of that constant reciprocal bearing of the whole upon the part and of the minute part upon the understanding of the whole which it has seemed always in my association with Lou Silberman to be his special genius to keep before the human interpreter.

II

One verse in which these problems of interpretation come to a head is Rom 10:4: *telos gar nomou christos eis dikaiosunēn panti tō pisteuonti.* This is variously translated as "For Christ is the end of the law, that every one who has faith may be justified" (RSV); "For Christ ends the law and brings righteousness for everyone who has faith" *(NEB);* "But now the Law has come to an end with Christ, and everyone who has faith may be justified" *(JB);* "For Christ, by realizing righteousness for every believer, proves to be the end of the law" (C. K. Barrett).[6]

The passage is a well-known, not to say notorious, crux primarily because of the lexical possibilities available for *telos* ("end"). Here they are mainly two: "termination" (as in Luke 1:33) or final state or "outcome." In this latter sense the word may, depending on context, refer to a "goal" intended in advance (1 Tim 1:5) or to a "consequence" or outcome reached quite apart from any deliberate intent on the part of the one who reaches it (Rom 6:21-22).[7] In the alternative translations just quoted *telos* is uniformly rendered by "end" not simply because the translators have chosen the first of these options but also because it preserves some of the ambivalence of the Greek term. It will be noted that no such uniformity marks the very diverse treatments given the prepositional phrase at the end of the verse.[8] The *RSV* rewords it with a purpose clause. The *NEB* and *JB* appear to think rather of result, though for the *JB* this result is clearly potential, a resulting possibility. Barrett treats the phrase as an expression of purpose or goal in his discussion, but he translates it as a modal parallel to the main clause as though it were a participial construction in Greek.[9]

Given these difficulties in the verse as it stands, it is no surprise that the major grounds for preferring one interpretation over another are taken from the context or related considerations. The crucial decisions are made elsewhere and this part of Paul's text is in fact and in practice understood within and from a wider whole. We need briefly to examine this context before we consider just how some of these decisions are made.

There is first of all the context preceding 10:4 and the issue where the present unit of Paul's argument may properly be said to begin. Rom 10:1, inasmuch as it makes a personal affirmation of Paul's concern for Israel and his identification with her, seems at first sight to be quite parallel to 9:1-5 and so also to be making a fresh start. If that is the case, 9:30-33, beginning as it does with the rhetorical question "What shall we say, then?," is a brief aside or interlude. But Paul does not this time follow the question by formulating a conclusion that might have been drawn from his own preceding argument only then to repudiate such a conclusion as wrong ("God forbid") and to go on to correct it, as he does in 9:14 and often. The "conclusion" here is supplied by Paul as a legitimate one that needs only further explanation and elaboration, which the next question and its reply in v 32 proceed to furnish. Moreover, this "conclusion" does not clearly and easily follow from the preceding argument at all, and Paul's explanation of it is clearly continued in 10:2-3. It turns out that the personal asseveration does not then open a new argument but is evoked by Paul's own statement about Israel in 9:32, "They have stumbled over the stumbling stone." Thus many commentators take 9:30 to be the beginning of a major section that runs through 10:21.[10]

The opening sentences of this section in 9:30-31 are on any reading of Paul's argument a remarkable statement. By skillful rhetorical use of "antithetical parallelism"[11] they underscore the presence of an historical paradox crying out to be made in some measure intelligible. It is important for just that reason not "to rewrite Paul's sentence for him according to our own notions of what he ought to have said."[12] What Paul writes is: "Gentiles, who did not pursue righteousness, (nonetheless) achieved righteousness, to be sure one that comes from faith; but Israel on the other hand, while (or though) pursuing a law of righteousness, did not attain to law." By very wide agreement among commentators, the language is unmistakably that of the race-course: achievement and attainment here are matters of catching up with the pursued quarry or rival or arriving at the aimed-for goal. The tripping of the next verse merely sustains the figure. "A law of righteousness"[13] must in this context have reference to a law that holds out the promise of righteousness in return for the effort given in its observance and pursuit. The paradox is not devoid of irony, but the irony lies in the unforeseen, in the reversal of normal expectations, and these in turn are formulated from what would have to be characterized as a Jewish rather than a Gentile perspective. The foil is provided by Gentiles who are not only indefinite (the article is absent) but also unidentified except by the trait of their non-pursuit of righteousness, just as in 2:14 they are identified simply (but twice in one verse) by their non-possession of the Torah. Of these it is said that they have achieved the *un*-sought-for goal, just as in 2:14 it was said of them that they do occasionally on their own *(physei)* and without the promptings of the Torah what it requires. To be sure, Paul adds, the righteousness these Gentiles have achieved is the sort that comes from faith. It could hardly be otherwise; their achievement of this un-sought-for goal is "apart from law," to echo 3:21. Against such a background it is then said of Israel (with what is now a modal rather than an adjectival participle) that either in spite of or alongside that very pursuit that distinguishes Jew from Gentile, of a divine instruction that Israel alone is distinguished for having and that holds out the promise of righteousness, her goal remains unattained—not the goal of the promised righteousness, it should be noted, but even more drastically the goal of the prior divine instruction. It is Torah itself that has inexplicably become the unattained goal, the destination not reached. One is compelled by such assertions to resort to the term dialectic in order to designate adequately not only the rhetoric operative here but the very notion of Torah which it conveys as well. Israel does not "have" this Torah so much as she pursues it. Israel is distinguished from the Gentiles by the pursuit of it—and distinguished from the Gentiles at the same time by the odd fact that her pursuit, unlike theirs, remains without consummation.

Normal expectations straightforwardly fulfilled are like the proverbial dead men; at least they ask no questions and demand no replies. But this unforeseen reversal is of another order. No sooner has Paul formulated it than he proceeds to try to make it intelligible with a new question and answer in v 32. But the most remarkable feature of the new verse is the simple fact that it is there at all. For by being there it shows that while vv 30-31 document the ironical reversal, in themselves they offer no word of resolution or explanation. The modal participle in *v* 31 cannot be translated "because of pursuing a law of righteousness;" like the adjectival participle in v 30, to which it corresponds, it is part of the puzzle and not its solution. The historical paradox is not caused by Israel's pursuit of the law.[14] Rather, Paul goes on, it is due in the first instance to a misunderstanding,[15] a false assumption with which the pursuit was undertaken. "Why? Because not deriving from faith, but as if derived from works" *(hoti ouk ek pisteōs all' hōs ex ergōn)*. The severe elliptical brevity of the explanation strips it down to its one basic essential, misunderstanding, but there is little doubt about Paul's meaning.[16]

Returning to the imagery of running pursuit in v 32b, Paul supplements this first accounting with the flat assertion, in language taken from Isaiah, "They have stumbled against the stone of stumbling." By at once expressly identifying the Scriptural source of this language with his usual formula "just as it is written" and offering the well-known and oft-discussed composite quotation from Isa 8:14 and 28:16 ("Behold I am laying a stone in Zion . . .") Paul takes the significant further step of implying that this unexpected outcome was no merely subjective vagary but was rooted in God's deliberate intent. If this seems to complicate Paul's explanation by reintroducing from chap. 9 the tension between divine purpose and instigation on the one hand and human response and accountability on the other, that is no more and no less than what is involved anyway in the mere appropriation of LXX terminology for "a stone of stumbling" and "a rock of offense."[17] The traditional language about such a stone combines the elements of an unavoidable obstruction and an avoidable encounter with it. Indeed the double form of the citation confirms this tension by setting alongside the offense the alternative possibility of believing trust, and assigning this equal sanction in the divine utterance. In the end, Paul's "explanation" is hardly less complex than the baffling and unexpected double reversal it was called forth to illuminate, and it is neither jarring nor surprising that the first verse of chap. 10 should consist, as we have seen, of a renewed asseveration by the apostle of his deep concern for his people and their salvation in the presence of this confounding God, both his and theirs.

It will be noted that we have left unspecified the matter of the application of the composite quotation from Isaiah. What did Paul have in mind as the stone which has been placed by God in Zion and which has confronted Israel with the alternatives of believing or stumbling? The line of thought Paul has been pursuing and the race-course imagery with which he has been working—in short, the context read on its own terms— suggests that the Torah is the rock placed by God in Zion. There is nothing in the antecedent context, in the whole of chap. 9 or all of Romans before it, to suggest anything else. Yet all seem to have missed Paul's intent; no commentary on Romans known to me departs from the unanimous opinion that for Paul this stone is Christ. There is no more striking example in the Pauline letters of a crucial exegetical decision made on grounds extrinsic to the text itself. The reason usually given for the latter interpretation is that Paul is drawing upon a tradition of early Christian use of these texts from Isa 8:14 and 28:16 which had already sufficiently established the identification of Christ as the stone so that Paul could take it for granted. Yet this argument has come under increasing attack and has, I think, been decisively undermined.[18] Otherwise, one must in order to sustain this interpretation simply read Paul as anticipating here his mention of Christ in 10:4. But this remains mere conjecture unless one makes additional assumptions: that Paul's view of Jewish reaction to the preaching of the cross (1 Cor 1:23) was already so generalized, so polarized, and so fixed, and his own thinking so exclusively Christological, that it was impossible for him to think that God would cause his people a theological and religious difficulty in any other way; or that *telos* in 10:4 means "abolishment," so that the cause of offense to the Jew is not the messianic claim of the Christians as such or the preaching of the cross but the fact that the Jew cannot accept God's abolishment of his Torah. The first assumption is refuted by chap. 9; the second falls by its own circularity. Except in the total absence of any alternatives, i.e. unless one is reduced to looking ahead because one cannot make sense of an unintelligible passage, Rom 10:4 has little evidential value for the meaning of 9:33.

If Paul makes a "new start" in 10:2-3,[19] it is a renewed attempt to shed light on just the state of affairs with which he began in 9:30-31, another try at reducing what obstinately remains a very intricate explanation to a more manageable dimension. He has no new subject in mind. This is clear from the fact that in v 3 he returns to the same verbal form (aorist third person plural) he used in 9:32; the same event or sequence of events is in view. Righteousness and justification, i.e. the question who may stand in God's presence and on what grounds, is still at stake as it was in 9:30-31. And though Paul has shifted the categories from pursuit and the failure of attainment to obedience and disobedience, the same reversal is being described. Now the foil is a deposition by Paul on behalf of his people: what distinguishes them is "zeal for God," nothing else than that eager and devoted commitment to the service of God and to living in accordance with his will and claim which elsewhere Paul alleged without apology or dissimulation to be his own proud legacy from his Jewish past (Phil 3:6). But now against that background there is the same baffling and unexpected outcome: "they did not submit to God's righteousness" (v 3). There is even something of the same dialectic as in 9:30-31, only without the complicating presence of the Gentiles it comes out much more straightforwardly: obedience, real and genuine in both its intention and its fervor, has turned out as disobedience. Why? Again the explanatory middle link in vv 2b and 3a has two sides: a passive one in a failure of recognition *(epignōsis)*,[20] a knowledge of God's righteousness that has aborted *(agnoein)*;[21] and a more active side in a contrary search to establish "one's own" righteousness.

Kuss[22] points out an important detail in the grammar of the verses we have been following, one to which we have tried to hold. Verses 2, 3, 4 (and 5 as well) all begin with the conjunction *gar* ("for"). V 2 gives the grounds for (i.e. explains) Paul's statement of involved concern by characterizing his people both positively and negatively; v 3 in turn explains v 2 by elaborating on both aspects of the analysis. V 4 next explains v 3; but how? If v 4 makes Christ God's termination of the Torah, it can "explain" as disobedience only continued adherence to law, the "zeal" of v 2 and the pursuit of 9:32; but these are not in themselves perverse for Paul. If v 4 makes Christ the termination of Torah, it can "explain" then not the main clause of v 3 but only its subordinate participle ("seeking to establish their own"), and then only on the secondary premise that there is no way for the Jew to live by Torah without seeking to establish his own righteousness. But then Paul could have spared himself all the dialectic of 9:30-10:3, just as he could have spared himself the defense of the law's holiness in 7:7-12. So to read 10:4

is to compel Paul into a simplistic antinomian position and to make unintelligible his present intricate argument. It also requires one arbitrarily to fill in an ellipsis in the verse (cf. n.8 above): "Christ is the end of the law *(as a means to)* righteousness . . ." In fact, however, Paul nowhere suggests that the way to obedience to God for the Israelite lies in abandoning the Torah. If, on the other hand, v 4 makes the crediting of righteousness to everyone who believes and trusts God the goal and intent of Torah, it explains directly and straightforwardly, without any need for supplementation by the reader out of his own baggage, why the failure to acknowledge God's righteousness and the attempt to establish one's own is an act of disobedience and defiance.

Paul's new explanation is no more simple than his earlier one. But the reader, no longer merely baffled, finds himself instead coming out into the clear on familiar Pauline terrain. In the first place, the language has become reminiscent of Phil 3:9 and the paradigmatic way Paul writes of himself there, contrasting two kinds of righteousness: one which belongs to God or comes from God as his gift and can only be recognized and acknowledged in faith, and the other which human beings strive to establish out of their own resources. But more significant than this echo of Phil 3:9 are those other passages from earlier parts of Paul's argument in Romans that now enter into and shape the recognition process. For to understand God's righteousness, to "attain to" it in faith (9:30), means also to submit to it, to acknowledge God as the one who defines righteousness as well as good and evil, truth and falsehood (3:4); it is to recognize his prerogative as well as his claim (3:6); it is to add to the knowledge of him the recognition of him as God with praise and thanksgiving (1:21); it is to believe after the manner of Abraham, trusting him to carry through what he has promised (4:21).

Indeed the coalescing of Paul's experience with his perception of his people and of his analysis of his people's experience with his own penetrates to a still deeper level. He gives here no hint whatsoever that in Israel's past the Torah was identified mistakenly, or was of demonic origin, or was corrupted in its transmission. There is no suggestion that her knowledge of God was unreal or ever diverted into idolatry and the worship of false gods. There is no indication that her zeal was half-hearted or cold, that it did not spring from genuine commitment. Yet, in spite of all that, a Torah given and "pursued" but not reached; a knowledge of God aborted in non-recognition; a zeal for God that has turned into disobedience. Where do we find ourselves if not back in Romans 7, at the heart of Paul's own experience with God's holy Torah and with the transcendent (*kath' hyperbolēn,* 7:13) capacity of sin to pervert his deepest commitment to it? "The very commandment which promised life proved to be death to me" (7:10). "I do not understand what I bring about; for it is not what I intend or desire that I put into practice, but the very thing I want to avoid" (7:15).

It was after all not only Paul's discovery of the *iustificatio impii,* of God's vindication of the sinner, in the death of Jesus (and hence of the irreconcilable contradiction between that death and justification through the law, Gal 2:21), but also, and perhaps for himself personally more importantly, this experience, interpreted in the light of the cross, of the power of sin to convert even his delight in the Torah into captivity (7:22-23) that raised to the level of an axiom in Paul's mind the conviction that no person's standing before God could be secured by observance of the law (Gal 2:16; 3:11; Rom 3:20, 28; 4:5; 11:16). Even more: in Romans 7 the holiness of God's Torah was so far beyond dispute for him that even this perverse use made of it by the power of sin to trick and to kill had to be seen as serving the divine purpose, namely to manifest the incalculable dimensions of that power. This point is made twice in 7:13, with two independent purpose clauses. (Unfortunately, the *RSV* here reduces the impact of these clauses by bringing them together and fusing them into one; worse, the *NEB* turns them into matter-of-fact result clauses, eliminating the divine purpose entirely; worst of all, the *JB* makes one a result clause but in keeping the other a purpose construction turns it into a reflexive and assigns the intent to sin itself.) Of course this simply develops a move already made in 5:21, where another purpose clause assigned a deliberate and ultimately redemptive design to the "increase" of sin by the law. The result is the most idiosyncratic feature of Paul's view of the law, the claim that, far from preserving its adherent from sin, it compounds sin.[23] Curiously, this feature has not infrequently been taken to show how far removed Paul had become from his Jewish roots; on the contrary, it shows how unshakable his attachment to Torah as God's and as gift really was.[24] And now—something completely missed in the conventional equation of the "stone" with Christ—just this peculiar but unmistakable signature of Pauline reflection and experience reappears in his backward look over Israel's corporate history when the law is identified as the "stone of stumbling" (9:32).

There is, to be sure, a difference. In Romans 7, speaking personally and for himself, Paul can thank God for a deliverance he has found in Jesus Christ. In Romans 10 and 11, speaking in solidarity with Israel, his thought can only come to rest in the future of God's irrevocable calling

(11:26, 29). But the difference in no way impugns the impartiality of God, who has treated all on the same terms and can be counted on to do so in the future (10:12-13; cf. 2:6-11; 4:11-12; 9:11, 16; and 11:28-32). The end result in the case of those who are "in Christ Jesus" (8:1, 2) has been that God has done what the law could not do to bring about the fulfillment of the law's just requirement (8:4), a new obedience to God and a submission to his will free of that hostility of the flesh that perverts obedience into the securing of a person's own righteousness (8:7-9). Paul does not yet say what the end result will be for Israel, but one can see that it too will be by faith (10:11; 11:23), and by calling upon the Lord, as Scripture says (10:13). In any case, that kind of righteousness which belongs to faith and to trust in the God of Abraham, and which Paul now sees from his Christian perspective to have been God's intent all along (4:11-12, 23-24; 9:33b; Gal 3:8) will be for Israel as it is for himself the Torah arrived at, the knowledge of God made authentic in recognition and thanksgiving, the performance and zeal that deserves the name of obedience, the not-so-obvious Jewish identity and circumcision that receives its praise and recognition from God and not from human beings (2:28-29). "For the intent and goal of the law, to lead to righteousness for everyone who believes, is (nothing different from) Christ."

With that we are back where we started. Before we leave Rom 10:4 we should note that in the next verse Paul goes on, with a new causal sentence, to demonstrate that the grounds for such an affirmation as he has just made are in turn to be found by turning to Scripture (10:5-13). With that a new stage is reached which we cannot follow here, although it is of very great significance for understanding the methods, intentions and assumptions of Paul's exegesis.[25]

One point, however, needs to be recognized and accounted for: 10:5-6 is widely used as evidence to show that in v 4 Paul uses *telos* in the sense of "abolition." The argument is essentially that the contrast these verses draws between "the righteousness which is based on the law" and "the righteousness based on faith" is so sharp and the resulting confrontation between the Moses who "writes" in v 5 and a personified faith-righteousness that "speaks" in v 6 so uncompromising that "law" and "Christ" in v 4 can only be mutually exclusive and Christ can in Paul's mind only mean the termination of Torah.[26] We have examined enough of the context of 10:4 to see that such an argument seriously dislocates the polarity from the place where Paul places it, and does this in such a way as to alter crucially Paul's view of the law. The two kinds of righteousness in vv 5-6 are indeed opposites, as irreconcilable as obedience and disobedience, as "submitting to God's righteousness" and "seeking to establish one's own" in v 3. They repeat the contrast between "from faith" and "from works" in 9:32. There is no compromise between an election "by grace" and one "by works" (11:6), between what depends "on the God who calls" and what "on works" (9:12), between what comes "as a gift" and what "as one's due" (4:4). But the law does not belong on the side of this polarity that is alien to God or opposed to God. When it is found to function there, it does so as a consequence of a fundamental and tragic misunderstanding (9:32), or as an instrument of human disobedience and failure to recognize God and his righteousness (10:3), or as an opportunity seized by the demonic power of sin (7:11) for its own nourishment. But even when it is found to function in these ways, it has not been torn out of God's hand and it does not cease to be his holy instrument, for ultimately it does not contradict even then but advances, however indirectly, the carrying out of God's purpose (Rom 5:20-21; 7:13; 11:32; Gal 3:21-22, 24). To make such a claim is not to deny the presence of evil, the power of sin, the tragedy of the distortion of the divine intent in the name of religion. It is rather precisely to take all these with utmost seriousness, yet not absolutely, to claim in them and beyond them the ultimate manifestation of God's righteousness, his impartial goodness, and his sovereignty. Of course this is for Paul the Christian to read history in a pattern or meaning derived from the crucifixion of Jesus. But it is also for Paul the Jewish Christian to trace in the movements of history the sovereignty of the God of Abraham, Isaac and Jacob, the God of Moses, the Judge and Comforter of the Exile, who is also the Father of the Crucified.

III

If such reflections and conclusions as these can claim significant warrant in Paul's own text, it is very difficult to avoid reflecting on the reasons why they are not only not very widely held but also in some quarters, and in the commentary literature generally, firmly opposed, sometimes vehemently. The issue is significant enough to merit a brief postscript.

One matter that we have not mentioned but that has special bearing upon the interpretation of 9:30-10:4 is its relation to 9:1-29. What is the nature of the transition between the body of chap. 9 and 9:30-33? On its face this is a very simple question: how is chap. 10 related to chap. 9? But answering it is one of the major decisions facing the interpreter of Romans 9-11. For, as Dahl has pointed out,[27] through most of its history the interpretation of these chapters has been dominated by the problem of theodicy. More specifically, in the wake of Augustine's preoccupation with the issue of the freedom of the will, Romans 9-11 has been read as a discussion of divine predestination and human responsibility. On the assumption that what primarily troubles Paul in these chapters is his own Jewish people's rejection of the proclamation of Jesus as the Messiah, the three chapters are read as three different and rather unrelated, not to say logically incompatible, attempts to explain and understand this *contemporary* turn of events, this "disobedience of Israel":[28] in 9, by attributing it to God's absolute sovereignty and freedom to elect and to reject (divine determinism); in 10, by attributing it to the Jews' own responsible refusal of the Christ (human freedom); and in 11, by describing it as a temporary expedient that makes possible the inclusion of the Gentiles in God's redemptive purpose and that therefore, frustrating God's sovereignty in appearance only, actually contributes to the salvation of "all Israel" (11:26) and the ultimate victory of God's purpose (not so much in spite of human resistance as in and through it, not wiping it out so much as using it). On such reading of course the transition from chap. 9 to chap. 10 (at 9:30) is abrupt.[29] The discontinuity is as sharp as the contradiction between determinism and freedom. If there is logical coherence here, it would have to be something like the coherence of "thesis" and "antithesis" on the way to "synthesis." But it is questionable whether Paul's argument moves through the stages of this popular but simple and vulgarized schema somehow left to religious language by Hegel. In any case, such reading of these chapters has had the effect through a large part of the history of the exegesis of Romans of isolating these chapters from the rest of the epistle and of creating unnecessary obstacles in the understanding of particular sections.

It is to be sure beyond doubt that the negative reaction of Jews to the Christian kerygma, especially in its contrast to the reception accorded by Gentiles, is one of the things on Paul's mind. It is no accident that Paul's use in 11:8 of language from Deut 29:3 and Isa 29:10 is very close in meaning ("eine Sinnparallele")[30] to the text from Isa 6:9-11 imbedded in the evangelists' reflections on Jewish response to the gospel (Matt 13:14-15; Mark 4:12; Luke 8:10; John 12:40; Acts 28:26-27). But the issue in chap. 9 does not begin there, as a matter of "the disobedience of Israel." For Paul—the Jew—this discussion begins in 9:6 with the matter of the consistency and reliability of God's word. This is not a new issue in the text of Romans. It is rather a piece of unfinished business left over from a previous stage in the argument, specifically from 3:1-4, just as 6:1-7:6 deals with an issue abruptly turned aside by the apostle and left unresolved in 3:5-8.[31] There, after bluntly pressing the point of God's impartiality, before which Jew and Greek stand on an equal footing, Paul had himself given expression to the question he most naturally expected from a Jew: "What then is the point of being a Jew?" (3:1) His answer, too brief to be anything but a pointer, had been to say that that issue and the matter of God's faithfulness and truth stand or fall together, and to suggest with a quotation from Ps 51:4 that the real issue in justification is *God*'s being "justified," i.e. acknowledged as true, even if every human being turns out to be a liar. Clearly Romans 9 pursues that matter first. But that means—and this is the point that bears on our discussion—that what occupies Paul is God's faithfulness over the long past and the consistency of his dealings with his people over past and present. As 9:11 and 16 clearly show, Paul is aware of the extent to which his own descriptions of justification "apart from law" depend for their credibility on the case that he can make for this faithfulness and consistency on God's part. It is not at all merely a matter of a contemporary turn of events. It is a matter of surveying and reviewing (without a chronological retelling) essential features of Israel's past from his Christian perspective, just as he had been driven earlier to review (without autobiographical sequence) certain aspects of his individual past as a paradigm of human existence under the Torah (chap. 7).

Thus what we meet in Rom 9:30-10:4 is not an apostate Jew accusing his kinsmen of disobeying God because they have not been won over to his new interpretation of God's righteousness, or of persisting in an anachronism because they cannot accept God's putative termination of his Torah, or of being so attached to Moses that they have been unable to follow the living God in his new revelations of himself in unexpected ways.[32] Rather, we encounter a Jewish Christian whose new religious identity depends on continuity with his old; who must, for his own sake and the sake of those who have made the move with him, as well as for the sake of the right understanding of his gospel on the part of Gentile Christians (11:13), undertake such a review. Just as he had pressed the matter of God's consistency in the problematic of descent from Abraham in chap. 9, so now in chap. 10 he had to pursue God's faithfulness in the dialectic of obedience and disobedience (including Gentile obedience and Jewish disobedience), of Jewish devotion to Torah and Jewish failure to attain to Torah, of the problem of a defiance of God in the midst of the greatest possible human zeal for God, in order to be able to discover in his own kerygma the presence of his Jewish God and an answer to the question about that God's intentions in the giving of Torah.

But these are not the only reasons why an interpretation of Rom 10:4

such as we have suggested here has not commended itself. At once the most vehement attack against all translations of *telos* in 10:4 as "goal" and the most eloquent defense of its rendering as "termination" has been made by Käsemann in his superb commentary.[33] There is much in his argument with which one must agree. This applies especially to his polemic against a Christian moralizing, "pedagogical" interpretation of the law in its relation to Christ that derives from a false translation of *paidagōgos* in Gal 3:24 as "tutor" rather than "custodian." Such an interpretation makes of both the Jewish Torah and Israel's history a preparatory schooling for Christian truth, a half-way step on the liberal road of progressive religious development climaxing in Christian piety. Such triumphalism among Christians is not only the soil on which a patronizing view of Judaism grows (and worse, where Christendom dominates, a questioning of the Jew's right to existence); it is irreconcilable with Paul's understanding of justification. For Paul the problem with *homo religiosus,* the religious human being, is not that he has been on the right track, only has not exerted himself sufficiently (Paul could then never have formulated the paradox of 9:30-31). Rather, human religious striving and "progress" has made more acute a fundamental problematic in man's relation to God, and God's gift of the Torah has deepened that crisis just where it has been obeyed (Gal 3:19-24). Here one can only agree with Käsemann.

The problem appears to me to lie elsewhere. Käsemann is quite ready to characterize Paul's understanding of the Jewish Torah in 9:30-31 as "dialectical,"[34] and reminds his readers that "Paul was a Jew, and remained one even as a Christian, in that he still allowed the Torah to be the kernel of the Old Testament."[35] Yet, when he comes to 10:4 he insists upon a unilateral and undialectical view of Torah that prohibits *telos* from meaning anything other than "termination." The reason is that "law and gospel mutually exclude one another in an entirely undialectical way;"[36] Christ and the Torah of Moses stand in the same kind of contrary relationship as Christ and Adam in 5:12-21, the one belonging to the new aeon and the other to the old.[37] In short, Käsemann's interpretation of Rom 10:4 rests on the premise that the Jewish Torah, the Mosaic law, belongs for Paul to the old aeon that must come, that has come, to an end in Christ. This is a kind of ultimate example of the way in which the understanding of 10:4 depends on decisions that one has made elsewhere.

What is it that casts this dark Manichaean shadow across the pages of Paul and of his commentators? Is this the flaw in an apocalyptic reading of Paul, that it proves impotent to deliver us wholly from our Protestant habit of reading Paul through the eyes of Luther? In any case, this premise does not stand up under scrutiny in the light of such passages as are usually adduced in its support, especially 5:20; 7:1-6; 8:2-4.

We have already alluded to the problem produced by the mislocation of the genuine Pauline polarity in relation to the Jewish Torah.[38] And we have also pointed out that the phrasing of Rom 8:2 ("the law of sin and death") is not to be understood apart from the dialectic of Romans 7 which it summarizes in shorthand form, in which God's holy law is described as having been used by sin in order to produce death.[39] Rom 8:3-4 shows that the counterpart in v 2 ("the law of the Spirit of life in Christ Jesus") is the same divine Torah brought to fulfillment through the life-giving power which it was itself unable to provide but which belongs to the Spirit. The contraries are sin and righteousness, death and life. Law and Spirit, however, are not related as such opposites but as powerlessness and life-giving power.

The case is similar in Rom 7:1-6. The first three verses are not unclear. In Paul's illustration, living with another man before her husband's death brings upon the woman the label and mark of an adulteress, the "scarlet letter." The very same action after the husband's death brings no such consequence. The law is not annulled by the husband's death, but the power of the law to *condemn* is broken—just the point that is resumed in 8:1 ("There is therefore now no condemnation for those who are in Christ Jesus"). That Paul wishes precisely to avoid suggesting that the law is no longer in effect is shown when he writes (literally translated): "she is annulled *(katērgētai)* from the law of the husband;" the Greek language is being strained to the breaking point to avoid the natural use of this verb, to avoid saying "the law of the husband has been cancelled." The whole purpose of 7:7-12 is to make clear that Paul wants no one to conclude that the Mosaic law is to be equated with the power of sin and to insist instead that as God's holy, righteous and good commandment it is not evil or demonic.

Finally there is the much more complex matter of the law in Rom 5:12-21. One thing is clear: in vv 20-21 the law intrudes itself as "the factor which disturbs the analogy in [the] contrast between Adam and Christ."[40] It functions for Paul on *both* sides of the divide between Adam and Christ, to make of death on the one hand not merely an inexorable fate inherited by all as a result of Adam's trespass alone but a condemnation deserved by the trespasses of all (v 13), and to make life on the other hand not merely a neutral consequence inherited by all as a result of Christ's obedience but a gift that has its character most of all in being undeserved and gracious. That is why it deepens the trespass in order to deepen all the more the ensuing grace, to show that death is the symptom and result of sin's rule and power, but just as surely to show that life in Christ is the symptom and sign of the rule of God's undeserved grace. The law defines for both the old and the new their character; it does not stand unambiguously on the side of the old.

One might very well ask what the consequences would be of a consistent Christian interpretation that insists on identifying the Mosaic Torah with the old aeon. What would that mean for the Christian's relationship to Judaism, to the Hebrew Scriptures, to the God of Moses? That consequence might not be as reprehensible as that other paternalizing view of Judaism as a lower order of religious commitment and behavior on its way to Christianity, but it surely would miss by an even wider mark Paul's deep engagement with the Judaism from which he came and to which he remained profoundly tied. To miss that engagement and so to abandon the structure which Paul gave to Christianity because of it would be, as Goguel observed in the passage referred to at the beginning of this essay, "to shake the very foundations of Christianity."

NOTES

[1]*The Birth of Christianity* (London: Allen & Unwin, 1953; French original, Paris: Payot, 1946) 195.

[2]Ibid., 195 and 194.

[3]N. A. Dahl, *Studies in Paul* (Minneapolis: Augsburg, 1977) 156; cf. 148.

[4]For the necessity and at the same time the problematic of using such modern terms in connection with Paul, the essential discussion for the present is E. Käsemann's essay "Justification and Salvation History in the Epistle to the Romans," *Perspectives on Paul* (Philadelphia: Fortress, 1971) 60-78.

[5]To the full commentary treatment by Käsemann, *An die Römer* (Tübingen: Mohr, 1973) 241-308, there must now be added the even longer discussion by O. Kuss, *Der Römerbrief*, Dritte Lieferung (Regensburg: Verlag Friedrich Pustet, 1978) 662-935; cf. 667-8 for a select bibliography of earlier special treatments of Romans 9-11. This literature is just now seeing an explosive growth; other major commentaries on Romans 9-11 in the context of the whole letter are being prepared for such series as ICC, Hermeneia, AB and EKKNT.

[6]*A Commentary on the Epistle to the Romans* (New York: Harper & Row, 1957) 195.

[7]Cf. *BAG*, 819. It should be noted that if one sets aside the more specialized meanings *telos* may have as "tax, duty" (Rom 13:7) or in stereotyped adverbial prepositional phrases such as *heōs telous* (2 Cor 1:13) or *eis telos* (1 Thess 2:16), all occurrences in the undisputed Pauline letters apart from Rom 10:4 fall into the second group (end as "outcome," "conclusion"). This preponderance of meaning is especially clear in 1 Cor 15:24; 2 Cor 3:13; 11:15; Phil 3:19. In these letters the word never means simply end as "cessation;" such a meaning is to be found in the whole of the traditional Pauline corpus only in Heb 7:3. These proportions clearly conform to the general picture of Greek usage provided by *LSJ*, 1772-4.

[8]All do connect the dative participle with the prepositional phrase rather than with the main clause. To construe it in the latter way ("in the judgment of every believer Christ has become the end of the law [as a way] to righteousness") might appear plausible in terms of classical usage (R. Kühner-B. Gerth, *Ausführliche Grammatik der griechischen Sprache*, Satzlehre, 1. Teil, 4. Aufl. [Leverkusen, 1955] 1. 421), but internal reasons are strongly against it. (a) Paul's use of the dative alone is never so purely "subjective"; cf. 1 Cor 1:18, the nearest parallel I can find. (b) The frequent close association of *pisteuein/pistis* with *dikaioun/dikaiosynē* throughout Paul's letters and in this context in 9:30; 10:6 speaks against separating them here. And (c) the need to supply the words in parentheses in order to yield some sense shows how awkward such a construal is.

[9]*Romans*, 197. Cf. 198: "He puts an end to the law, not by destroying all that the law stood for but by realizing it." Such a strained modal translation is the price he seems to believe himself compelled to pay for the choice of a final meaning for *telos*. It is, however, not a necessary price. Leenhardt (*L'Epitre de Saint Paul aux Romains* [Neuchatel: Delachaux & Niestlé, 1957] 151) translates easily with a

purpose clause: "Christ est cependant but et terme de la loi, pour mettre quiconque croit au bénéfice de ce jugement de grâce." This shows, too, that in the other direction a natural final translation of the prepositional phrase (as purpose or result) does not require in its wake interpreting *telos* as "termination," as in *RSV*, *NEB* and *JB*.

[10]So Käsemann, *Römer*, 264-5; Kuss, *Römerbrief*, 740-748. Dahl, *Studies*, 147, calls 9:30-33 a "provisional summary" that "functions as a transition to the following section," but significantly he goes on to say that what it summarizes is not the preceding argument of chap 9 but "Paul's view of the contemporary stituation." Rom 10:1-3 seems to him to make a new start because "only at this point does Paul explain what prompts the sorrow and anguish about which he spoke in 9:1-3" and Dahl finds that explanation in v 3. But v 3 is nothing else than Paul's interpretation of 9:32. For Dahl both verses have to do with the Jews' rejection of Jesus as Messiah, so even on his terms 9:30-33 functions as a "transition" mainly by introducing new elements for the next stage of Paul's argument (cf. 143, n 24).

[11]Käsemann, *Römer*, 265.

[12]C.E.B. Cranfield, "Some Notes on Romans 9:30-33," *Jesus und Paulus: Festschrift für Werner Georg Kümmel* (Göttingen: Vandenhoeck & Ruprecht, 1975) 36. A good example of such re-writing is found in H. Lietzmann, *An die Römer* (Tübingen: Mohr, 1971) 94, but others abound in the commentary literature on these verses as already in the manuscript variants and conjectural emendations to the text.

[13]*nomos dikaiōsynēs* is a *hapax legomenon* in the NT; in the LXX it occurs only once (Wis 2:11) and then clearly *in malam partem*.

[14]On this detail Cranfield is quite correct ("Notes," 39). But to go on, as he does, triumphantly to declare "fundamental agreement" between Paul and Jesus on the law is a sharp abridgment of Paul's complex reflections on the law and can only result in caricature. There is nothing in the tradition of Jesus' teaching to compare with Rom 5:20; 7:13; or Gal 3:21-22.

[15]H. J. Schoeps, who in his very instructive book on Paul's theology climaxes his discussion of Paul's treatment of the law with a whole section on the fundamental Pauline misunderstanding of the Torah, never once mentions this verse of Romans (*Paul: The Theology of the Apostle in the Light of Jewish Religious History* [London: Lutterworth, 1961]).

[16]Both Käsemann (*Römer*, 265) and Kuss (*Römerbrief*, 745) refer to L. Radermacher's discussion of the expressly Greek nuancing of the verse (*Neutestamentliche Grammatik* [Tübingen: Mohr, 1925] 26) in the absence of any mention of it in *BDF*. There can be little doubt, in view of Paul's common use of these contrasting prepositional phrases, that the governing word intended but only implied is either the substantive "righteousness" or a cognate verbal form such as "being justified."

[17]Cf. G. Stählin, *"skandalon k.t.l.,"* *TWNT* 7 (1964) 341-2. The parallel *proskomma* adds the further nuance of "being taken unawares."

[18]John E. Toews, *The Law in Paul's Letter to the Romans: A Study of Romans 9:30-10:13* (Dissertation, Northwestern University, 1977). One central argument of this dissertation, that Rom 9:33 is not a messianic stone testimonium, was presented by Toews in a paper on "Romans 9:33 and the Testimonia Hypothesis" to the Pauline Epistles Section of the Society of Biblical Literature meeting in New Orleans on November 20, 1978. In this paper he showed that the Christian Christological use of Isa 8:14 everywhere else presupposes the use of Ps 118:22, just what is absent in Rom 9:33. For a general view of the state of the discussion on the so-called "testimonia," cf. J. A. Fitzmyer, " '4Q Testimonia' and the New Testament," in his *Essays on the Semitic Background of the New Testament* (Missoula: Scholars' Press, 1974) 59-89. Klyne R. Snodgrass ("I Peter II. 1-10: Its Formation and Literary Affinities," *NTS* 24 [1977-78] 97-106) shows that the connection of Isa 8:14 and 28:16 was made already in Jewish tradition, and that the *ep' autō* of Rom 9:33 is not the result of Christian interpolation; this means that this phrase cannot be taken as evidence for a Christological application by Paul.

[19]Dahl, *Studies*, 147.

[20] *epignōsis* occurs in the undisputed Pauline letters here and Rom 1:28; 3:20; Phil 1:9; and Philm 6. The contexts always show the presence of the connotation "recognition" or "acknowledgment" (e.g. in Phil 1:9 the parallel term is *aisthēsis*).

[21]Cf. R. Bultmann, "*agnoeō*," *TWNT* 1 (1949) 116-117.

[22]*Römerbrief*, 748.

[23]There is a remarkable Biblical precedent for Paul's view in Ezek 20:25, where concern with the holiness of God himself yields a unique reflection on the statutes and ordinances that, intended for life (vv 11, 13, 21), lead to death. The concrete allusion is to Exod 22:28 and the enigma of a divine judgment operating in the command itself (W. Zimmerli, *Ezechiel* 1 [Neukirchen: Neukirchener Verlag, 1969] 449: "Die paulinische Erkenntnis vom Wesen des Gesetzes [Rö 5,20; 7,13; Gal 3,19] ist hier in einer eigentümlich begrenzten Formulierung von ferne zu ahnen").

[24]Schoeps *(Paul*, 182), after remarking on the precedents in Jewish tradition for the claim that the law brings knowledge of sin, goes on to say that no Jew can follow Paul when he concludes from this that the law is a law unto death, and then refers to Rom 8:2-3 and Gal 3:21. But even the Jew Paul does not draw such a conclusion in the verses referred to. In Rom 8:2 the phrase "the law of sin and death" is a short-hand summation of Paul's account in 7:7-12 of (God's) law used by sin to produce death; v 4 goes on to refer to what God has done to turn this state of affairs around in order that "the just requirement of the law might be fulfilled." Gal 3:21 voices Paul's conviction that the law is powerless to make alive, but that is not yet to say that the *law* (in distinction from the *letter*, 2 Cor 3:6) kills; the very next verse explicitly makes the function of "scripture," to "consign all things to sin," subservient to the execution of the promise. The negative effects of the law are for Paul always *pen*ultimate.

[25]Cf. M. J. Suggs, " 'The Word is Near You'; Romans 10:6-10 within the

Purpose of the Letter," *Christian History and Interpretation: Studies Presented to John Knox* (Cambridge: University Press, 1967) 289-312.

[26]E.g. Käsemann, *Römer*, 272; on the other side, F. Flückiger, "Christus, des Gesetzes *telos*," *TZ* 11 (1955) 155-156.

[27]*Studies*, 142-3.

[28]The phrase occurs, for instance, in the opening sentence of Cranfield, "Notes," 34. Its use here, where Cranfield is summarizing 9:6-29, illustrates the problem we are addressing. How does one come on careful reading of Romans 9 to speak at all about "Israel's disobedience," especially in the light of v 11? What must such an interpreter be bringing with him, and whence?

[29]Dahl himself (*Studies*, 148) sees 10:4-21 to be an important digression, in some ways logically prior to chap. 9.

[30]Kuss, *Römerbrief*, 791.

[31]Cf. Dahl, *Studies*, 139. I owe my initial recognition of this feature of Romans and its significance to the valuable little commentary by E. Gaugler, *Der Brief an die Römer* (2 vols.; Zürich: Zwingli-Verlag, 1945-52) 1. 71.

[32]The language used here echoes that used by Kuss, *Römerbrief*, 741. It is very doubtful that we should read Romans 10 as an attack ("Generalangriff") on Judaism at all, as Kuss does (753).

[33]*Römer*, 269-71; cf. also "The Spirit and the Letter," *Perspectives on Paul* (Philadelphia: Fortress, 1971) 138-166.

[34]*Römer*, 265; *Perspectives*, 159.

[35]*Perspectives*, 154.

[36]*Römer*, 269.

[37]Ibid., 270.

[38]See p. 68 above.

[39]See n. 24 above.

[40]Dahl, *Studies*, 91.

SOME COMMENTS ON PROVIDENCE IN PHILO

SAMUEL SANDMEL†

THE UNIVERSITY OF CHICAGO DIVINITY SCHOOL, CHICAGO, ILLINOIS
60637

PHILO's treatises relating to the anti-Jewish riots of 38 in Alexandria are two: *Against Flaccus* and *On the Embassy to Gaius*. They are normally studied together, since they both deal with an ordeal suffered by the Alexandrian Jewish community. *Against Flaccus* seems earlier than *On the Embassy,* but only by a few years. In part the two treatises overlap in content, namely in the description which Philo gives of the uncontrolled disorders which Flaccus, the Roman governor, had not quelled. The distinction in the treatises is that of the chosen subject, namely, the misdeeds of Flaccus in Alexandria on the one hand and the imperial madness of Gaius Caligula on the other. Philo had headed the delegation to Gaius to protest against the anti-Jewish activities. Accordingly, *Against Flaccus* is an account of the misdeeds that led to the sending of the deputation, while *Embassy* describes the high-handed treatment of the Jewish delegation.

The ending of the later treatise, *On the Embassy to Gaius,* has long been recognized as curious. It runs as follows: "So now I have told in a summary way the cause of the enmity which Gaius had for the whole nation of the Jews, but I must also describe the palinode." Whatever a palinode might be, it is strikingly absent. Possibly Philo wrote it, but it got lost; possibly Philo never got around to writing it.

The word *palinodia* is one of infrequent occurrence and therefore lexicographers assert that its precise meaning is obscure. Where it appears elsewhere in Philo, it seems to mean "recantation." Such a meaning fits very poorly here, though the effort has been made by some scholars to make it fit.

Towards the end of *Against Flaccus,* at #102, Philo begins to describe the abrupt turn in Flaccus' career, that from high honor to abject humiliation and cruel punishment. He introduces this section with the words that "God, it is clear, takes care for human affairs." A few lines later Philo says that justice, "the champion and defender of the wronged, the avenger of unholy men and deeds, began to enter the lists" against Flaccus. Thereafter Philo proceeds to furnish the details about the downfall of Flaccus, leading to Philo's conclusion that what happened to Flaccus "was caused, I am convinced, by his treatment of the Jews." The beginning of the downfall of Flaccus had coincided with the festival of Booths, which the Alexandrian Jews had been prevented from observing. Then when the Jews learned that Flaccus had been arrested, "with hands outstretched to heaven, they sang hymns and led songs of triumph to God who watches over human affairs." Philo next proceeds to reproduce the substance of a prayer which praises God for suddenly bringing down the enemy of the Jews. This divine intervention occurred, so he writes, not in some distant place, forcing those whom he ill-treated to "hear it by report and have less keen pleasure," but rather, "here, close at hand, almost before the eyes of the wronged." To the two circumstances, first, that Flaccus was arrested, and second, that the arrest took place near-by, and that on the festival of Booths, there was added a third circumstance, which, so Philo says, was "brought about by divine providence" (125), namely, that when Flaccus was brought to Italy for the imperial inquiry into his misdeeds, there appeared to testify against him two Gentile Alexandrians who earlier had been loyal henchmen. Their testimony was the stronger because these Alexandrians "saw that he [God] who presided over human affairs was [Flaccus'] mortal enemy." Philo proceeds to say that God "assumed the guise of a judge, so as not to appear to condemn anyone by anticipation and without trial . . ." Thereafter Philo gives his summary of what he has already written: "I have described these events at length, not in order to recall long past iniquities, but to extol the justice which watches over human affairs." He then relates that Flaccus, having been convicted and punished by exile to the "unblessed" island of Andros, went insane. Once, at a midnight, he turned his eyes to heaven, crying, "King of gods and men, You do not, then, disregard the Jewish nation, and they do not misrepresent your providence . . ." Philo goes on, in this prayer, which was composed, of course, by Philo, to depict the acute miseries which Flaccus had already come to suffer. Then two assassins, sent from Rome to execute Flaccus, arrived at Andros. When they fell on him with swords drawn, his resistance made it impossible "to apply their swords directly, but . . . downwards and sidewards. He caused himself to suffer more severely; and, with his hands, feet, head, breast, and sides stabbed and cut to bits, he lay carved like a sacrificial victim. For it was the will of justice that the butcheries which she wrought on his single body should be as numerous as the number of the Jews he unlawfully put to death." Finally, Philo writes that the fate of Flaccus[1] is an indubitable proof that the help which God can give was not withheld from the Jewish nation.

Though Philo does not here use the term palinode, the last portion of *Against Flaccus* briefly reviewed can be regarded as one; it is a theological conclusion to an essay which stands in balance with the earlier exposition of "the facts." If the ending of *Against Flaccus* is indeed a sort of palinode, then it is not hard to imagine what the palinode missing from *Embassy* provided: an account with full details of the murder and attendant sufferings of Gaius, these linked to Philo's views of justice and God's providential care of Jews.

Embassy begins with a prologue, a meditation, as it were, on the contrast between nature *(physics)* and fortune *(tyche)*. By *physis* Philo means the true reality behind the universe which the gifted mind comes to understand, while *tyche* is an event, an accidental occurrence, which the fallible senses encounter; in Philo's words, "The eyes of the body discern what is manifest and close at hand, but reason reaches to the unseen and the future." That is to say, there can be a difference between some event now, in our time, and the meaning of that same event when it is set into the full context of the past and the future.

But even present-day events, says Philo, can bring about a reasonable conviction, this despite the deplorable circumstances that some people have come to disbelieve in divine providence in general, and in God's providence respecting the Jews in particular. Now, if the observation of righteous elderly men can spur a respect for them, even greater respect should exist for these righteous men who have risen into the fullest possible knowledge of God. Skepticism about providence arises in part out of human limitations; these Philo here briefly spells out: the failure to recognize providence rests on the inability of reason to ascend all the way to God *(To Ōn)* in his essence. Indeed, even the attendant *dynameis* ("powers") of God are beyond the understanding of many people.

What Philo is here saying in telescoped form is elsewhere fully expounded: God, in his essence, is unknowable. Aspects of God are attainable by reason. One aspect is God as creator, this contained in Scripture in the word *theos;* another aspect is God as ruler, contained in the biblical word *kyrios*. The further characteristics of *theos* include providence; those of *kyrios* include divine rewards and punishments. In reality, so Philo goes on to say, the punitive aspect of God is subsumed within the category of rewards, for two reasons: one, no law can be complete without honors and benefits; and, two, the punishment of others "often admonishes and calls them to wisdom . . ." Finally, "penalties are good for the morals of the multitude, who fear to suffer . . ."

From this general meditative prologue Philo turns immediately in *Embassy* to review the career of Gaius Caligula. In doing so he abstains almost completely from hearkening back to his introductory words, doing so only twice, and then only passingly.[2] That is to say, the introduction to *Embassy* is in the nature of a thesis, with the expectation that the ensuing exposition is to demonstrate the correctness of the thesis, and will do so by explicit inferences and conclusions and relevant contentions. These are what are absent from the missing palinode. Presumably the substance of the palinode, if it was ever written, was Philo's explicit inferences from the data he has provided. While it would have been desirable for the palinode, assuming it was written, to have survived, it is not too difficult to guess what it would have contained, namely, a description of the horrible death of Caligula, kindred to that undergone by Flaccus.

The distinction made by Philo between *tyche* and *physis* might here merit some exposition, however labored it might seem. Let us imagine a village at the foot of a mountain. A huge boulder, loosened by rain, begins to descend directly onto the village. It strikes a huge oak tree which alters the path of the boulder, and so diverts it that it does not fall onto the village. Residents of the village proceed to give an explanation for what took place, namely, that by accident that oak tree altered the path of the boulder. Resource to *physis,* through utilizing right reason, would yield the conclusion that it was by divine providence that the oak tree was there, and by this deliberate providential intervention the path of the boulder was altered. *Tyche* is the explanation for an event which the senses offer; *physis* is the explanation which reason, going beyond the senses and into the domain of metaphysical inquiry, offers.

As is well known, the doctrine of providence leads inevitably into the problem of theodicy. The principal objection to a doctrine of providence, this in a range of other objections, is that the experience of disasters by the human race, ranging from one man's personal misfortune to a collective community or national calamity, like the Holocaust, seems to refute providence. This is especially so because the adjective beneficent is universally applied to providence. Even punitive providence is in the final analysis beneficent, but providence devoid of beneficence is an impossibility.

The surviving fragments of Philo's treatise *On Providence* present Philo's retort to a certain Alexander[3] who has "refuted" the idea of beneficent providence through a mention of instances wherein divine justice, a concomitant of providence, has been singularly absent. Philo's retort to Alexander goes along the following lines: God, not being a tyrant, but a kindly sovereign, governs earth and heaven with justice. He is to the world what a father is to his family, caring even for wastrel children, allowing them ample opportunity for reformation and merciful acceptance. The lot of the wicked is never happiness, since the acquisition of wealth and possessions is empty, and without divine respect. Physicians ministering to a sick king strip him of his fine clothes to examine his body. On the other hand, philosophers are concerned with man's soul, not with his body, however powerful his physique. Socrates, concerned as he was for virtue and not for possessions, was content to live a life of poverty. On the other hand, those men whom Alexander had cited by name as wicked but prosperous men were ultimately all victims of divine justice. The justice of God is not like that of man, or of a human tribunal. God "penetrates noiselessly into the recesses of the soul . . . inspects our motives in their native reality and at once distinguishes the counterfeit from the genuine." Human justice "has many pitfalls, the delusions of the senses, the malignancy of the passions . . ."

But, Philo goes on to say, a temporary period of human tyranny is not without its uses, nor is the punishment of men necessarily detrimental. "In all properly enacted laws, punishment is included, and those who enacted them are universally praised, for punishment has the same relation to law as a tyrant has to a people." God wishes "to purify our race"; wickedness cannot be purged away "without some ruthless soul to do it." Just as a state maintains appointed executioners to deal with murderers, traitors, and temple robbers, so also God sets up tyrants over cities "inundated with violence." But thereafter God crowns the punishment by bringing tyrants themselves to justice.

At times, in place of tyrants, God uses famine, pestilence, or earthquake or other "divine visitations" as part of his purpose of promoting virtue. The effect of storms of wind and rain may be some harm to a few, but they benefit mankind as a whole, for through these God "purges the earth with water and the whole sublunary area with breezes." The disadvantaged few are only "a small fraction, and his care is for the whole human race."

Just as students can as yet not explain "the belt of the Milky Way," but must not shrink from trying to learn, so too they must try to understand the phenomena of disasters such as earthquakes and storms. But it is wrong to regard these as maleficent visitations of God.[4] "Nothing evil at all is caused by God."

Then what causes earthquakes and storms? "Changes in the elements"! These, however, are not primary works of nature itself, but, rather, a sequel to nature's essential works. They are only attendant circumstances. Those good people who perish in disasters may not truly have been good in the eyes of God. But divine providence, so says Philo, deals with the most important of things, not with "some chance individual of the obscure and insignificant kind"[5] (53-55).

Since the problem of theodicy is beyond reasonable solution, we should not expect to find Philo solving it. What we do find, however, is somewhat striking in its general superficiality, a quality usually not found in Philo. The only contention he does not introduce that he might have is that what man regards as evil may actually be good.[6] He comes closest to this in his contention reproduced above, that good arises out of punishment.

Most surprising of all is the absence of any concern for the unfortunate individual. If a storm purges the air, where is his sympathy for the person killed by that storm?

So far as I know, it remains unexpressed. Perhaps the thought never occurred to Philo. Or else, in his hewing to the line of providence as beneficent, he is quite willing to overlook historical events that could refute or damage his contention. He expresses unreserved indignation at the misdeeds of those who did violence against the Jews of Alexandria, but he seems to make no effort to sympathize with the sufferings undergone by these Jews.

Philo, then, has a good bit to say about providence. But one needs to question the quality of what he says. Or, perhaps the problem is such that what Philo does say is the most that he felt able to say.

In rabbinic literature there is a recurrent notion, that of *yisurin shel 'ahava*. It is derived from biblical passages the import of which is that "whom God loves, he chastens." One passage runs: "If a man sees that *yisurin* ("afflictions") come upon him, let him examine his actions [to determine if he deserved what he experienced]. If, on examining his actions, he finds himself innocent, let him ascribe his afflictions to neglect of the Torah. But if he is innocent of neglect of the Torah, let him be certain that he is undergoing afflictions of love."[7]

Still another passage comes to mind. The suffering sage Hanina said, "I would gladly do without the love for the sake of doing without the *yisurin*."[8]

I know of nothing in Philo like this concern for the suffering.

NOTES

[1] The Greek of the last sentence has the word *kai*. It is conjectured (see F. H. Colson, *Philo*, LCIX, 295, footnote a) that *Against Flaccus* ensued on a conjectured, similar work, unhappily lost, describing the downfall of Sejanus.

[2] One instance relates to the statue of Zeus which Caligula ordered to be placed in the Temple. The statue was made in Phoenicea, that is, within the area subject to Petronius, the Roman governor of Syria, rather than made in Rome, outside Petronius' jurisdiction. However, Petronius was able to ascribe his deliberate delay in executing Caligula's command to the slowness of the construction of the statue. The decision for the statue to be constructed in Phoenicea was "in my opinion through the providence of God, who unseen by us stretched out his hand to protect the wronged" (*Embassy*, 220). The context of the other (*ibid.*, 335) is that when Caligula rescinded the command about the statue, he added an injunction that those who interfered with people [pagans] bent on setting up statues in his honor were to be punished. This added injunction could have had far-reaching damaging consequences, "but by a dispensation of the providence and watchful care of God, not a single person . . . gave any provocation to violence."

[3] This Alexander is often inferred to be Tiberius Julius Alexander, Philo's nephew, who, an apostate, rose to unusual eminence in the Roman military world. Alexander served as the Roman procurator of Judea and then as a hostile prefect of Egypt. See "Alexander, Tiberius Julius," *Jewish Encyclopedia*, I, 357-358.

[4] The contention (*Prov.* 53ff.) seemingly contradicts what is above (41). F. H. Colson, Loeb edition, IX, 546 tries, in my opinion without success, to harmonize the contradiction. My opinion is that in refining his view, Philo trespasses into a contradiction he is unaware of.

[5] There then ensues in the treatise a section in which Philo responds to Alexander's denial of providence which had cited the instance of people killed by wild animals. Philo replies that if people leave their peaceful homes and wander into the lairs of these beasts, they should blame themselves; the same is true of spectators at a chariot race who, instead of remaining in their seats, trespass onto the race track and are crushed as "a proper reward for their folly" (58). He responds to Alexander's contention that the land of the Cyclops was fertile and Greece barren (this circumstance arguing against providence) by asserting that the relative lack of fertility in Greece resulted in finer men, citing Heroclitus, "where the land is dry, the soul is best and wisest." In the rest of the fragment Philo praises vegetarianism and those lawgivers who enacted restraints respecting the eating of animals. Flowers, he says, were made for health, not for pleasure. Though their scent is in itself beneficial, they are the more so when they are used in compounding drugs. Just as neither man nor woman alone can engender new life, their union qualifies them to do together what neither can do separately (59-72).

[6] See Gen 50:20.

[7] Berachat 5a.

[8] *Canticles Rabba*, II, to ch 2, verse 16.

JEREMIAH AND THE DIMENSIONS OF THE MORAL LIFE

DOUGLAS A. KNIGHT
VANDERBILT DIVINITY SCHOOL, NASHVILLE, TN 37240

IN continuity with his prophetic predecessors, Jeremiah considered it one of his primary tasks to make the people of Judah aware of their faults. This is among the divine charges he receives:

> I have made you an assayer of my people,
>   that you should know and assay their conduct *(derek)*. (Jer 6:27)

As a prophet of both the preexilic and exilic periods, Jeremiah felt compelled to speak out against the people's religious and moral practices, to declare God's imminent judgment against them if they did not repent and reform, eventually to announce that their failure so to reform meant that God's punishment no longer could be diverted, and then finally after the cataclysm to aid the people in understanding it and in preparing for the future. For him as for all the prophets the morality and religion of the people are intimately intertwined, with both subject to divine scrutiny according to the standards and expectations that have been made known to the people since ancient times. Jeremiah moves easily between the religious and moral spheres in his critique of Judah. The people's rebellion against God incorporates both, for each sphere is in essence rooted in the other.

It is common for us to differentiate between morality and religion, and this can be appropriate in our study of ancient Israel so long as we do not lose sight of their interdependence in the biblical view. We consider religion to encompass primarily those acts and attitudes ordered toward God, while morality consists of human behavior and postures ordered toward humanity. With morality we observe persons conducting themselves, either individually or in concert with others, according to value or right. The ethicist analyzes such activity while attempting to address especially three fundamental issues that recur throughout the long history of the discipline: the nature and locus of the good; the nature of the moral agent; and the function of norms and principles in moral judgment.[1] As a part of this, it may be possible to construct a theory of moral agency, a systematic and ordered display of all aspects operating in the processes of the moral life. This would aim to clarify all dimensions of existence which impinge upon the process of moral acting.[2]

Jeremiah himself has no interest in developing a theory of moral agency. His concerns are much more practical and direct: to bring the people's faults to their attention and to persuade them of the course of action which they should immediately adopt. Nonetheless, it is reasonable to assume that the prophet indeed had a clear conception of the moral nature of the people who deserved the divine judgment. Whether or not he would have been capable of consciously and systematically articulating the various elements of this conception as it relates to moral agency is of little concern to us. It is equally inappropriate for us to expect that Jeremiah, any more than any other individual, operated throughout his whole lifetime with a single and consistent view of the moral actors around him. As events moved closer to the fall of Jerusalem, the people's intransigence in the face of his calls for repentance evoked from Jeremiah an increasingly pessimistic evaluation of their capability for moral rectitude and religious loyalty to YHWH. His assessment may not even be radically reversed in his later pronouncements of hope and deliverance, as we shall see.

To gain an understanding of Jeremiah's view of the moral life, we need to examine in sequence six fundamental conditions of the moral agent. These are all elements that contribute to the makeup of human existence inasmuch as they characterize human nature and human community. As such, they bear on one's moral judgment and conduct. Our method involves an inductive approach to Jeremiah's conception of the moral life through an analysis of all possible texts which make some reference, however obliquely, to any of these conditions. The sources for this are thus the utterances generally recognized to be Jeremianic, together with, in a more cautious and critical fashion, the prose narratives that stem from Jeremiah's biographer. Deuteronomistic and other later additions to this collection are generally disregarded; they belong to the theology and ethics of the Book of Jeremiah, but less so to the theological anthropology of the historical Jeremiah.

I.   The Conditions of the Moral Agent

What is the nature of the moral agent according to Jeremiah? Are there human characteristics of a fundamental nature that affect one's moral action? To what extent is the individual subject to influences from without? Is it indeed appropriate to hold the agent fully responsible for all actions and choices? To achieve resolution of these problems one needs to focus on several conditions of the moral agent. Such conditions are conceived here not as empirical components of life but as ideal types of various aspects of life as it is played out in the actual contexts of existence. Such typologies can aid us in illuminating the complexities of life, but it would be unwarranted to force these distinctions or to advocate the radical autonomy of any from the others. This is especially the case for Hebraic anthropology which does not strive for an ordered, segmented systematization of human life, but rather for an understanding of human existence.

1) Rationality

For Jeremiah, the moral agent's characteristics of rationality, volition, and affectivity are mentioned usually in his utterances directed to the people as a whole. However, he seems to consider them not as social attributes but as properties of the individual. It is not the corporate entity that is rational, volitional, or affective in the first instance. Rather, the persons comprising the society possess these characteristics as individuals. To be sure, they may be sharing them in common and are also affecting each other's moral qualities; this is the factor of sociality, to be addressed below, for which Jeremiah can pronounce judgment on the whole people. Yet with respect to the other three aspects he is speaking to Judah essentially as a collectivity of agents who each respectively demonstrates these certain traits. Only occasionally does he single out persons, primarily kings and prophets, for direct and specific comment.

Jeremiah's view of rationality is not dissimilar from that which is evident from other pages of the Hebrew Bible.[3] Accordingly, the heart figures prominently, especially in the Deuteronomistic passages, as the image for the intellectual and rational functions, including those that are categorized best as will, intentions, and conscience. Jeremiah recognizes fully the people's capacity to think, deliberate, and understand. For him the problem lies in their tendency to overlook or misunderstand evidence, especially relating to God's acts in the past, and to use their minds instead for ill.

For Jeremiah, the people's thinking is especially evident. He pictures them at several points deceiving their neighbors (9:5 [H 9:4]; 9:8 [H 9:7]; 17:9)—a deliberate act of the mind guided by hidden intentions of the will.[4] Some of this may indeed be well intentioned, as with those who counsel "šālôm šālôm" when there is no peace (6:13f.; 8:10f.; see also

23:16f.). At other points the people are scheming for their own self-interests, either to rid themselves of Jeremiah (11:19f.; 12:6) or to devise ways to benefit from exploiting others, as is stated in the utterance against Jehoiakim:

> For your eyes and your heart (= mind) do not exist
> > but for your own gain
> > and for shedding innocent blood
> > and for practicing oppression and maltreatment. (22:17)

Their calculating also takes the form of political machinations (2:18, 36f.; perhaps also 4:30). Only at one point does Jeremiah come close to accusing the people of irrationality or at least of mindless behavior, and that is when he compares their cultic loyalties to the aimless meanderings of a young female camel in heat (2:23f.). Yet in his preaching Jeremiah makes direct appeals to the people's reason in an attempt to get them to reform their ways (see especially 2:10-13; 10:1-10; 36:3; 44:15-23, perhaps Deuteronomistic).

While their minds remain active, the people seem to lack the proper understanding of the course of history and of God's demands, according to Jeremiah. They purport to be wise (8:8), but they do not give evidence of the quality of perception that results from receptive hearing of God's word (5:21-23; 6:10; and in more pronounced form in Deuteronomistic passages such as 11:8 and 32:33). Such perception may only come retrospectively, if not indeed eschatologically: "In the latter days you will understand this" (30:24b). In the meantime the people continue in their naïveté (4:22; 10:14; 3:4f.; also 7:9, the Deuteronomistic report of Jeremiah's "Temple Sermon").

This lack of proper understanding seems, according to Jeremiah, to be primarily due to the people's self-deception. In the face of flagrant oppression they avow their innocence and expect that YHWH's anger will be short-lived (2:34f.) or that YHWH[5] will not even be observing them (12:4). They even fail to have the necessary insight to perceive the corrective[6] purpose of God's punishment (2:30a; 5:3; 15:7; cf. 2:19; 6:8; 10:24; 31:18). Their misreading of the course of history and tradition is similar to their neighbors' unjustified trust in past securities: the Moabites' reliance on their works and treasures (48:7a); the Ammonites', on their supplies (49:4b); and the Edomites', on their reputation for causing calamity (49:8, 16). Yet Jeremiah is not willing to believe that the people are unaware of their guilt:

Judah's sin is written with an iron stylus,
    with a diamond point it is engraved on the tablet of their heart
    and on the horns of their altars. (17:1)

Such a phrase as "engraved on the tablet of their heart" refers to a condition of permanent consciousness concerning this matter;[7] the people are not able to ignore or forget their sin. In the same manner they should remember God's faithfulness and gracious acts for them (2:5-8), just as a young woman would give attention to her jewelry or a bride to her sash (girdle?) (2:32).

As disturbing as anything for Jeremiah is the sense of direction which the people have established in their minds. This is associated directly with their will, to be treated in the next section. Jeremiah observes the people in a state of continual revolt. Although once pure, they have turned away from God and stayed away (2:21; 8:4f.), and now no longer know how to do otherwise (4:22; 2:25). Morally, this is associated with their self-serving, oppressive inclinations (5:26-28; 6:6f., 13; 9:4-6 [H 9:3-5]; 22:17). The shift in direction can be seen both throughout the course of history (2:2-13) and in an individual case such as the Deuteronomistic description of the people's freeing their slaves and then forcing them back into their service (34:8-16).

Thus Jeremiah acknowledges fully the people's capacity for rational and intellectual functioning. They can think, plan, scheme, know, understand, have insight, be conscious of the surrounding state of affairs, remember, and set a direction for their lives. They are to be criticized, however, for the conclusions they draw on the basis of their interpretation of the evidence from history and tradition, for they do not seem to grasp that it is vitally important to follow the demands of God in order to receive his blessings. Above all, they have developed a stubbornness complementing their will and desires, and this accounts as much as anything for their repeated moral and religious faults. Yet fundamentally, the prophet—perhaps out of exasperation from having tried so long to reason with the people, yet also in good accord with the biblical stance (e.g., Prov 15:11; 24:12; Psa 44:21; 139:23)—acknowledges that only God can possibly examine the human mind (Jer 11:20; 12:3; 20:12) and understand it:

The mind *(lēb)* is more insidious than all things,
    and incurably corrupt. Who understands it?
I YHWH search the mind *(lēb)*
    and examine the affections *(kĕlāyôt)*,

> in order to repay everyone according to one's conduct,
> according to the fruit of one's deeds. (17:9f.)

2) Volition

Jeremiah is more intensely critical of the aspects associated with the human will than with any other condition of the moral agent. We do not find him attacking the people for lack of will, i.e. for indifference, apathy, or even laziness. On the contrary, his primary concern is that they have developed a disposition, a willful purpose, and a preferred course of action that are all contrary to the will of YHWH. These are associated, of course, with choice, decision, and planning, parts of the process of moral acting. At this point we need to look more carefully at the nature of this will and of its consequences for moral action.

Hebraic thought does not differentiate sharply between understanding and will as human activities. They are closely related and interdependent inasmuch as the mind is capable of setting a direction for living while the will needs the rational capacities in order to plan and reach its desired end. This relationship between reason and will is seen clearly in the linguistic proximity between "perceiving" and "choosing" and between "hearing" and "obeying."[8] Similarly, stubbornness is seen as an intransigence of both the mind and the will. Nonetheless, the will can at times become so habitual and "second-nature" that the proclivity borders on ethical neutrality,[9] as Jeremiah seems to recognize in his quotation of his audience about their driving force:

> No, it is hopeless!
> For I have loved strangers,
> and after them I must go. (2:25b)

This does not constitute a valid excuse for the people, according to Jeremiah. Rather, it is a subtle instance of the pernicious power of routinized sin, with the doer becoming the victim in the end. At any rate, the prophet certainly considers the will to be, as a rule, an expression of human choice,[10] even though in two instances the conquerors' will to destroy is explicitly attributed to YHWH (51:1, 11).

Jeremiah perceives both moral and religious dimensions of the people's will. Morally, they are greedy for dishonest gain (6:13; 8:10; Jehoiakim in 22:17; note also the proverb in 17:11). In order to achieve this they are willing to practice oppression (5:26; 6:6f.; 9:6 [H 9:5]; 21:12; 22:17), to deceive and deal treacherously (e.g., 5:27; 9:5f. [H 9:4f.]), and to subvert justice in the lawcourt (5:28; 21:12). Presumably these tactics could be successfully accomplished only by a limited number within the society, as Jeremiah intimates in his reference to "the wicked ones among my people" (5:26). Yet at another point his search for "a doer of justice and a seeker of truth" turns up no one, neither among the poor nor among the great (5:1-5). The inclination toward pleasure and lust can certainly be commonly shared among all social levels, and Jeremiah observes it rampant (5:7f.). The moral will among the people is complemented by the religious will, and Jeremiah cannot speak forcefully and often enough about the dispositions of the people in this regard: apostasy, idolatry, rebellion against YHWH, and abandonment of the ancient covenantal devotion (e.g., 2:2).

As troublesome for Jeremiah as the objects of their will is the tenacity with which they adhere to their preferences. Whatever Jeremiah's relation to the Josianic reform might have been—if he was even functioning as a prophet during it[11]—he was certainly struck by its superficial effect on the people. Even in the face of deteriorating political affairs in the two decades prior to the fall of Jerusalem, the Judahites are depicted by Jeremiah as refusing to turn from their willful course. This stubbornness becomes a recurring motif in the pronouncements of both Jeremiah (5:23; 6:28; 13:10; 23:17) and the Deuteronomists (7:24; 11:8; 16:12; 18:12; and perhaps also 3:17 and 9:14 [H 9:13]; cf. also Deut 29:19 [H 29:18]).[12] The typical expression for this conjoins "stubborn" with "heart," and in these contexts the heart must be referring more to the human will than to the mind. The people refuse to listen to YHWH's word (5:21; 6:10; 19:15; 36:24f.), to take correction (2:30; 5:3; 15:7), or to refrain from this injustice (9:6 [H 9:5]; cf. 22:16). Indeed, their conscience seems to have dulled in the process, for no one is troubled (12:11) or ashamed (3:3) because of their practices: "They do not even know how to blush!" (6:15; similarly 8:12).

It does not come as unexpected, then, that Jeremiah concludes that it will take a decisive, radical act to effect a change of the people's will. Again envisioning the heart as the seat of the will, he challenges the people:

> Circumcise yourselves to YHWH,
> and remove the foreskins of your hearts. (4:4)

When they fail to respond (9:25f.), there appears to be no other hope but that YHWH himself will act to change the people's hearts (31:33). This is the expectation of Ezekiel also (Ezek 11:19 and 36:26; cf. 18:31), as well as of the Deuteronomistic redactors of the Book of Jeremiah (24:7; 32:39f.; cf. 3:10 and 29:13).

3) Affectivity

Mental life and activity are not restricted to rational, intellectual, and volitional functions. There exists also a range of feelings and moods that spring from the state of consciousness. These are commonly designated emotions and are to be distinguished from the purely physiological sensations of touch, contact, temperature, pressure, or physical pain or pleasure. Affectivity is a condition of the moral agent inasmuch as the emotions can have a direct as well as an indirect impact upon the choices and conduct of a person. It stands in dialectical relationship with the other conditions, with no necessary tyranny of one over the others. The emotions can serve as a goal in stimulating a project, just as they can at other points play a secondary or even insignificant role in favor of other functions of the mind. There has been, to be sure, considerable controversy in the disciplines, especially in psychology and ethics, about the relative ordering of the emotions to each other and about the relation of affectivity especially to rationality and volition. This is a philosophical problem which has not yet been resolved after more than two millennia of attention, and it is not our intent to take it up in this context. So far as the ancient Hebrews were concerned, it is possible to address the subject of emotions directly, yet these are not to be divorced radically from the other dimensions of life, all of which we are considering under the rubrics of conditions of the moral agent.

Jeremiah has frequent reference to affectivity in his analysis of the people's morality. For him the emotions displayed by them are entirely consistent with what he can determine about their reason and will. They fall roughly into two groupings: those associated with the period prior to the divine punishment and those connected with the time of doom.

Prior to the doom Jeremiah notes five primary emotions: lustful desire, greed, callous unconcern for others, pride, and a gullible love of security. The lustful desire is invariably linked to images of whoredom. Unfortunately, it is often difficult, if not impossible, to determine whether references to sexual lusts and prostitution are descriptions of actual harlotry or rather are figurative allusions to religious apostasy. One is tempted to see actual prostitution as the object of prophetic scorn in such passages as 2:25, 33; 4:30 (or are all three of these texts allusions to Judah's political machinations?); and 5:8—although two of these sayings (2:25; 5:8) are presently in contexts where worship of other gods is the issue. Apostasy is more clearly identified as harlotry in 2:20, while the whoring image is strong enough in 3:1f. as to make the interpretation somewhat uncertain. Yet whether actual or figurative, the practices are for Jeremiah indicative of a determined striving and unlimited desire that have diverted the people from a course of action pleasing to YHWH. The same can be said of the greed which the people display, a lust for profit and for luxury (6:13 = 8:10; 5:26-28; 22:17, Jehoiakim) which they pursue with whatever deceit and treachery may be needed. This involves as well an habitual attitude of callousness, a self-serving complacency about the hurt that they might in the process be inflicting on others (5:3, 27f.; 6:7; 9:6 [H 9:5]; 12:11). Their obstinacy has indeed reached such a point of insensitivity that they can no longer even blush or be ashamed about their religious and moral behavior (3:3; 5:3; 6:15 = 8:12). The charge of pride is not levied often against Judah—explicitly only in 9:23 [H 9:22]; 13:9; and 13:15—although it may well be implicit in other utterances. Jeremiah refers to his insolent opponents who advocate flight to Egypt after the murder of Gedaliah (43:2), and beyond this it is arrogance and presumption that become major grounds for proclamations of doom against foreign nations: Moab (48:14-20, 26, 29f., 42), Edom (49:16), and Babylon (50:29, 31f.). The fifth emotion affecting the people's choices and behavior is a strong desire for security, a naïve optimism that prohibits them from coming to terms with the historical and theological realities that Jeremiah sees so clearly. This is especially associated with the message of the false prophets:

> The prophets prophesy in deceit,
>   and the priests rule on their own authority.
> My people love it like this.
>   But what will you do when it ends? (5:31)

The people seem eager to hear the prophets and priests who preach peace and well-being before the catastrophe (5:12; 6:14 = 8:11; 14:13; 23:17) and early restoration or deliverance after the demise of Judah begins (chaps. 27-28; 37:9).[13]

Emotions associated with the doom itself and with its aftermath are virtually the reverse of those which had been dominant in the decades preceding. It is often difficult to determine whether these are actual exilic descriptions or rather are preexilic projections by Jeremiah, for many of his utterances about the judgment and also about hope for the future were quite possibly spoken earlier with the intention of dramatically informing the people about what they will experience—also emotionally—if they refuse to change their ways.[14]

Fear and despair characterize the people as the destruction approaches. In sharp contrast to the lust and greed that guided their previous behavior, the people are now overwhelmed by an anguish that reaches to the foundation of their existence. At several points Jeremiah expresses this with the image of a woman in labor (4:31; 6:24; 13:21; 22:23; 30:6; cf. 15:8f.; 50:37), elsewhere with a direct reference to the failure of courage, especially among the rulers (4:9; 25:34; contrast this with the king's obstinate lack of fear in 36:24f.). The despair may be occasioned by the drought (14:1-6) or by the onslaught of the enemy (6:1-5; 18:22; 14:17-15:4, perhaps a community lament with Jeremiah as a participant).

The exilic situation itself elicits sorrow and longing. Again as with the fear, these emotions are depicted as being so great as virtually to overcome the people. Sorrow and weeping (cultic?) are associated with mourning (9:17-22 [H 9:16-21]; 22:10; 31:15), perhaps reminiscent of the grief expressed just prior to the fall of Jerusalem (30:12-15 in its independent form before it was conjoined to the "therefore" sentence in its present context). Concomitant with the sorrow is a longing to be restored to the land, a single-minded desire of the languishing soul (31:25; 50:19). Jeremiah responds with words of hope, but he also counsels them to learn to accept their punishment (30:11bβ) and not to abandon the normal functions of life (29:4-7). In his pronouncements about the future restoration the prophet anticipates that the people's sorrow will be replaced with an equally overwhelming sense of joy (chaps. 30-31 passim; 33:9-11).

It is intriguing to observe that some of these same emotions characterizing the people in the later years are precisely the ones which mark Jeremiah himself in his earlier ministry: fear (implied in 1:17; in 37:20; and in several of the Confessions) and sorrow or grief (8:18-9:1 [H 8:18-23]; 13:17; 20:18), as well as indignation (15:17) and anger (especially in the Confessions). At the root of his ministry is the frustration of dealing with a people who no longer practice *ḥesed* (2:2), the fundamental posture of the covenantal people that necessarily integrates all of the conditions of the moral agent. Instead the people's state of being has become broken, with any of the conditions—including here affectivity—becoming distorted and dominant in an unacceptable fashion.

4) Sociality

An additional condition of the moral agent is sociality, the natural tendency of individuals to bind themselves to others and in this shared context of existence to develop structures of meaning, understanding, interaction, and continuity.[15] For our purposes here we can distinguish between two aspects for our attention: the social character of human existence, and the community as moral agent.

The social character of human existence stipulates that persons cannot live out their lives atomistically, devoid of significant relationship with others. For moral agency this means that over a period of time people devise in concert—often unconsciously—coherent systems of values, codes of accepted behavior, meaning constructs, structures of responsibility and accountability, and patterns of affecting and reacting to each other. Jeremiah does not treat these matters explicitly, at least not as fundamental issues, but he refers enough to various types of social interaction to permit one to conclude that he is aware of the importance of sociality. He seems to assume a uniformity or commonality among the people, for his search for a just person turns up no one (5:1-5).[16] He is intensely critical of the effect that certain persons have over others, viz. the leaders (prophets, priests, rulers, scribes, and sages) in offering unfounded assurances that misguide the people (5:12, 31; 6:13f.; 8:8-11; 14:13; 23:9-32; 26:7-23; 28:1-4, 15). Jeremiah's repeated reference to the wickedness around him derives from the widespread faults associated with rationality, volition, and affectivity—values and behavioral patterns which are learned and reinforced in the social arena. The prophet appears to be condemning sociality as such in the proverb, "Cursed is the person who trusts in humanity" (17:5aα), but the primary intention of this wisdom saying is not so much to comment on human community but rather to affirm the system of divine retribution (see also 12:1-4). Jeremiah, who felt compelled to sit alone (15:17; also 16:1-13, Deuteronomistic) when he might well have preferred otherwise, is not opposed to sociality—but to *his* society. Thus in response to the proverb about the eating of sour grapes (31:29f.), he does not advocate a radical individualism in which no single person is responsible to or for anyone else, but rather he offers a rebuttal against a fatalistic system in which a new generation, such as the exilic one, would necessarily have its existence determined exclusively by its predecessors. The community very much remains—indeed is presupposed—in this.

An additional dimension to sociality is the emergence of the corporate body as an entity itself. A society which exists over time and through social contract becomes more than the sum total of its members. It acquires a character and a direction, and thus may be considered a "moral agent" itself, albeit not with all of the above-mentioned conditions that mark the individual agent. For a society is not simply the individual writ large, although there will be some congruences. The Hebrew Bible typically stresses the important role of the community, both for its members and before God. Consequently, it is an especially serious flaw for Jeremiah to observe that the fabric of the community has decayed (13:1-11). He sees neighbor deceiving neighbor (e.g., 9:4-8 [H 9:3-7]), wealthy and powerful oppressing the weak (2:34; 5:26-28), and their leaders taking them astray (see above paragraph). Thus the key indicators of the strength of a society—public interdependence, social justice, and political responsibility—are all sorely deficient. It comes as little surprise that the Deuteronomists select the Rechabites as a model of a social group that has an unwavering commitment to a set of values and to its own identity (chap. 35).

5) Temporality and Historicality

Of similar importance for an understanding of moral agency is the rootedness of persons in time and history.[17] No one is able to conduct life *solely* in relation to some principle of the good, or to some imperative of duty, or to some higher (e.g., ethereal) order of existence. The self is located in a certain present and with a specific as well as general past and future, contexts which can range from narrow to broad, even to the point finally of embracing the history of humanity. Who we are, how we view life, where our fundamental values lie, how we interpret and react to historical and natural stimuli—all of these are significantly influenced by our social as well as personal biography. This does not amount to a rigid determinism, however, for we retain the freedom to alter our place in this context through a new understanding of or response to it. Thus for the moral life we can ascertain three key dimensions of temporality and historicality: a sense of being in time; the interpretation of history; and the necessity of response.

The sense of being in time involves the agent's relation to past, present, and future. Each person typically has a primary orientation to the present. It is in the here and now that we experience routine and crisis, and to our present we subordinate our interest in both past and future. Consistent with the other prophets, Jeremiah focuses his attention above all on the contemporary situation of the people. The whole thrust of his message is to help his compatriots understand what is happening around them and what consequently is expected of them. This message changes as he perceives the events developing: from a cautious optimism that the people may reform, to a pessimism because of their intransigence, and finally to a realistic encouragement for them after the destruction and exile. His references to the past (e.g., the long history of rebellion, 2:5, 2:20, 23:27; or the good path that has been shown them, 6:16, 18:15, 22:15f.) or to the future (e.g., the repeated proclamations of doom) are not made for their own sake but in order to enhance the understanding of the present, and in this sense past and future are primarily extensions of the present. This allows him to render fundamental evaluations of the people (e.g., 4:22; 8:5) and to find grounds for hope (e.g., the survival of a remnant in 4:27; 5:10; 30:11; 46:28).

Yet according to the Hebrew Bible the fundamental relation to time coheres with the relation to history, whereby both are viewed *sub specie divinitatis*. At this point the factor of interpretation becomes crucial. Of the two levels of interpretation, Jeremiah provides virtually no direct information about the first, viz. the manner in which each new generation and each individual receive from the past the symbolic and conceptual mechanisms of understanding, acting, and expressing. It may be implicit in his observations about the continuity throughout generations in the people's inclination to evil. But the second level of interpretation, involving the express attribution of meaning to significant occurrences or phenomena, receives direct attention. This constitutes in fact a point of conflict between the prophet and the people. In most cases the people interpret the past for their benefit, as a guarantee of their continued security and prosperity, while Jeremiah sees it as a threat that YHWH, in his freedom, will visit the people in terrifying ways because of their wrongs.[18] Such is the case for the saying, "Every jar will be filled with wine" (13:12-14); for the tradition about the inviolability of Zion (8:19f.); for the belief that God will not punish his people (5:12; 21:13); and for the discrepancy between the message of the false prophets and that of Jeremiah (chaps. 23 and 28). We see a graphic dispute over interpretation also in the largely Deuteronomistic account about the worship of the queen of heaven (44:15-28). Similarly, Jeremiah presents the people with a distinct interpretation of the current events which the people refuse to accept as foreboding disaster, and during the exile he presents them with hope and determination when the future looks bleak to them (e.g., chap. 29).

All of the dimensions of the moral life according to Jeremiah converge at this point to underscore the urgency of response. This is keyed to the events of the current situation, especially the crises which demand fitting responses if the people are to survive. The problem in this regard for Jeremiah lies in convincing the people of the presence of the crisis and of the appropriate way to react to it. It is to be noted that the response must be contextually determined, as is evident from Jeremiah's at one point pleading with the people to repent in order to divert disaster (3:12f., 22; 4:1-4, 14; 26:2-6, 13) and later advising surrender in order to preserve life (speaking to King Zedekiah in 38:14-23; and to the people in 21:8-10, the latter being Deuteronomistic in revision but certainly Jeremianic in origin; 38:2 is a Deuteronomistic or later gloss).

6) Moral Freedom

In light of the significance of the above five conditions, what remains of the human's ability to choose? Ethicists range between two poles in dealing with this issue of moral freedom: from considering the agent as a victim of any or all of these determinants, to regarding the person as essentially "self-made." Jeremiah, like other prophets, presupposes the moral freedom of humans. This scarcely appears as an explicit subject in his utterances, yet it is foundational to his ethic. The people act of their own accord and thus are to be held fully accountable for their choices. The Deuteronomists schematize this in terms of the need to decide between two paths, the one of obedience and the other of disobedience, and they make it clear that the people's decision will be the determining factor for their own fate (see, e.g., Jer 18:7-11; 21:8f.; 22:3-5; 25:5f.; 35:15). Jeremiah is close to such an either/or. His appeals to the people are tempered only by his realistic assessment of their fundamental characteristics, those discussed in the sections above. Yet for him such characteristics do not lessen the people's accountability—but only help to explain their repeated failure to respond appropriately to God's demands.

However, for Jeremiah this freedom to choose and act does not mean that the people possess an absolute independence from YHWH. In fact, he criticizes directly such a notion among the people with a word from YHWH:

> Have I been a wilderness to Israel,
>   or a land of deep darkness?
> Why then has my people said, "We are free (lit., we roam unbridled)!
>   We will come to you no more." (2:31)

While the people have the right of choice, they cannot cancel the fact of their covenantal relationship with YHWH, and they will be punished if they so attempt. This status as God's people belongs to their very nature, and in one striking passage Jeremiah cannot fathom that they act contrary to their essence any more than that natural phenomena themselves would change (18:13-17, of which the key verse 14 is unfortunately quite corrupt; see also 8:7 and 2:10-12).

Jeremiah, then, adopts an equivocal position on the question of moral freedom. The people are free to choose in the sense that there is nothing intrinsic to their nature or to their community that compels them, whether consciously or unconsciously, to a certain course of moral action. None of the above conditions is necessarily or uniformly deterministic in this sense. Yet on the other hand, according to Jeremiah, the people do not face a morally indifferent world. At this point theology converges on ethics. YHWH has long been related intimately to Israel, and the people refuse to honor the implications of this at their own peril. The concept of moral freedom thereby becomes substantially modified by the need for responsibility to a relationship. Jeremiah shares with the rest of the Hebrew Bible the essential position that such a responsibility does not lead to forfeiture of being but rather to fulfillment of life. Freedom and promise become juxtaposed, just as are value and obligation.

II. The Ambiguity of Hope

The above conditions combine to constitute the moral agent. Without assigning priority to any one over the others, Jeremiah views human life as a confluence of all factors, each with its own importance and each in conformity with the others. He does not consider the possibility of a person divided within, e.g. torn between will and reason. The conditions reflect each other and contribute to each other.

For this reason Jeremiah finds it possible, having taken all conditions into consideration, to move to the point of rendering a fundamental evaluation of the people. We should emphasize, however, that this evaluation is neither unitary nor universal. In the first place, it can change as the political events develop and also as Jeremiah becomes increasingly aware of the people's intransigence. Certainly the exilic message is different at this point from the preexilic assessment. Secondly, Jeremiah is addressing *that* covenantal people at *that* time. We find no indication that he intends for his observations to apply to later generations of believers, much less to all of humanity—even though later persons may themselves be inclined to make such an application. Jeremiah is seeking to understand his consociates—the factors affecting their responses (i.e., all of the above conditions of the moral agent), the ways they relate to each other and to God, their fundamental values and loyalties—in short, the nature of their existence.

The most striking generalizations about the people stem from the pre-disaster years when Jeremiah has become convinced that the people are incorrigible: they are degenerate (2:21), shameless (3:3; 6:15 = 8:12), thoroughly wicked (3:5), foolish and stupid (4:22; 10:14), oppressive and violent (2:34; 5:26-28), unreceptive (5:21), untrustworthy (9:4f. [H 9:3f.]), good for nothing (13:1-10), habitual in their ways (8:4-6; 13:23), corrupt (17:9), incurable (30:12-15). His earlier hope for their reform (e.g., 3:22; 4:1-4; 5:1-6) is thus replaced with a cynical conclusion:

> Can the Ethiopian change his skin,
>   or the leopard its spots?
> Then you also would be able to do good,
>   who are trained in evil. (13:23)

They fail even to respond to chastisement (2:30; 5:3; 15:7). The picture of the repentant people especially in chaps. 30-31 is in marked contrast.

Inevitably, this raises a related question: What are the nature and locus of the good, and to what extent is the moral agent capable of knowing and doing the good? The former question would require prolonged attention if it is to be answered for Jeremiah and, beyond his utterances, for the Hebrew Bible on the whole. But the latter issue is more within our reach on the basis of the present analysis of Jeremiah's view of the moral agent. First, Jeremiah emphasizes that the good does not reside fundamentally within the human being (10:23). A person cannot know it immediately and alone; it is for God to assist in this knowing and doing. Second, the prophet affirms that the good has been experienced by the people in their past and that they can learn it now by examining their history (6:16; cf. 18:15). Third, the moral agent embraces the good only in the context of faithfulness to YHWH (2:19; 8:8f.; 17:5-8) and his law (2:8; 6:19; 8:7), a loyalty which finds expression through the maintenance of the community by means of practicing justice and truth (22:16; 9:3,6 [H 9:2,5]). Fourth, the good is not presented to humans as a vague, general value or obligation. Rather, people experience it in the concrete—in the affairs of normal life and in the crises of troubled times. Choice and decision are required, both over the prolonged period and at the crucial moments of tension. Fifth, because the good is present in the concrete, it does not have to be assigned to one of two typical poles: teleology or deontology. There is a conflation of end and ought in this ethic, with subjective, objective, and transcendental motivations[19] all potentially operative at different points in the moral process or in the moral life. For Jeremiah, then, people normally have the capacity to know and do the good. It was *his* generation that refused.

With this, his words of hope, especially those in chaps. 30-31, acquire a touch of irony and sadness. There appears to be no hope for reform so long as the people do not receive the final, decisive punishment of conquest and exile. Only thereafter are they ready to weep and return to YHWH. These proclamations of deliverance are notably devoid of references to morality, although it is certainly implicit to the understanding of the restored community. Only 31:31-34 stands out in this regard,[20] with a theological anthropology which at its root may well be consistent with Jeremiah's pre-disaster evaluation of the moral agent. The prophet seems unwilling to expect that the people's loyalties and conduct can change without a direct incursion by God, parallel to his movement of political events from doom to deliverance. With the establishment of the new covenant, faithfulness to the law must become a part of human nature, grafted onto the mind and the will. Jeremiah is advocating the recovery of a moral sense, indeed of morality itself as well as religious faithfulness. Yet he remains realistic that the people will be incapable of effecting this permanently, independent of divine measures. The actual conditions of the moral agents will always be potentially problematical in this regard. To be sure, it is precisely this fact which contributes so substantially to the divine/human drama.

NOTES

[1]For a summary of these classical issues in ethics, see James M. Gustafson, *Christian Ethics and the Community* (Philadelphia: Pilgrim, 1971), 84-100; and *Christ and the Moral Life* (New York: Harper & Row, 1968), 1-10.

[2]A theory of moral agency has not yet been fully attempted, although much of the groundwork for it has been laid. The present essay does not aim, in its limited scope, to construct such a theory. It represents, rather, a first attempt to develop rubrics for analyzing the structure of the moral agent and to apply these to Jeremiah's prophetic utterances.

[3]A discussion of the Hebrew understanding of rationality is available in Hans Walter Wolff, *Anthropology of the Old Testament* (Philadelphia: Fortress, 1974), 40-58.

[4]Interestingly, Jeremiah himself is willing to engage in deception at King Zedekiah's bidding (38:24-27), although this seems somewhat coordinated with the event described by his biographer in 37:20.

[5]The MT of 12:4 leaves some doubt whether the subject of *yir'eh* is YHWH or Jeremiah. The LXX preserves the explicit mention of YHWH while also reading "ways" for "latter ends." See the commentaries, ad loc.

[6]Using the same word *ysr*, the Deuteronomists extend the sense of disciplining to instructing: 7:28; 17:23; 32:33; 35:13f.

[7]Wolff, *Anthropology*, 48.

[8]Wolff, *Anthropology*, 51.

[9]Wolff, *Anthropology*, 38.

[10]The Deuteronomists describe the free choice of slaves in 34:16.

[11]For arguments in favor of a low chronology for Jeremiah, see J. Philip Hyatt, introduction and exegesis on the Book of Jeremiah, *The Interpreter's Bible*, vol. 5 (New York/Nashville: Abingdon, 1956), 778-80, 797-98; and William L. Holladay, "The Background of Jeremiah's Self-Understanding: Moses, Samuel, and Psalm 22", *JBL* 83 (1964) 153-64; and his *Jeremiah: Spokesman Out of Time* (Philadelphia: Pilgrim, 1974).

[12]To express stubbornness the Deuteronomists invariably use *šrr* whereas Jeremiah employs *srr* in the first two texts mentioned and *šrr* in the latter two.

[13]In 4:10 Jeremiah charges YHWH with misleading the people with such comforting messages, although he does not at all clarify whether he has in mind the general promises of the past (e.g., Gen 12:1-3; 2 Sam 7:8-16) or the lying spirit sent to the false prophets (1 Kgs 22:22f.). Most commentators, perhaps disturbed by theological implications of this, prefer to emend the text to read, "and they will say." However, the text-critical evidence for this is insufficient, and the more difficult reading should be retained.

[14]This is not adequately considered by Raitt in his periodization of Jeremiah's oracles of doom and deliverance; Thomas M. Raitt, *A Theology of Exile: Judgment/Deliverance in Jeremiah and Ezekiel* (Philadelphia: Fortress, 1977).

[15]For detailed discussion of sociality, see especially Alfred Schutz, *The*

Phenomenology of the Social World (Evanston: Northwestern University, 1967; German edition, 1932); Alfred Schutz and Thomas Luckmann, *The Structures of the Life-World* (Evanston: Northwestern University, 1973); Peter L. Berger and Thomas Luckmann, *The Social Construction of Reality: A Treatise in the Sociology of Knowledge* (Garden City: Doubleday, 1966); and H. Richard Niebuhr, *The Responsible Self: An Essay in Christian Moral Philosophy* (New York: Harper & Row, 1963).

[16]Such uniformity may indeed be expressed as a rhetorical device. An actual division among the people seems clear at least in 5:26a and in his references to a remnant (4:27; 5:10; 30:11; 46:28), although the latter are not pictured as deserving deliverance because of their faith or good deeds.

[17]For an analysis of the nature and importance of temporality and historicality, see especially the works cited in note 15 above.

[18]On this phenomenon of interpretation in the prophetic literature, see especially Walther Zimmerli, "Prophetic Proclamation and Reinterpretation," in *Tradition and Theology in the Old Testament*, ed. Douglas A. Knight (Philadelphia: Fortress, 1977), 69-100.

[19]The various types of motivations are divided into these three categories in Heinz-Horst Schrey, *Einführung in die Ethik* (Darmstadt: Wissenschaftliche Buchgesellschaft, 1972).

[20]Date and authorship of 31:31-34, like most of chaps. 30-31, are contested. Rudolph considers that this material was proclaimed in the period of Josiah's reform and directed originally to the exiles of the Northern Kingdom, while Weiser sets it even earlier in the time before the reform; cf. Wilhelm Rudolph, *Jeremia*, 3rd ed., HAT 12 (Tübingen: Mohr, 1968), 188f., 201-04; Artur Weiser, *Das Buch Jeremia*, 6th ed., ATD 20-21 (Göttingen: Vandenhoeck & Ruprecht, 1969), 264-67, 285-88. E. W. Nicholson, on the other hand, considers it an exilic composition by the Deuteronomists; *Preaching to the Exiles: A Study of the Prose Tradition in the Book of Jeremiah* (Oxford: Blackwell, 1970), 82-84. The position taken here is that it is essentially Jeremianic and was originally intended by him for all exiles, both Israelites and Judahites, following the fall of Jerusalem. Its similarities to Deuteronomistic language and theology stem from its later revision by this group. Yet fundamentally it shares more with the view of the moral agent evident elsewhere in Jeremianic utterances.

AFTER THE EXILE:
GOD AND HISTORY IN THE BOOKS OF CHRONICLES AND ESTHER

SANDRA BETH BERG

UNIVERSITY OF NORTHERN IOWA, CEDAR FALLS, IOWA 50613

THE Babylonian exile profoundly affected the totality of ancient Israelite life, a fact commonly acknowledged in scholarly literature. Less frequently noted, however, is the theological significance of the return from exile. This event was no less decisive for the development of Israelite thought.[1]

The postexilic era began with Deutero-Isaiah's hopeful pronouncements of Babylon's imminent overthrow, coupled with Israel's triumphant return from exile. But for the prophet, this restoration signified more than a *heilsgeschichtliche* event. Using the mythopoetic language of creation, Deutero-Isaiah envisioned the restoration as transforming the very structures of human life and the natural realm. Undiscouraged by the apparent delays following the return, large segments of the postexilic community retained their hope in the promise of a new age. Thus, for example, Haggai and Zechariah still awaited Yahweh's abundant blessings, although divine grace now became contingent upon completion of the new Temple (Hag 1:2-11; Zech 1:7-17). Despite increasing doubts, Trito-Isaiah proclaimed the transformation of the land and the establishment of a new Jerusalem (cf. Isa 60:1-7; 61:5-11; 62:1-12; 65:19-25), while Obadiah promised the imminent glorification of Zion and the destruction of its enemies (cf. vv 15-21).

The postexilic era, accordingly, began with proclamations of a new age about to dawn. Despite disappointments and delays, the returned exiles continued to affirm the significance of the restoration. The return, with its Zion-centered eschatology, remained an important concern well into the fifth century, when Nehemiah begged permission to return to Judah (Neh 1:3-4; 2:5). Much of the biblical literature from the Persian period, then, reflects the theological importance of the restoration, and the centrality of Zion.

Yet this Zion-oriented view posed two theological problems for some postexilic Jews. First, since both the biblical and extra-biblical sources indicate that not all Israelites chose to return to the land,[2] the significance of the restoration and the centrality of Zion obviously posed existential problems for those Jews who chose to remain in "exile." Secondly, the promised abundance of divine grace failed to materialize, even for Jews who returned to Judah. The reality of the restoration as an historical event did not obviate the difficulties of being a subject people. Hence, God's great acts in history seemed increasingly less applicable to the present age,[3] and the questions of where God was to be found, and His relationship to the elect people, became pressing concerns.

The present study investigates some of the ways in which these issues were addressed by two postexilic theologians,[4] the authors of Chronicles and Esther. The following remarks are offered in modest recognition of, and gratitude for, Lou Silberman's contributions to the human struggle to find God, and to understand what it means to be His people.

Most recent attention to the postexilic period has been devoted toward historical reconstruction. On the one hand, the lacunae in our knowledge of the Persian period make this interest both understandable and commendable. In fact, the literature itself encourages this historical pursuit: 1-2 Chronicles, Ezra, Nehemiah, Esther, and to some extent, Daniel 2-6, purportedly record the events leading to, and encompassing, the period following the overthrow of Babylon. On the other hand, the scholarly preoccupation with historical reconstruction often leads to an evaluation of the texts in terms of their historical accuracy alone. Accordingly, it is not surprising that the Books of Chronicles and Esther frequently come under attack.[5]

Yet one should not suppose that the value of these two works directly depends upon their historicity. Even were we able to verify the accounts as historically reliable in every detail, their theological significance would remain unproved. Conversely, if Chronicles and Esther were completely fictitious, their respective theologies still would demand consideration. Our primary concern must remain with the theological significance of events as these books portray them.[6]

This investigation therefore diverges somewhat from most examinations of Chronicles and Esther; its concern lies neither with the historicity of events, nor with the specific reasons which motivated the writing of these "histories," but rather with what Chronicles and Esther indicate about the divine-human encounter. A further concern is to note some of the religious motifs present in Palestine and the diaspora during this formative, albeit still obscure, phase of Israelite history.[7]

I. The Books of Chronicles

The questions of date and redaction require consideration prior to any discussion of Chronicles' portrayal of events. Was Chr's history composed by one individual, or does it result from several, distinct stages of development? Does one assign a date to the original composition, or to the redaction of Chr's history as now found in the MT? Are the Books of Ezra and Nehemiah a part of Chr's work and to be considered along with 1-2 Chronicles?

This latter question obviously affects the *terminus ad quem* of the work and therefore may be addressed first. While no consensus has been reached regarding the relationship of 1-2 Chronicles, Ezra and Nehemiah, Sara Japhet's recent arguments against the inclusion of the Ezra-Nehemiah materials remain impressive.[8] To the linguistic and stylistic data amassed by Japhet may be added various analyses of Chr's theology.[9] Recent investigations by David Noel Freedman, James D. Newsome, Jr., and T. Willi indicate that the theological emphases of 1-2 Chronicles differ significantly from those of Ezra-Nehemiah.[10] Each of these scholars independently concludes that a different literary and theological perspective dominates the two collections of materials. Hence, there is reasonable basis for the exclusion of Ezra-Nehemiah from Chr's history.

This conclusion helps to establish the date of Chr's work, but it does not solve the problem. That problem is complicated further by comparisons of the MT with the LXX. Again, comparing the Qumran manuscripts of 1-2 Samuel with Chronicles raises additional questions about Chr's *Vorlage.*[11] Nevertheless, it seems best to focus upon the "history" of Israel in 1-2 Chronicles,[12] as preserved, in the main, by the MT.[13]

Those scholars who exclude the Ezra-Nehemiah materials tend to date Chronicles between 515-335 B.C.E.[14] A sixth-century date often is favored, since Chr fails to address the fortunes of Zerubbabel and his successors, despite his great interest in the Davidic dynasty and the establishment of the Temple cult.[15] If Chr's account, however, includes 1 Chr 1-9,[16] 1 Chr 3:17-24 advises against so early a date.[17] Moreover, Chr's selective treatment of Israel's and Judah's histories—even his interest in an age presumably earlier than his own—suggests caution in evaluating his failure to discuss Zerubbabel and his successors, for the events encompassed by Chronicles may be limited by Chr's specific theological concerns, as much as by the period during which he wrote. Chr's interest in David and the Temple, in fact, could represent a response to rising doubts about the theological significance of the restoration. If Chronicles indeed reflects such a concern, a somewhat later date seems reasonable.[18]

As Freedman notes, the primary objective of Chr in compiling his work is far from clear. Yet, at the same time,

it is not difficult to isolate the major themes which run through the history: the author is above all a legitimist, and he is concerned with the divinely appointed institutions and duly authorized personnel which administer them in behalf of the people of Israel. Thus, his interest focuses on the kingdom of Judah, its capital city Jerusalem, and at the very center the temple; with respect to personnel, on the monarchy and the priesthood, or more particularly David and his dynasty, the high priest Zadok, his descendants, and ultimately all those belonging to Aaron and Levi.[19]

These central concerns, of course, reflect significant facets of Israelite life prior to the exile.[20] Chr's interests are understandable if he addressed a community still struggling with the problems of life as a subject people—particularly if that community had expressed its disappointment in the failure of the expected transformations in the human and natural realms to materialize.

The prominence of the Davidic monarchy and of the Temple, with their related concerns, is notable in Chr's theology. Yet Chr's theology is not one sans *theós*.[21] On the contrary, David's rise to power is divinely sanctioned (cf. 1 Chr 10:13-14; 13:3),[22] as is the eventual building of the Temple (cf. 1 Chr 17:1-15; 2 Chr 1-7, especially 5:11-14). For Chr, Yahweh's control of history does not conclude with David's anointment, nor with the establishment of the Temple cult. Rather, Yahweh continues to act in Israel's history throughout the account. Even the concluding passage of 2 Chr 36:22-23 indicates that Cyrus' authorization for the return ultimately resides with Yahweh. Much of 1-2 Chronicles, in fact, suggests God's close supervision of, and participation in, Israel's history—almost to the point of manipulation.[23]

Closely linked to God's active control of history is Chr's concept of immediate retribution.[24] Thus, for example, Saul loses the kingdom because of his disobedience (1 Chr 10:13-14); Shishak plunders Jerusalem because Rehoboam abandons Yahweh's law (2 Chr 12:1); and Uzziah suffers leprosy because of a cultic encroachment (2 Chr 26:16-23). Conversely, the villainous Manasseh enjoys a particularly long reign because he humbles himself before Yahweh and reforms the cult (2 Chr 33:11-20).

Yahweh's words in 2 Chr 7:13-20 summarize, to a large extent, Chr's portrayal of God's relationship with His people:

When I close up the heavens so that it does not rain and command the locust to crop the land, or send a pestilence against my people, and then my people, over whom my name is called, humble themselves, pray and seek my presence, and turn back from their evil ways, I will listen from the heavens, forgive their sin, and restore their land. . . . But if you turn aside, forsake my statutes and my commandments which I have set before you, and go to serve other gods and worship them, I will uproot you [MT: them] from my land which I gave to you [MT: them]. . . .

Yahweh judges each generation individually, and each monarch begins with a clean slate, earning immediate reward or punishment. For Chr, the most serious and flagrant of sins is idolatry, although the nature of this apostasy can vary. Foremost is the abandonment of faith in Yahweh, this through the worship of other gods. In Chronicles, both Northern and Southern kings prove idolatrous in this way. Jeroboam's worship of satyrs and calves at the "high places" presents a paradigmatic example of this form of infidelity (cf. 2 Chr 11:14-15). His apostasy is underscored by Chr's suggestion in 2 Chr 11:16 that those who remained faithful to Yahweh abandoned the Northern Kingdom and moved to Judah.

Chr, however, depicts the Southern kings, too, as idolatrous, in spite of his generally favorable view of the Judean monarchy. For example, Rehoboam is attacked by Shishak of Egypt because Rehoboam abandons Yahweh (2 Chr 12:1-6). Jehoram's sins result in an incurable disease and constant attacks upon his kingdom by surrounding peoples (2 Chr 21:2-10). Moreover, Jehoram's career concludes with his unlamented death and his burial outside the royal cemetery (cf. 2 Chr 21:20). Joash's reign begins well (2 Chr 24:1-16), but he rejects Yahweh in order to worship other gods. His actions bring about a victorious invasion by Aram, although Judah's military strength is superior. Joash himself is murdered in a conspiracy against him (2 Chr 24:25-26). These examples could be multiplied, but will suffice to indicate that the God of Chronicles does not tolerate worship of false gods.[25]

Yet in Chronicles, idolatry includes more than the worship of other gods. Each kingdom, North and South, contributes its own unique form of iniquity.

Respecting the North, the very existence of a separate, non-Davidic monarchy is considered idolatrous. For Chr, Israel, under Jeroboam, was conceived in idolatry, although the apostasy of the North extended beyond the reign of its first king. Given the character of Rehoboam's rule—one no less idolatrous than that of Jeroboam—the formation of a new kingdom could not be condemned. Yet with the accession of Abijah, whom Chr favors, any possible justification for a Northern Kingdom disappears. Under Abijah, Yahweh is faithfully worshipped in Judah (2

Chr 13:10-11). Moreover, Yahweh "has given eternal dominion over Israel to David and his sons by a covenant of salt" (v 5). Chr thus implies that continued rebellion against Southern rule becomes tantamount to rebellion against Yahweh's rule (vv 8, 11b-12). The defeat of the North in the ensuing battle confirms that the North has rejected Yahweh by rejecting Yahweh's appointed regent. Hence, the existence itself of the Northern Kingdom points toward its idolatrous nature. This view is maintained throughout Chr's portrayal of Israel's subsequent history.[26]

Chr, nonetheless, does not automatically dismiss the Israelites from consideration as Yahweh's people.[27] Rather, they are excluded only so long as they rebel against the South. Chr indeed relates that Yahweh's faithful returned to Judah (e.g., 2 Chr 11:13-17; 15:9), and Hezekiah's invitation to the Israelites to celebrate the Passover in Judah envisions the possibility of a complete restoration of the United Kingdom (cf. 2 Chr 30:8-11).[28] For Chr, Israel's continued refusal to reunite with Judah—particularly in light of the opportunities to do so—affirms that the exclusion of the Israelites from the elect people is by their own choice.

The North's rejection of Davidic rule is idolatrous in a further sense, since it entails a self-imposed exile from Jerusalem and its Temple. To even the most casual reader of Chronicles, the interest in the Temple and its attendant personnel is unmistakable.[29] Chr copiously records the planning of the Temple (cf. 1 Chr 21-29), its building (cf. 2 Chr 2-7) and the various reforms of its cult (e.g., 2 Chr 29-31). 2 Chronicles 7:1-3 suggests that God's glory filled the Temple (cf. 2 Chr 5:11-14), making the Temple His earthly dwelling, although Chr is at pains to indicate that Yahweh's presence is not restricted to the Temple (cf. 2 Chr 6:18). Nonetheless, for Chr, God's presence in the Temple is real, and we therefore are not surprised that Chr never mentions any sanctuaries outside Jerusalem. We hear nothing of Bethel or of Dan because only one legitimate locale exists for the Yahwistic cult.[30] In short, the Jerusalem Temple was "the life center of the people of God, the hub of the Lord's kingdom on earth."[31] By remaining apart from Judah and its central sanctuary, the Northern Kingdom once more manifested its rejection of Yahweh.

This transgression on the part of the North clearly cannot apply to the Southern Kingdom. Chr, however, does not consider David's successors to be without sin. On the contrary, Judah's kings display their own brand of idolatry by their dependence upon sources other than Yahweh.

Chr indicts various Southern Kings for their worship of other gods, although this form of trespass is not the only one for which they stand guilty. Saul set the example for his Davidic successors; thus 1 Chronicles 10:13-14 suggests that Saul failed to fulfill the divine word, and that he relied upon a medium.[32] For Chr, these two transgressions are related, and both justify Yahweh's transferral of the realm to David. In contrast to Saul, David often seems faultless in Chronicles. Such a characterization, however, is not completely accurate. Even David provokes Yahweh's wrath, and, ironically, for the same reasons as Saul.

1 Chronicles 21 describes David's attempts to undertake a census. What prompts Yahweh's displeasure is not the actual numbering of the people, but the purpose of that numbering.[33] As 1 Chr 21:5 makes clear, the census is for human military purposes, and to Chr, this suggests a less than total dependence upon Yahweh. David's census also contrasts with his earlier reliance upon Yahweh—a complete trust which resulted in impressive military victories (cf. 1 Chr 14:10-17; 18:6, 13).[34] Hence, even David experiences divine retribution for his reliance upon human resources. Yet David's punishment appropriately terminates with his offering of sacrifices at the newly-built altar, for his actions signify both an acknowledgment of his sin, and his unlimited recognition of Yahweh's sovereignty.[35]

On the whole, Chr views the Southern kingdom favorably and emphasizes that Judah joyfully fulfilled its cultic obligations.[36] Nonetheless, various Judean kings are guilty of reliance upon non-Yahwistic agencies, even when they do not worship other gods. Like David before them, several Judean monarchs apostasize by placing their trust in human alliances. For example, Chr portrays Asa's early years as peaceful and prosperous because the king instituted religious reforms and sought Yahweh's assistance in his battles (2 Chr 14-15). There is little doubt that the words of Azariah the prophet to Asa express Chr's own view: "If you seek Him, He will let himself be found by you; but if you abandon Him, He will abandon you" (2 Chr 15:2). Yet later in his reign, Asa forms a coalition with the Syrians against Baasha of Israel. He is rebuked by Hanani, whose prophetic word condemns Asa to continuous war and personal illness. Asa is condemned, not because he allied himself with a non-Judean power, but simply because he sought human assistance.[37] From Chr's perspective, Asa should have placed the fate of his kingdom under Yahweh's care (cf. 2 Chr 16:7-9). Even Jehoshaphat, one of Chr's favorite kings, is criticized for his alliance with Ahab. Despite Jehoshaphat's efforts to suppress worship of the Asheroth, he incurs Yahweh's wrath for seeking human allies (2 Chr 19:2-3). The prophetic censure of Jehoshaphat's alliances is repeated in the (misplaced?) pericope of 2 Chr 20:35-37. Jehoshaphat's maritime venture, of course, ends in disaster.[38]

Throughout 2 Chronicles, Judah's success depends solely upon

Yahweh, and human alliances are to be avoided.[39] Even too great a dependence upon the nation's own strength demonstrates insufficient faith, for military victories bear no relation to the size of one's army. As John Goldingay notes, "one man with God is a majority (cf. 2 Ch 13; 25.5-12)—indeed the one doesn't necessarily even have to fight (20.20-24)! Conversely, a majority without God will fail (24.24)."[40]

It should again be observed that Chr's appraisal of the Israelite and Judean kings points to only some of his concerns. Nonetheless, Chr's evaluation of the Northern and Southern kings is consistent enough to permit some conclusions regarding his perceptions of the divine-human encounter. First, Yahweh remains in firm control of historical events, even to the point of appearing manipulative. Moreover, God is accessible to the community through prayer and, especially, through the Temple cult. Secondly, Chr sees the elect community as represented best by Judah, under the leadership of the divinely-appointed Davidic dynasty. Those who fail to accept Judean rule—particularly when there are opportunities to do so—rebel against Yahweh. Those who choose to remain in "exile" reject God and will incur divine wrath. Southern kings, however, also sin by failing to trust completely in God. In particular, Chr censures not only the worship of other gods, but also any dependence upon human allies. For this Palestinian theologian, then, the chosen people consists of those who seek God by accepting His appointed king and cult, and who rely only upon Yahweh.

II. The Book of Esther

The Book of Esther offers an interesting contrast to Chr's view of the divine-human encounter. Whereas Chr addressed a Palestinian community which struggled with the theological import of the postexilic era, the Book of Esther provides a diaspora perspective.[41] In addition, Esther was written at a time more or less contemporaneous with Chronicles.[42]

But where are the implications of Chr's views for the diaspora? Like the Northern Kingdom in Chronicles, the Jewish community depicted in Esther would seem to rebel against Yahweh by choosing to remain in "exile." This rebellion against God, however, would be compounded by further apostasy: the Book of Esther betrays no interest in either Judah or its cult.[43] It also lacks any obvious interest in Yahweh or in the divine control of historical events.[44] A frequent observation concerning Esther is that it never mentions God.[45] Complete dependence upon Yahweh would seem precluded by the simple fact that Yahweh does not appear in the story. Rather, the scroll focuses upon the actions of its human protagonists, all of whom function within the structures of Persian court life. Esther thereby points to a reliance upon human agencies, and appears antithetical to Chr's view that one should depend only upon Yahweh.

Even at first glance, the Palestinian and diaspora estimations of God's relationship with His people, as perceived by Chronicles and Esther, significantly diverge. Indeed, a closer examination of the Book of Esther verifies these general impressions. Yet at the same time, the interests of these two "historians" coincide at significant points and suggest common concerns. As in Chr's history, the Book of Esther focuses upon a period which antedates the writer's own time.[46] The portrayal of events in Esther is no less stylized than in Chronicles, and "history" is accommodated to a particular pattern. Michael Fox's recent study of Esther's literary structure[47] demonstrates that events conform to a peripetetic principle.[48]

Several scholars note the astonishing series of coincidences in the scroll.[49] For example, through a series of remarkably fortuitous events, Haman unwittingly volunteers the method by which his adversary, Mordecai, is honored by the king. Yet Haman had come to court to seek the death of Mordecai. Later, Haman's inopportune plea for his own life occurs at the precise moment the king returns to Esther's banquet. This coincidence leads to Haman's death upon the gallows he intended for Mordecai. Throughout the story, peripety is at play, and events lead to the opposite of what we initially expect.

The peripetetic nature of events, however, is not restricted to the coincidences in the story. Rather, the narrated events are organized into

a symmetrical series of theses and antitheses, situations and their reversals. The theses are situations portending disaster for the Jews and success for their enemies, situations which could be expected to lead, in the natural course of events, to the Jews' destruction. But events do not run their natural course, but lead to the antitheses, which are the exact opposites of the result potential in the theses.[50]

For example, we may compare the following pairs of theses/antitheses:[51]

Thesis		*Antithesis*	
3:1	After these things King Ahashuerus promoted Haman son of Hammedatha, the Agagite, and advanced him above all his fellow ministers.	10:3	For Mordecai the Jew was next in rank to King Ahashuerus and great among the Jews. . . .

3:10 And the king took off his ring from his hand and gave it to Haman, son of Hammedatha, the Agagite, the enemy of the Jews.

8:2a And the king took off his ring, which he had taken away from Haman, and gave it to Mordecai.

3:12 The king's scribes were summoned on the 13th day of the first month, and it was written just as Haman had commanded to the king's satraps and to the governors who were over every province and to the ministers of every people, to each province according to its script and to every people according to its language. In the name of King Ahashuerus it was written, and it was sealed with the ring of the king.

8:9-10a The king's scribes were summoned at that time on the 23rd day of the third month, the month of Sivan, and it was written just as Mordecai had commanded to the Jews and to the satraps, the governors, and the ministers of the provinces which are from India to Kush, 127 provinces, to each province according to its script and to each people according to its language, and to the Jews according to their script and their language. He wrote it in the name of King Ahashuerus and sealed it with the ring of the king.

3:13 The letters were sent by couriers to all the king's provinces, to annihilate, to slay, and to destroy all the Jews, both young and old, infants and women, in one day, on the 13th day of the 12th month, the month of Adar, and to take their spoil as plunder.

8:10b-12 And he sent letters by the couriers, mounted on royal steeds . . . wherein the king allowed the Jews in every city to assemble and to stand up for their lives; to annihilate, to slay, and to destroy all the forces of the people and the provinces who were harassing them,

		(even) infants and women, and to take their spoil as plunder, in one day in all the provinces of King Ahashuerus, on the 13th day of the 12th month, the month of Adar.
3:14 A copy of the writings was to be given out as a decree in every province, published to all the peoples, to be ready for that day.	8:13	A copy of the writings was to be given out as a decree in every province, published to all the peoples, that the Jews should be ready on that day to deliver themselves from their enemies.

This series of thesis/antithesis continues throughout the tale.[52] Fox finds the thesis series beginning in chapter 3, and proceeding to 6:9, where the antithesis sequence begins. Yet the unexpected reversal of events actually begins much earlier. In Esther 4, we find the always-obedient heroine (e.g., 2:10, 20) suddenly issuing her own commands to Mordecai.[53] By contrast, Mordecai does "everything which Esther commanded him" (4:17). From this point on, Esther becomes the initiator of events, reversing our images of the protagonists. Esther 5:1 begins a reversal in the fortunes of the *dramatis personae*, which follows upon Mordecai's conversation with Esther. Esther goes uninvited before the king, and the Persian administration's previous responses to law-breakers[54] suggest that her action will not be welcomed. Yet Esther's unsummoned appearance—contrary to our expectations—is not punished. Rather, Esther wins Ahasuerus' favor, symbolized by the extension of his scepter. In addition, Ahasuerus promises that her petition will be granted, "even up to half the kingdom" (5:3). Esther 6:1 initiates the reversal of Mordecai's personal fortunes, and the succeeding chapters describe the unexpected transformation of the Jewish community from a people about to be annihilated, to one that is feared (cf. 8:17).

The peripetetic principle which governs the portrayal of events, however, becomes apparent only after Esther agrees to risk her own life, in the hope that her people might be saved (cf. 4:13-16). Mordecai's assurance that help for the Jews would appear, and his observation that Esther's ascension to royal power is fortuitously suited to "a time such as this" (4:14), intimate that history consists of more than mere coincidence or a random series of events. Mordecai's words in 4:13-14, when viewed along with the structure of the book, point to a hidden causality behind the surface of events.[55]

The Book of Esther does not mention God, even by circumlocution. To an ancient Jewish audience, however, the agency responsible for the order of events would seem obvious. Other examples of peripety in the Hebrew Bible point to God's control of history,[56] and Esther's audience presumably also would attribute the reversal of events to Yahweh.

Avoidance of any direct reference to Yahweh suggests that the peripetetic pattern of events was not intended to *prove* God's control of history. Apart from the fact that this understanding probably was assumed by an ancient audience, it would have been more natural for the narrator simply to depict Yahweh's unambiguous and undeniable control of history. The theological emphasis of the tale consequently must lie elsewhere.

The Book of Esther does not ignore the presence of divine activity. Rather, it suggests that Yahweh's control of history remains behind the surface of human events. Because Yahweh's control of history is neither overt nor easily discerned, the determination of the shape and direction of history shifts to humanity. While Yahweh ultimately shapes events, humans share in the determination of their fate. Hence, the unexpected reversal of events begins *only* after Esther assumes the initiative and undertakes actions to save her people. Similarly, the narrator avoids direct reference to the deity precisely in order to accentuate human responsibility in shaping history, and because God's control of history remains hidden.

This emphasis upon individual responsibility for the successful outcome of events also clarifies Mordecai's words to Esther in 4:13-14. In view of the hidden causality behind events, Mordecai insists that Esther must assume the initiative in saving their people. The Book of Esther thereby presents a dialectical theology where Yahweh's ultimate, but hidden, control of history stands in creative tension with human responsibility. The future of the Jewish community resides not only with God, but with both God and humanity.

Arndt Meinhold calls attention to a different type of hidden theology in Esther.[57] He notes the use of the expression, "fear of Mordecai," in Esth

9:3, and the similar phrase, "fear of the Jews," in Esth 8:17 (cf. 9:2). Meinhold argues that these references to "fear" recall expressions such as "fear of Isaac" (cf. Gen 31:42) and "fear of Yahweh" (cf. 1 Sam 11:7; Isa 2:10, 19, 21). These earlier "fear of X" expressions represent indirect references to Yahweh's intervention in history on behalf of His elect people. The recollection of Yahweh's past performance serves as the source of the "fear" instilled in Israel's enemies (cf. Deut 2:25; 11:25; 1 Chr 14:17). In the Book of Esther, the "fear of Yahweh," which lies behind the expressions, "fear of Mordecai" and "fear of the Jews," is not articulated overtly. Nonetheless, the unstated recognition of Yahweh's power still remains the vital force behind these expressions.

The implicit theology of the Book of Esther suggests that its author understood the Jewish community of Susa to constitute the chosen people.[58] The story's allusions to earlier Israelite traditions,[59] and even Mordecai's introduction in Esth 2:5, affirm the continuity between the pre-exilic and the Susa communities. The importance of Susa's Jewish community even seems to surpass that of Jerusalem, for the events at Susa affect *all* Jews of the empire, including those in Palestine (e.g., Esth 3:8, 12-14; 8:9-13; 9:2-3, 12, 16, 20-23, 27-31).

The concept of election in Esther is brought into fuller relief when we consider the scroll's dating of events. Haman's lots were cast in the first month, i.e., Nisan, and the impending destruction of the Jews was promulgated on the thirteenth day of that month. News of Haman's edict reached the Jews as they anticipated and prepared for the Passover celebration. This irony is underscored by Esther's appearance before the king on the "the third day" (Esth 5:1), presumably on Nisan 15. We later learn that the Jews battled their adversaries on Adar 13 and 14, celebrating their victory on Adar 14 and 15.

The scroll portrays the anticipated destruction of the Jews during the Passover season, and their subsequent deliverance exactly one month before the Passover observance.[60] Purim thereby anticipates Passover and constitutes, in some sense, a parallel with this formative event.[61] The events at Susa indicate that Yahweh continues to act on behalf of His chosen people, and the Book of Esther affirms the reality of the *Heilsge-schichte* for the postexilic diaspora.

III. Conclusions

In the period after the exile, the people of Israel was buffeted by forces over which it had limited influence. The danger of despair was fought by the postexilic prophets, and in their own ways, by the authors of Chronicles and Esther. Both accounts reveal that historical events assume a meaningful and orderly direction, and that divine guidance may be discerned in the pattern and nature of events. Chronicles and Esther, however, also disclose that the assurance that history will prove beneficial to the people of Israel is not total; it is conditional. The human response to events assumes a particular importance, and determines, in part, the shape of history.

Chronicles and Esther thus reinterpret earlier events, suggesting the proper relationship between God and His chosen people. They differ radically, however, in their respective approaches to this concern.

Chr finds Yahweh's elect best represented by those who rely solely upon God, accepting His appointed king and cult. Those who refuse to join this community rebel against God. By contrast, the Book of Esther affirms God's continued actions on behalf of diaspora Judaism. "Exile" would appear to lack any geographical connotations.

Chronicles and Esther also diverge in their views of the proper relationship between God and the elect community. In Chronicles, Yahweh's control of history dominates the account and appears manipulative. Chr thus suggests that anything less than total dependence upon the deity is idolatrous. In Esther, an opposite position is taken. Because Yahweh's control of history is neither overt nor easily discerned, the narrator stresses the importance of human initiative.

Chronicles and Esther, then, suggest antithetical perspectives, vis à vis the question of divine and/or human initiative in shaping history. Yet the very fact that both accounts assume such extreme positions implies the importance of this problem for the postexilic age. Both accounts struggle with the problem of God's continued presence in history, and both seek to demonstrate Israel's proper response to God's ultimate control of events. Hence, despite their divergences, Chronicles and Esther display common concerns which transcend the geographical and theological diversities of postexilic Israel.

NOTES

[1]Peter R. Ackroyd's, *Exile and Restoration* (OTL; Philadelphia: Westminister, 1968) remains among the best statements of the restoration's significance for Israelite thought. Ackroyd's study, perhaps more than any other single work, calls attention to the influences of the restoration upon Israel's theology.

[2]For example, the Books of Esther and Daniel presuppose a diaspora setting, as do various other segments of the postexilic literature. The texts from Elephantine similarly indicate that not all Jews chose to return to Palestine. On the Elephantine colony, see Bezalel Porton, *Archives from Elephantine* (Berkeley/Los Angeles: University of California, 1968).

[3]Most of the literature from this period increasingly emphasizes God's past or future acts in history. Rarely does the present age suggest the *Heilsgeschichte*.

[4]The religious pluralism of the postexilic period requires one to vary the questions which are posed in assessing Chronicles and Esther.

[5]Virtually all recent studies of Chronicles and Esther comment upon their historical improbabilities, inaccuracies, exaggerated numbers and stylized portrayals of events. Even those scholars who express interest in the theological significance of these works, do so within the context of the historicity of the texts.

With respect to the Book of Esther, see the writer's *The Book of Esther: Motifs, Themes and Structure* (SBLDS 44; Missoula, Montana: Scholars Press, 1979) chap. I.

The following quotations indicate a common juxtaposition of theological and historical evaluations in studies of Chronicles:

". . . Archaeological and historical studies have now rendered it more respectable and have shown it to be at times more accurate than some of its parallel sources. Naturally the Chronicler had a particular purpose in mind and, where he found more than one source to draw from for a story he wanted to use, he followed the one most harmonious and adequate for his purpose" (Jacob M. Myers, *I Chronicles* [AB 12; Garden City, N.Y.: Doubleday, 1965] xv; see also, xx, xlix; idem, *II Chronicles* [AB 13; Garden City, N.Y.: Doubleday, 1965] xx, xiv).

Robert North, "Does Archaeology Prove Chronicles' Sources?", *A Light unto my Path* [Festschrift Jacob M. Myers], ed. Howard N. Bream, Ralph D. Heim and Carey A. Moore (Philadelphia: Temple University, 1974) 392, comments:

". . . No single use of extrabiblical sources by the Chronicler has ever been proved. From this further follows not the fact but the undeniable possibility that any information communicated to us only by the Chronicler may be due in every case to his own legitimate theological inference or paraphrase from the canonical Scripture."

See also Frederick L. Moriarty, "The Chronicler's Account of Hezekiah's Reform," *CBQ* 27 (1965) 401; Paul D. Hanson, *The Dawn of Apocalyptic* (Philadelphia: Fortress, 1975) 273; John Goldingay, "The Chronicler as Theologian," *BTB* 5 (1975) 99-108.

[6]Of assistance here are the comments of Peter R. Ackroyd, *The Age of the Chronicler* (Auckland: Colloquium—The Australian and New Zealand Theological Review, 1970) 47, and Werner E. Lemke, "The Synoptic Problem in the Chronicler's History," *HTR* 58 (1965) 363, n. 44.

A significant contribution to the evaluation of Esther's "history" as theology is offered by Michael Fox. Fox's study, "The Structure of the Book of Esther," forthcoming in a Festschrift to I. L. Seeligmann, is discussed below.

[7]The theological concerns of Palestinian and diaspora communities did not always coincide. An obvious example here would be the Book of Esther, which lacks any interest in Palestine or its cultic institutions. The differing concerns of diaspora and Palestinian Jews continued into the hellenistic period, explaining the lack of any diaspora rebellion at the time of the Maccabean revolt. Unfortunately, very few scholars note the possibility of differing concerns in Palestine and the diaspora, and I know of no major study which seeks to compare the two.

[8]"The Ideology of the Book of Chronicles and its Place in Biblical Thought" (Ph.D. dissertation (Heb), Hebrew University of Jerusalem, 1973); idem, "The Supposed Common Authorship of Chronicles and Ezra-Nehemiah Investigated Anew," *VT* 18 (1968) 330-71. Japhet's views most recently are followed by H. G. M. Williamson, *Israel in the Books of Chronicles* (Cambridge: Cambridge University, 1977); and David L. Petersen, *Late Israelite Prophecy,* (SBLMS 23; Missoula, Montana: Scholars Press, 1977) 57-58.

[9]Williamson, 5-86, reviews Japhet's arguments and adds several of his own. His consideration of the extent of Chr's work, which also includes a thorough review of recent studies, compares the "ideology" of 1-2 Chronicles with that of Ezra and Nehemiah.

[10]Freedman, "The Chronicler's Purpose," *CBQ* 23 (1961) 439-40; Newsome, "The Chronicler's View of Prophecy" (Ph.D. dissertation, Vanderbilt University, 1973) 273-74; idem, "Toward a New Understanding of the Chronicler and His Purposes," *JBL* 94 (1975) 201-17; Willi, *Die Chronik als Auslegung* (FRLANT 106; Göttingen: Vandenhoeck & Ruprecht, 1972) 176-84.

[11]See Lemke, 349-63, and Myers, *I Chronicles,* lxxxvi-xc. Myers sometimes goes rather far by theorizing that the differences between Chronicles and Samuel-Kings result from Chr's differing *Vorlage*. Chr presumably preserved or altered his sources according to their compatibility with his own views. Hence, any differences between Chronicles and the account found in Samuel-Kings perhaps should be credited to Chr himself, rather than to a hypothetical *Vorlage*.

[12]Scholarly theories regarding the redaction of Chronicles tend toward three prevailing views. Scholars such as Myers, *I-II Chronicles,* see the work as basically the product of one hand. Others, like K. Galling, *Die Bücher der Chronik, Esra, Nehemiah* (ATD 12; Göttingen: Vandenhoeck & Ruprecht, 1954) 14-17, and Peter R. Ackroyd, "The Theology of the Chronicler," *LexTQ* 8 (1973) 102-3, favor two authors. The first was responsible for 1-2 Chronicles; a second, for the reworking of these books with Ezra and Nehemiah. Still others find

evidence for extensive redactional activity. Among these are Adam C. Welch, *The Work of the Chronicler* (London: Oxford University, 1939); W. Rudolph, *Chronikbücher* (HAT 21; Tübingen: J. C. B. Mohr, 1955); Frank Moore Cross, "A Reconstruction of the Judean Restoration," *JBL* 94 (1975) 4-18; and Petersen, *Late Israelite Prophecy*, 60. I favor the second position mentioned, and my concern here is with the author of 1-2 Chronicles.

[13]Note also that the MT—not a still hypothetical *Vorlage*—is included in our sacred scriptures, and demands our concern.

[14]Early dates are favored by Freedman, 441; Petersen, 58-60; see also Cross, 4-18, and Newsome, "Toward a New Understanding of the Chronicler and His Purposes," 201-17. On the other hand, Williamson, 86, concludes that Chr should be dated "at some point within the fourth century B.C." Since the publication of W. F. Albright's "The Date and Personality of the Chronicler," *JBL* 40 (1921) 104-24, only a few scholars maintain a hellenistic date.

[15]E.g., Freedman, 441.

[16]Some scholars view 1 Chr 1-9 as a later addition to Chr's work. This position was championed by Adam C. Welch, *Post-Exilic Judaism* (Edinburgh/London: William Blackwood, 1935) 186-87, and more recently revived by Cross, 11-14. The integrity of 1 Chr 1-9, however, is accepted by most scholars, although some secondary expansions are deemed possible. For a review of the evidence, see Marshall D. Johnson, *The Purpose of the Biblical Genealogies* (SNTSMS 8; Cambridge: Cambridge University, 1969) 37-76, and Williamson, 71-82.

[17]Williamson, 83-84.

[18]My own evaluation of the evidence favors a mid-fourth century date for the present form of the MT. While an earlier date bears upon Chr's purposes in writing his account, it would not substantially affect his portrayal of the divine-human encounter.

[19]"The Chronicler's Purpose," 436.

[20]One might add Chr's interest in prophecy. See the discussions of Newsome, "The Chronicler's View of Prophecy," and Petersen, *Late Israelite Prophecy*.

[21]Robert North, "Theology of the Chronicler," *JBL* 82 (1963) 381.

[22]Also cf. 1 Chr 11:3 with the parallel account in 2 Sam 5:1-5. Chr makes clear that David's rise to power resulted from Yahweh's will. Once God ordained David as king, the death of Saul, the acceptance of David by a united people, and the conquest of Jerusalem, rapidly follow. The succession of events takes considerably more time in 2 Samuel.

[23]Newsome, "Toward a New Understanding of the Chronicler and His Purposes," 207-8; but see the comments of W. Rudolph, "Problems of the Books of Chronicles," *VT* 4 (1954) 404-6.

Chr's concern to show how the purposes of God govern Israel's entire history already is expressed in the first of the genealogical lists. Chr begins with the creation and cites the descendants of Adam, partially in preparation for the divine appointment of David. Chr's interest in the worshipping community similarly reflects his belief that God remains active and accessible to the believer. Full discussions of Chr's views of worship are found in Gerhard von Rad, "The Levitical Sermon in I and II Chronicles," *The Problem of the Hexateuch and Other Essays* (New York: McGraw-Hill, 1966) 280; Myers, *I Chronicles*, lxvii-lxxiii.

[24] See Gerhard von Rad, *Old Testament Theology*, I (New York/Evanston: Harper & Row, 1962) 347-54; R. North, "Theology of the Chronicler," 372-74.

[25] For Chr, there can be no question as to the exclusivity of Yahwistic worship. For example, he describes the cessation of Temple worship during the reigns of Athaliah, Ahaz and, perhaps, Joash. Worship of Yahweh excludes any worship of other gods and, conversely, worship of other gods seems to preclude any worship of Yahweh!

[26] For example, cf. 2 Chr 10:19; 19:2-3; 25:7. Also see Myers, *II Chronicles*, 80-81, and Williamson, 111-13.

[27] Contra Rudolf Mosis, *Untersuchungen zur Theologie des chronistischen Geschichtswerkes* (Freiburger theologische Studien 92; Freiburg: Herder, 1973) 68-69, 172-73. Also see the recent essay by Roddy L. Braun, "A Reconsideration of the Chronicler's Attitude Toward the North," *JBL* 96 (1977) 59-62.

[28] Also cf. David's speech in 1 Chr 13:2: ". . . let us send for our kinsmen who remain in all the districts of Israel, and also to the priests and Levites in the cities where they have common lands, that they may join us."

[29] Most commentaries contain ample discussion of Chr's interest in the Temple cult. Additional remarks may be found in Roddy L. Braun, "The Message of Chronicles: Rally 'Round the Temple," *CTM* 42 (1971) 502-14.

[30] Chr also reinforces the centrality of the Jerusalem Temple in a more subtle fashion, e.g., the celebration of the Passover at Jerusalem under both Hezekiah and Josiah. Myers, *I Chronicles*, xxxiv, describes this double celebration as "just one more plank in the religious structure of the Judean capital as the official cult place. . . ."

[31] Myers, *I Chronicles*, lxviii.

[32] See the discussion of Peter R. Ackroyd, "The Chronicler as Exegete," *JSOT* 2 (1977) 7-8.

[33] For example, no negative judgment is attached to the numbering of the Levites in 1 Chr 23, nor to the genealogical classifications in the opening chapters of 1 Chronicles.

[34] Also of interest is 1 Chr 27:23-24, which lists two reasons for the incomplete census records, apart from the observation that those under twenty were not counted. The first reason concerns David's trust in Yahweh; the second, God's wrath at the taking of the census. While 1 Chronicles 23 and 27 seem to conflict, both accounts point to the view that a military census is antithetical to trust in Yahweh. Similarly, 1 Chr 5:18-22 can point to a military census, but the victories over the Hagrites clearly are due to a reliance upon Yahweh (cf. v 20).

[35] This altar, built at Ornan's threshing floor, becomes the future site of the Jerusalem Temple. That this altar should be connected with the end of the plague

seems appropriate, since the Temple marks Yahweh's presence among His people.

[36]Wilhelm Rudolph, "Problems of the Books of Chronicles," 408.

[37]Myers, *II Chronicles*, 95, further notes that the primary interest in Asa's disease "centers in the observation that he consulted physicians, rather than Yahweh, about healing."

[38]1 Kings 22:47-49 seems to suggest that the destruction of Jehoshaphat's fleet preceded Ahaziah's offer of assistance. Whether the transposition of events originates with Chr is not clear, although the present order of 1 Chr 20:35-37 suits his theological perspective.

[39]E.g., 2 Chr 25:5-13; 35:20-24; cf. 28:16-18; 36:12. For further discussion, see Welch, *The Work of the Chronicler*, 44-46; and Newsome, "The Chronicler's View of Prophecy," 110-29, 152-54.

[40]"The Chronicler as Theologian," 121.

[41]The view that Esther was produced by a diaspora community is commonly held. The reader is referred to the various commentaries on the book for further discussion.

[42]Most scholars date Esther sometime during the Persian period, and its Hebrew style frequently is compared to Chronicles. I have argued elsewhere that an earlier form of the narrative may come from Persian times, but the present form of the MT probably comes from the early hellenistic period; see chapter VI of *The Book of Esther: Motifs, Themes and Structure*.

In that study, I also suggest that a dominant motif in the Book of Esther concerns kingship. This motif perhaps provides a further point of comparison between Esther and Chronicles.

[43]Unlike, for example, the Book of Nehemiah, which suggests continued interest in Judean affairs.

[44]Nor do we find any overt mention of the covenant, prayer, dietary regulations or similar concerns which might suggest the recognition of Yahweh's active involvement in the life of His people.

[45]Various commentators see Mordecai's suggestion in Esth 4:14 that help will come from another source as a veiled allusion to God. Hans Bardtke, *Das Buch Esther* (KAT 17/5; Gütersloh: Gütersloher Verlagshaus Gerd Mohn, 1963) 333, however, correctly observes that such an interpretation conflicts with the tenor of the narrative. The most judicious reading of Esth 4:14 is that of Peter R. Ackroyd, "Two Hebrew Notes," *ASTI* 5 (1967) 82-86. Ackroyd argues that too little notice is taken of the adjective in the phrase *mqwm 'hr*. If *mqwm* is a metonym for God, we are forced into the untenable reading, "from another God." It is much more natural to take the phrase in a non-religious sense. Mordecai suggests less concern for the source of assistance, than the assurance that help is forthcoming. Hence, care should be exercised in interpreting *mqwm* as an allusion to God.

[46]See note 42 above.

[47]Cited above in note 6. I am grateful to Professor Fox for a copy of his article, prior to its publication. The analysis of Esther's structure which follows relies heavily upon Fox's views.

[48]That is, the unexpected reversal of affairs, such that the opposite of what one expects occurs.

[49]To cite only a few, see Bernhard W. Anderson, "The Place of the Book of Esther in the Christian Bible," *JR* 30 (1950) 36; Werner Dommershausen, *Die Estherrolle* (SBM 6; Stuttgart: Katholisches Bibelwerk, 1968) 157-58; Carey A. Moore, *Esther* (AB 7B; Garden City, N.Y.: Doubleday, 1971) 66-67; see also Abraham D. Cohen, " 'Hu Ha-goral': The Religious Significance of Esther," *Judaism* 23 (1974) 87-94.

[50]Fox, "The Structure of the Book of Esther."

[51]The following examples are taken from Fox, although not every example he cites is equally convincing. I present a fuller discussion of Esther's structure in *The Book of Esther: Motifs, Themes and Structure*, 103-21. See especially 119, n. 42.

[52]For example, cf. 3:15/8:14-15b; 4:1/8:15a; 4:3/8:17a; 5:14a/6:13b-14; 6:6-9/6:10. Note that the sequence of events does not present a precise chiasm. Moreover, the reversals are of a general nature, sometimes reflected in the style of narration, other times in the content of events.

[53]Note the use of *tswh*, applied to Esther in 4:10, 17. Also see the discussion of Bruce W. Jones, "Two Misconceptions about the Book of Esther," *CBQ* 39 (1977) 172-77.

[54]The narrator introduces his audience to the importance of obeying the law early in his tale. Esth 1:19 and 8:8 indicate that once issued, the king's law could not be rescinded. At the banquet of Esth 1:5-9, even noncompulsory drinking is regulated by law: *hshtyh kdt 'yn 'ns* (1:8). Moreover, both Vashti's and Mordecai's disobedience of imperial law is severely punished. Esther's future appears particularly dismal since "there is one penalty for anyone, man or woman, who approaches the king inside the inner court without having been summoned: to be put to death. . ." (4:11).

[55]A point well argued by Yehezkel Kaufmann, *The Religion of Israel* ([Heb] Jerusalem/Tel Aviv: Bialik Institute and Dvir, 1956) 8.445-47.

[56]Fox lists numerous examples throughout the Hebrew Bible.

[57]"Theologische Erwägungen zum Buch Esther," forthcoming in *TZ*. My sincere thanks to Dr. Meinhold for a copy of his essay.

[58]See the remarks of Anderson, 37, and Dommershausen, 14.

[59]Notably, the reworking of Saulide traditions, and a reinterpretation of the Joseph story. On the former, see W. McKane, "A Note on Esther IX and I Samuel XV," *JTS* (1961) 260-61. The relationship between the Joseph and Esther stories is discussed by Arndt Meinhold, "Die Gattung der Josephsgeschichte und des Estherbuches: Diasporanovelle, I, II," *ZAW* 87 (1975) 306-24; 88 (1976) 79-93; see also Berg, 123-65.

[60]Abraham D. Cohen, 90, notes that during the period of the Second Temple, the fourteenth as well as the fifteenth of Nisan involved observance of paschal rites. Also see the discussion of J. B. Segal, "Intercalation and the Hebrew Calendar," *VT* 7 (1957) 297-98. Segal argues that Purim always precedes Passover

by exactly one month, even during leap-years. He further suggests that Purim's fixed position in relation to Passover already was established by the second century B.C.E.

[61]Gillis Gerleman further maintains that the Book of Esther was meant as a parallel to the exodus account. His views are found in *Studien zu Esther* (BibS (N) 48; Neukirchen-Vluyn: Neukirchener Verlag des Erziehungsvereins GmbH, 1966), and *Esther* (BKAT 21; Neukirchen-Vluyn: Neukirchener Verlag, 1970-1973).

PROPHECIES OF FUTURE GREATNESS: THE CONTRIBUTION OF GRECO-ROMAN BIOGRAPHIES TO AN UNDERSTANDING OF LUKE 1:5-4:15

CHARLES H. TALBERT

WAKE FOREST UNIVERSITY, WINSTON-SALEM, NORTH CAROLINA 27109

WHAT handle can the interpreter grasp to bring Luke 1:5-4:15 within the sphere of our understanding? Since the question of the sources of Luke 1-2 is well nigh impossible to answer[1] and that of Luke 3:1-4:15 has become increasingly difficult,[2] no argument can be framed with confidence on the basis of a comparison of the final form of the Gospel with its sources. An alternate route, the one chosen in this paper, is to attempt to indicate how a Greco-Roman reader/hearer of Luke-Acts would have understood Luke 1:5-4:15.[3]

Before taking this route, however, it is necessary to justify the focus on 1:5-4:15 as a coherent unit within the Third Gospel. A survey of the contents of the early chapters of Luke seems to support the focus. Before 1:5-4:15 we find the prologue (1:1-4); after it there is the frontispiece of the public ministry (4:16-30). Within 1:5-4:15 is a unit dealing with John the Baptist and Jesus in three episodes:[4] (1) 1:5-56, the annunciations of the births of John and Jesus; (2) 1:57-2:52, the births and early lives of the Baptist and Mary's son; and (3) 3:1-4:15, the adult ministry of John and the prelude to Jesus' public career. Each of these three episodes is built around a series of correspondences between the material about John and that dealing with Jesus that reflects the Lukan artistry; each is concerned to portray Jesus' superiority over John the Baptist. In all three episodes John is depicted as a prophet (1:16-17; 1:76; 3:1-6), not the Messiah (3:15ff.), whereas Jesus is pictured in all three as the Davidic Messiah (1:32-33; 1:69; 2:4, 11; 3:23-38) and Son of God (1:35; 2:49; 3:22). This internal coherence argues for 1:5-4:15's being a single thought unit in the Lukan narrative.

The major objection to such a claim is the possibility that the Third Gospel once began with 3:1ff.[5] Three reasons have recently been ad-

vanced to support this contention. First, there are alleged historiographi-
cal parallels to 3:1ff. in other Greek writings which argue for this
passage's having been the original opening of the Lukan Gospel. Second,
Acts 1:1, 22 may be interpreted to mean that the Gospel once began with
the baptism of Jesus. Third, the placing of the genealogy in the third
chapter of Luke makes more sense if that had been done before an infancy
narrative had been prefixed. This problem, I think, is more apparent than
real. On the one hand, the reasons for thinking that the Third Gospel
originally began with 3:1ff. are not compelling.[6] (1) The evidence of the
first argument cuts both ways. Of the two examples cited by Raymond
Brown, the first (Josephus, *War*, 2.14.4 §284) comes in the middle of
Josephus' narrative, not at the start of any main section. The second
parallel (Thucydides, *History*, 2.2.1) may be the beginning of a section but
is certainly not the start of the document as a whole. Given these facts, we
may acknowledge that 3:1ff. is the beginning of the third episode of the
unit 1:5-4:15. One should note, however, that 1:5 gives a similar, if not as
elaborate, beginning for the first episode; and 1:26-27 and 2:1ff. give
analogous beginnings in the first and second episodes for the material that
relates to Jesus. The first argument is not persuasive. (2) The second
argument depends on a given interpretation of Acts 1:1, 22. It seems just
as plausible, however, to take Acts' reference to the baptism of John as a
marker for the beginning of the adult career of Jesus as for the start of the
Gospel. (3) Finally, the position of the genealogy is due to theological
considerations. It is integral to the unit which begins with the baptism and
ends with the temptation narrative and which focuses on the Son of God.[7]
There is no need to resort to the hypothesis of the Third Gospel's
beginning at 3:1ff. to account for its presence in chapter 3 rather than in
chapters 1-2. On the other hand, the issue before us ultimately has nothing
to do with earlier stages in the Third Gospel's development but with the
question whether or not *in the present form* of Luke, 1:5-4:15 is a coherent
narrative unit. The answer to that, I think, is "yes." This paper will focus,
then, on Luke 1:5-4:15 as a unit within the Lukan Gospel which treats the
life of Jesus prior to his public career.

What is the thrust of the material about Jesus in Luke 1:5-4:15?
Anticipations of Jesus' destiny predominate. These anticipations are
given in various forms. (1) There are two angelophanies.[8] (a) In the first,
Luke 1:26-38, the angel Gabriel comes to Mary not only to announce the
miraculous conception (1:35a) but also to tell of the child's destiny.

He will be great, and will be called the Son of the Most High; and the Lord God will give to him the throne of his father David, and he will reign over the house of Jacob forever; and of his kingdom there will be no end. (1:32-33, RSV) . . . and the child to be born will be called holy, the Son of God. (1:35b)

(b) In the second, Luke 2:8-20, an angel of the Lord appears to the shepherds in the field announcing the birth of one who would be a Savior, Christ the Lord (2:11).

(2) There are four prophecies. (a) Luke 1:67-79, the first, is a prophecy of Zechariah when he was filled with the Holy Spirit (67). In the context of his predictions about John (76-79), there is praise to God for raising up a "horn of salvation" in the "house of his servant David" (69). This, of course, refers in its Lukan context to Jesus. (b) Luke 2:25-35, the second, gives us the prophecy of Simeon, to whom it had been revealed that he should not taste death before he had seen the Lord's Christ (26). In the Spirit, on seeing Jesus he blesses God.

> Lord, now lettest thou thy servant depart in peace,
>   according to thy word;
> for mine eyes have seen thy salvation which thou hast prepared
>   in the presence of all peoples,
> a light for revelation to the Gentiles,
>   and for glory to thy people Israel. (2:29-32, RSV)

(c) In the third, Luke 2:36-38, we hear of the prophetess Anna who spoke of Jesus "to all who were looking for the redemption of Jerusalem" (38). (d) Finally, Luke 3:16-17 gives John the Baptist's messianic preaching. He speaks of the mightier one who is coming who will baptize with the Holy Spirit and with fire, a prophecy the author of Luke-Acts apparently believed was fulfilled at Pentecost (Acts 2:3-4, 33).

(3) Closely related to the series of four prophecies is Luke 1:41, 42-45, which consists of a portent followed by a prophetic interpretation. When the pregnant Elizabeth heard the greeting of Mary, the babe leaped in her womb. Filled with the Holy Spirit, Elizabeth then exclaimed: "Why is this granted to me, that the mother of my Lord should come to me? For behold, when the voice of your greeting came to my ears, the babe in my womb leaped for joy" (43-44, RSV).[9]

(4) Luke 3:21-22 has similarities to 1:41-45. It too has an event that is prophetic in nature followed by a verbal interpretation. Though not usually read as such, Luke 3:21-22 is a prayer scene consisting of a vision followed by an audition which interprets it. The Third Evangelist has

turned the narrative of Jesus' baptism into an episode of prayer in which there are an accompanying vision and audition. This is typically Lukan. (a) The Lukan emphasis on the prayer life of Jesus is well known (e.g., Luke 3:21; 5:16; 6:12; 9:18; 9:28-29; 11:1; 22:32; 22:39-46; 23:34; 23:46).[10] (b) It is also characteristic of the Evangelist to have prayer accompanied by visions and auditions.[11] For example, Luke 9:28-36 mentions that Jesus was praying, that a heavenly apparition occurred—Moses and Elijah appeared—and an interpretative audition followed—"this is my Son. . . ." Acts 10 offers another excellent example. In this chapter both Cornelius and Peter are involved in prayer; both have visions; both receive auditions which interpret what is seen. The same tendency may be found elsewhere in Acts 12:5ff.; 1:14 plus 2:1ff.; Luke 22:39-46; 1:10ff. In Luke 3:21-22 while Jesus is praying there is a heavenly apparition. The Holy Spirit descends in bodily form as a dove upon him.[12] The symbolism of the dove in Mediterranean antiquity (i.e., the beneficence of the deity in love)[13] is then interpreted by a *bath qol:* "You are my Son, my beloved, in you I am well pleased."[14] Here is another anticipation of Jesus' destiny, one that will become more striking when viewed in the context of the pagan practice of divination by means of the flight of birds. In Luke 1:5-4:15, therefore, angelophanies, prophecies in the Jewish sense of the word, a portent followed by an interpretation, and a vision plus an audition combine to give numerous verbal anticipations of Jesus' destiny.

Three other pericopes also deserve attention. There are two stories about the youth in which Jesus displays his wisdom and prowess (2:41-51; 4:1-13). In the episode of the twelve year old Jesus in the temple, the wisdom of the lad predominates.[15] In the test in the wilderness, the young Son of God demonstrates his spiritual power by means of his wise use of scripture and thereby defeats his adversary. Finally, there is the genealogy (3:23-38) which traces Jesus' lineage back through David to the father of the human race, Adam, and through him to God.[16] The impact of this material will be felt fully only after our foray into the Greco-Roman milieu of Luke-Acts.

How would such material—verbal anticipations of Jesus' destiny, stories of a young prodigy, and a genealogy—have been understood by a Greco-Roman reader? The question can be sharpened. Elsewhere I have argued that Luke-Acts belongs to a type of biography in antiquity which has the life of a philosopher who is a founder of a school followed by a narrative (or list) of his successors and selected other disciples.[17] The very form (a + b) would have been a clue to the readers/hearers about what to expect. In this light, how would a Greco-Roman listener hear a biography which had in its beginnings the components we have found in the Third Gospel in 1:5-4:15?

Suetonius' *Lives of the Twelve Caesars* is a good place to begin. In his "Life of Augustus" there is one section (94), set aside for "an account of the omens which occurred before he was born, on the very day of his birth, and afterwards. . . ." In this unit one finds at least fourteen omens which include: (a) portents interpreted by predictions (6 of the 14 items) which belong in the same general category as Luke 1:41-45; (b) dreams (3 of the 14 items)—e.g., a man dreamed of the savior of the Roman people, then on meeting Augustus for the first time, declared he was the boy about whom he had dreamed (cf. Luke 2:25-35); (c) prophecies (2 of 14 items), that is, verbal anticipations of the child's greatness and destiny (cf. the prophecies of Luke 1-3); (d) childhood prodigies (2 of 14 items), which tell us already that such childhood exploits were regarded as omens of the youth's destiny (cf. Luke 2:41-51; 4:1-13); (e) reference to a miraculous conception by Apollo (1 of 14 items), though the treatment of Augustus' family belongs to another section of the narrative about his pre-public life. In this section of omens from the beginning of Augustus' life we find all of the types of material that we noted in Luke 1:5-4:15 except a genealogy. It is interesting to note that here, as in Luke 1:5-4:15, the main thrust is on anticipations of the hero's destiny. His "Life of Augustus" is, moreover, typical of Suetonius' efforts.

In his "Life of Tiberius" 14, Suetonius speaks of Tiberius' "strong and unwavering confidence in his destiny, which he had conceived from his early years because of omens and predictions." There follow seven such omens and predictions, all of which belong to the category of prophecies. There are no childhood prodigies, nor is there a miraculous conception. In 1-4 we hear of the stock from which Tiberius derived his origins.

Suetonius' "Life of Claudius" 1-2 treats the emperor's ancestry. In 7 there is one portent of a prophetic nature. When Claudius entered the Forum for the first time carrying the fasces, an eagle lighted upon his shoulder. This was regarded as prophetic because of the Roman use of the flight of birds of omen to discern the decrees of Fate.[18] A classic case, as described by Plutarch, is that of Numa who was chosen king after Romulus.[19] Numa said that before assuming the kingship his authority must first be ratified by Heaven. So the chief of the augurs turned the veiled head of Numa toward the south, while he, standing behind him with his right hand on his head, prayed aloud and turned his eyes in all directions to observe whatever birds or other omens might be sent from the gods. When the proper birds approached, then Numa put on his royal robes and went down where he was received as the "most beloved of the gods" *(theophilestaton)*. In such a thought world, the Lukan baptismal narrative would have been viewed as an omen of Jesus' status as the beloved Son of God.

Three other Lives from Suetonius' work will suffice. In the "Life of Nero" 1-6, the emperor's family is treated. In 6 we are told that omens at his birth led to "direful predictions." Four examples follow, including one on the day of his purification (cf. Luke 2:22ff.). In the "Life of Vespasian" 1-2, Suetonius treats the emperor's family line. At the beginning of 5 we hear that Vespasian began to hope for imperial dignity "because of the following portents." At least fifteen examples follow, including the prophecy of Josephus when he was captured during the first Jewish Revolt against Rome. Suetonius' "Life of Titus" includes both prophecies of his future rule (2 and 5:2) and a note about his youthful excellencies in body and mind (3). From Suetonius' *Lives of the Twelve Caesars* one can conclude that this biographer believed a Life should include something about a hero's family lineage, prophecies of his future greatness, and examples of childhood prodigies as part of his prepublic career. Sometimes there might be a reference to a miraculous conception. Is Suetonius to be considered typical of the Greco-Roman biographical tradition in this regard? The answer is "yes."

Portents, prophecies, and omens are widely used in biographical literature of Mediterranean antiquity for the period of a hero's life before he enters upon his public career. For example, Quintus Curtius,[20] Plutarch,[21] Philostratus,[22] Pseudo-Callisthenes,[23] the *Historiae Augustae*,[24] and the biographical section in Josephus' *Antiquities* dealing with Moses[25] all contain this type of information in the pre-public lives of great men. A.D. Nock rightly said: "It was normally expected that a great man would be heralded by signs and prophecies."[26] The convention, being subject to perversion, could be ridiculed in satire, as in Lucian's *Alexander the False Prophet*. Before Alexander and his partner Cocconas entered into their public routine, they went, says Lucian, to Chalcedon and buried bronze tablets, stating that very soon Asclepios and his father Apollo would come to Pontus and settle. When the tablets were found, the people voted to build a temple. Alexander then came proclaiming an oracle that he was the scion of Perseus. Next a Sibylline prediction of his activity was produced. This series of prophecies set the stage for the false prophet's public activity. Such prophecies are a convention in biographical literature.

Childhood prodigies are just as frequently a part of the Lives of great men in Mediterranean civilization. It was a commonplace of Hellenistic biography to relate tales of the precocious intelligence and of the unusual power and authority of the youths of destiny.[27] Quintus Curtius,[28] Plutarch,[29] Philostratus,[30] Pseudo-Callisthenes,[31] the *Historiae Augustae*,[32] Josephus,[33] and Philo[34] reflect the practice.

References to miraculous conceptions are also an integral part of the biographical tradition, especially when the hero's Life is told in terms of the myth of the immortals.[35] Quintus Curtius,[36] Plutarch,[37] Philostratus,[38] and Pseudo-Callisthenes[39] give abundant examples of this tendency.

Finally, one expects to find material on the hero's family lineage which may eventuate in a genealogy. One may compare Plutarch,[40] Philostratus,[41] the *Historiae Augustae,*[42] and Josephus.[43]

The point is made. The biographical tradition of the Greco-Roman world would have conditioned a person in the Mediterranean region at the end of the first century C.E. to expect an account of the hero's career before he embarked on his public activity which included material on his family background, perhaps a reference to a miraculous conception, along with omens and other predictions of his future greatness, including childhood prodigies. When the reader confronted Luke 1:5-4:15, this narrative unit fulfilled these expectations in a remarkable way.

What was the purpose of such material in the narrative of a hero's life prior to his public career? For the sake of analysis, it will help if we divide the materials into two categories: omens, portents, and prophecies on the one hand, and birth, family, and childhood prodigies on the other. (1) Many Greco-Roman people believed that there existed a divine order of things which could be known by humans either through the initiative of the gods (i.e., revelation of when they were either angry or benevolent) or through the initiative of human beings skilled in unlocking such secrets (e.g., astrology). The prophecies of the biographies fit into this context. When Philostratus says of the portent at the birth of Apollonius, "No doubt the gods were giving a revelation—an omen of his brilliance, his exaltation above earthly things, his closeness to heaven,"[44] he was speaking of the belief that Tacitus alludes to with reference to Vespasian. Certain events, says Tacitus, revealed "the favour of heaven and a certain partiality of the gods toward him."[45] Through omens the gods revealed their preferences. Tacitus also tells how astrologers could, on their initiative, uncover fate. He says that Otho accepted the astrologer Ptolemy's "prophecies as if they were genuine warnings of fate disclosed by Ptolemy's skill. . . ."[46] In a similar manner Suetonius can say that Domitian knew the very hour and manner of his death because "in his youth astrologers had predicted all this to him. . . ."[47] Since either divine initiative or human skill could reveal one's destiny, Suetonius could write of Augustus:

Having reached this point, it will not be out of place to add an account of the omens which occurred before he was born, on the very day of his birth, and afterwards, from which it was possible to anticipate and perceive his future greatness and uninterrupted good fortune.[48]

Sometimes, of course, such omens were not believed until after their fulfillment. Tacitus tells us that the secrets of Fate and the signs and omens which predestined (*destinatum*) Vespasian and his sons for power "we believed only after his success was secured."[49] And even a disregard of omens often pointed to acceptance of the assumption that there existed a higher order which was revealed through signs. So Tacitus tells us that Galba's disregard for omens was due to the fact that we "cannot avoid the fixed decrees of fate, by whatever signs revealed."[50] Given this way of thinking, it is to be expected that a biography of a great man would often contain one or more omens of the destiny allotted the individual and that they would be given during the period prior to his public career.

(2) When we focus on the family lineage, birth, and childhood of the hero, we find sometimes an emphasis on the supernatural dimensions of them, sometimes an emphasis on their natural character. On the one hand, sometimes a miraculous conception is joined with the theme of its manifestation in youthful prowess. For example, in Plutarch's "Life of Romulus," Numitor beholds Remus' superiority in stature and strength in body and notes that his acts correspond with his looks, when as yet the twins' identity was unknown. From this, Plutarch says, he grasped the truth of Remus' identity—that is, he was a divinely conceived child of a noble family.[51] Or in his "Theseus," Plutarch remarks about the youthful triumphs of the hero who was offering "noble deeds and achievements as the manifesting mark of his noble birth."[52] On the other hand, sometimes the youth's behavior is understood as a natural phenomenon as in Plutarch's "Demetrius." He gives a story of Demetrius' boyhood and says: "This . . . is an illustration of the strong natural bent of Demetrius towards kindness and justice."[53] Whether the emphasis is on the supernatural or the natural, such stories of youthful behavior were taken as anticipations of the hero's future character. Plutarch says of Alcibiades: "His character, in later life, displayed . . . many strong passions. . . . This is clear from the stories recorded of his boyhood."[54]

Again, the biographical tradition used a combination of birth, family, and boyhood stories to give anticipations about the future life of the hero. It would not be amiss to say that all of these components functioned also as prophecies of the character of the public career of the subject of the biography. If this was their purpose in the Greco-Roman biographies, then this is how a reader/hearer of Luke would most probably have taken the material of a similar nature in Luke 1:5-4:15.[55]

Virtually the totality of the material about Jesus in Luke 1:5-4:15 would have been regarded as an anticipation of his later public greatness. The angelophanies, the prophecies of a Jewish type, the portent plus its interpretation, the vision plus its audition, the two stories of childhood prodigies, and the genealogy (and miraculous conception) would combine to foretell/foreshadow the type of person Jesus would be in his public ministry which began at Luke 4:16-30.[56] By writing in this way, the Evangelist was simply following the conventions of Greco-Roman biographical literature.

The Jewish cast to Luke's material[57] is no obstacle to this thesis. Philo's *Life of Moses*, the biographical section on the career of Moses in Josephus' *Antiquities*, and Josephus' autobiography show that the Hellenistic biographical tradition made its impact on Judaism before and alongside of its impact on Christianity. Charles Perrot's collection of haggadic materials relating to the infancy/childhood of Noah, Abraham, Isaac, Samson, Samuel, Elijah, and Moses makes the same point.[58] The tendency in Mediterranean culture at large provoked a renewed interest in the early lives of heroes in Jewish circles which surfaced in the haggadah. To find material with a Jewish cast but presented in the mold of biographical convention is no impossibility, therefore. It is again rather what one would expect in an early Christian gospel.

Are we justified in speaking of a genre of an account of the pre-public careers of great men in Mediterranean antiquity? I think so. If so, then it would be a bit more inclusive than the recognized genre of infancy narratives of famous men.[59] In any case, the evidence assembled in this paper has enabled us to see that Luke made use of the conventional form of expression in his time and place for telling the story of the pre-public life of a hero.[60]

Mediterranean culture usually assumed that there was a divine order with some type of predetermined plan for human life. This order or plan was disclosed either through divine or human initiative in "prophecy" of some sort. Prophecy, both oral and written, belonged to the propaganda strategies of Mediterranean religion generally.[61] It was not the preserve of

Jewish and Christian traditions only. In using the argument from prophecy, then, Christians were merely working within the framework of common cultural assumptions. The particulars varied but the underlying structural assumptions were similar.[62]

NOTES

[1]For a concise survey of the discussion, see Raymond E. Brown, *The Birth of the Messiah* (Garden City, NY: Doubleday, 1977) 244-50; Charles H. Talbert, *Literary Patterns, Theological Themes and the Genre of Luke-Acts* (SBLMS 20; Missoula: Scholars Press, 1974), 45, 50.

[2]Cf. Joseph B. Tyson, "Source Criticism of the Gospel of Luke," in *Perspectives on Luke-Acts*, ed. Charles H. Talbert. ABPRSSS, 5 (Danville, Va.: Association of Baptist Professors of Religion, 1978) 24-39.

[3]This type of approach has proved effective at other points in the study of Luke-Acts: e.g., G. B. Miles and G. Trompf, "Luke and Antiphon: The Theology of Acts 27-28 in the Light of Pagan Beliefs about Divine Retribution, Pollution, and Shipwreck," *HTR* 69 (1976) 259-67; Fred Veltman, "The Defense Speeches of Paul in Acts," in *Perspectives on Luke-Acts*, 243-56; Vernon K. Robbins, "By Land and By Sea: The We-Passages and Ancient Sea Voyages," in *Perspectives on Luke-Acts*, 215-42.

[4]Talbert, *Literary Patterns*, 44-48.

[5]Most recently, Raymond E. Brown, "Luke's Method in the Annunciation Narrative of Chapter One," in *No Famine in the Land*, ed. J. W. Flanagan and A. W. Robinson (Missoula: Scholars Press, 1975) 180; *The Birth of the Messiah*, 240.

[6]Cf. Paul S. Minear, "Luke's Use of the Birth Stories," in *Studies in Luke-Acts*, ed. L. E. Keck and J. L. Martyn (Nashville: Abingdon, 1966) 111-30.

[7]Talbert, *Literary Patterns*, 117-18.

[8]On the form of these two narratives see G. F. Wood, "The Form and Composition of the Lucan Annunciation Narratives," STD Thesis, Catholic University of America, 1962; Benjamin Hubbard, "Commissioning Stories in Luke-Acts: A Study of Their Antecedents, Form and Content," *Semeia*, 8 (1977) 103-26.

[9]Cf. Gen 25:22-23. John Drury, *Tradition and Design in Luke* (Atlanta: John Knox, 1976) 60, says: "In both instances the phenomenon is prophetic."

[10]Cf. Allison Trites, "The Prayer Motif in Luke-Acts," in *Perspectives on Luke-Acts*, 168-86.

[11]Cf. 2 Esdr 9:26ff.; 2 Bar 21:1ff. for Jewish parallels.

[12]Leander E. Keck, "The Spirit and the Dove," *NTS* 17 (1970-71) 63-67, argues that *hōs peristeran* originally was adverbial, specifying the action of the Spirit. On Hellenistic soil there was a shift from adverbial to adjectival meaning, clearly evident in Luke. In the Third Gospel it is the dove-like form that is meant.

[13]E. R. Goodenough, *Jewish Symbols in the Greco-Roman Period* (New York: Pantheon Books, 1953-) VIII, 40-41, after a survey of the uses of the dove in pagan, Jewish, and Christian tradition, concludes: "Beneath the variety of settings the dove itself shows a unity, and that unity, we may now see, lies essentially in the fact that the dove represents the beneficence of divinity in love, the loving character of divine life itself."

[14]Ultimately the textual question must be settled by determining the mind of the

Evangelist. If Luke 1-2 is an integral part of the Gospel, then Luke 1:35 indicates Jesus was not begotten Son of God at his baptism. The Western reading is thereby excluded.

[15]Henk J. de Jonge, "Sonship, Wisdom, Infancy: Luke 2:41-51a," *NTS* 24 (1978) 317-54.

[16]Rodney T. Hood, "The Genealogies of Jesus," in *Early Christian Origins*, ed. A. P. Wikgren (Chicago: Quadrangle Books, 1961) 1-15, still seems to me to offer the best clue to Luke's genealogy.

[17]Talbert, *Literary Patterns*, chapter 8; *What Is A Gospel? The Genre of the Canonical Gospels* (Philadelphia: Fortress Press, 1977).

[18]Cf. Plutarch, "Romulus," 9 and Livy 1:7:1 for the use of such means to settle the quarrel between Romulus and Remus. Plutarch, in this context, speaks of the continuing Roman practice of taking auguries from the flight of birds.

[19]Plutarch, "Numa," 7:1-3.

[20]Quintus Curtius, *History of Alexander*, 1 (a portent plus an interpretative prophecy).

[21]Plutarch, "Romulus," 2:4; "Pericles," 6:2-3; "Alexander," 3:1, 4-5; "Caius Marius," 3:3-4:1; "Lycurgus," 5, etc.

[22]Philostratus, *Life of Apollonius of Tyana*, 1:5.

[23]Pseudo-Callisthenes, *Alexander Romance*.

[24]"Hadrian," 2:4, 8, 9; "Severus," 1:7-8; "Antonius Pius," 3:1-5.

[25]*Antiquities*, 2.9.2-3 §215-16. John Drury, *Tradition and Design in Luke's Gospel*, 47, says: "The resemblance of this to the prophetic canticles in Luke 1 and 2 needs no advertisement." Cf. also 1 Enoch 106:13-19 (prophecy about Noah's destiny at his birth) and the Genesis Aprocryphon 2 which has a similar story about Noah.

[26]A. D. Nock, *Conversion* (Oxford University Press, 1933) 240.

[27]de Jonge, "Sonship, Wisdom, Infancy: Luke 2:41-51a," 341.

[28]Quintus Curtius, *History of Alexander*, 1.

[29]Plutarch, "Romulus," 8 (overthrow of a tyrant); 6; "Alexander," 5:1 (wisdom); "Solon," 2; "Themistocles," 2:1; "Cicero," 2:2; "Theseus," 6:4 (prowess and wisdom); "Dion," 4:2.

[30]Philostratus, *Life of Apollonius*, 1:7:11.

[31]Pseudo-Callisthenes, *Alexander Romance* (a number of childhood wonders, e.g., one of wisdom, one of strength, one of self-control, one of peacemaking, two of reliance on persuasion instead of war, one of respect for his father).

[32]"Severus," 1:4.

[33]*Antiquities*, 2.9.6 §231; 2.9.7 §233; 2.10.1-2 §238ff. Cf. also 1 Enoch 106:11 where Noah blesses God while still in the hands of the midwife.

[34]*Life of Moses*, 1:5:20-24; 1:6:25-29. Cf. also Jubilees 11-12 (childhood prodigies of Abraham).

[35]Charles H. Talbert, "The Concept of Immortals in Mediterranean Antiquity," *JBL* 94 (1975) 419-36.

[36]Quintus Curtius, *History of Alexander*, 1.

[37]Plutarch, "Theseus," 2, 6, 36:3 (begotten by Poseidon); "Romulus," 2:5; 4:2; "Alexander," 3:1-2.

[38]Philostratus, *Life of Apollonius*, 1:4:6.

[39]Pseudo-Callisthenes, *Alexander Romance*.

[40]Plutarch, "Theseus," 3; "Fabius Maximus," 1; "Brutus," 1-2; "Pyrrhus," 1; "Lycurgus," 1:4 (genealogy tracing his lineage back to Heracles).

[41]Philostratus, *Life of Apollonius*, 1:4.

[42]"Hadrian," 1:1-2; "Antonius Pius," 1:1-7.

[43]*Antiquities* 2.9.6 §229 (genealogy tracing Moses back to Abraham); *Life* 1 (the genealogy of Josephus).

[44]Philostratus, *Life of Apollonius*, 1:5 (LCL).

[45]Tacitus, *Histories*, 4:81.

[46]Tacitus, *Histories*, 1:22.

[47]Suetonius, "Domitian," 14.

[48]Suetonius, "Augustus," 94 (LCL).

[49]Tacitus, *Histories*, 1:10.

[50]Tacitus, *Histories*, 1:18.

[51]Plutarch, "Romulus," 7:3-4.

[52]Plutarch, "Theseus," 7.

[53]Plutarch, "Demetrius," 4:4.

[54]Plutarch, "Alcibiades," 2:1.

[55]John Drury, *Tradition and Design*, 131, says the order of the temptations in Luke places the Jerusalem temptation last because Jerusalem is the end and goal of Luke's gospel. "The temptations are thus made prophetic of Jesus' course."

[56]Raymond Brown, *The Birth of the Messiah*, 28, 481-82 (following Laurentin, *Jesus*, 147-58) recognizes this principle for Luke 2:41-51. This essay suggests the principle holds for the totality of Luke 1:5-4:15 as it relates to Jesus.

[57]E.g., echoes of Old Testament material that are often called midrashic and the use of an annunciation form characteristic of the Jewish scriptures.

[58]Charles Perrot, "Les recits d'enfance dans la haggada," *RdSR* 55 (1967) 481-518, especially 507.

[59]Raymond Brown, *The Birth of the Messiah*, 561, says the first two chapters of the Third Gospel belong to the genre of "infancy narratives of famous men."

[60]As always, the question of genre is separable from the question of historicity. Cf. Charles H. Talbert, "Oral and Independent or Literary and Interdependent? A Response to Albert B. Lord," in *The Relationships among the Gospels: An Interdisciplinary Dialogue*, ed. W. O. Walker, Jr. (San Antonio: Trinity University Press, 1978) 99-100.

[61]A. D. Nock, *Conversion*, 250.

THE VISION OF JERUSALEM IN EZEKIEL 8-11: A HOLISTIC INTERPRETATION

MOSHE GREENBERG

THE HEBREW UNIVERSITY, JERUSALEM, ISRAEL

I. Reflections on interpretation

TWO opposed axioms have served, historically, for the interpretation of the Bible, one theological, the other historical-analogical. The theological maintains that without insight gained from faith in the divine origin of Scripture, its message cannot be understood. Faith is rewarded by grace, whose light illumines the meaning of Scripture. A modern Catholic states the axiom as follows:

> . . . the Church has always maintained . . . that . . . all natural knowledge, even the maximum of natural knowledge, will never succeed in understanding the Word of God as it should be understood . . . If the light of grace and the holy desire for what is good, inspired by grace, do not enlighten and animate the reader of the Bible. The vitally essential . . . content of the divine message can be . . . more clearly perceived by a simple and upright soul responding to God's call . . . than by a very erudite and, humanly speaking, very acute scholar who is impervious to the things of God.[1]

Historically, the product of this axiom has usually been an exegesis that puts into Scripture what ought to be believed rather than attending to what it says. The reaction, which reached fullest articulation in ch vii of Spinoza's THEOLOGICAL-POLITICAL TRACTATE (first printing, 1670), insisted that nothing but what Scripture itself revealed of its sense might be used in interpreting it. The ordinary process of induction, so fruitful in arriving at an understanding of nature, was adequate for—was indeed the only legitimate basis of—interpreting the Bible.

> . . . the method of interpreting Scripture does not differ from the method of interpreting nature . . . For as the interpretation of nature consists in drawing up a

history (=a systematic account of the data) of nature and therefrom inferring definitions of natural phenomena, so Scriptural interpretation necessarily proceeds by drawing up a true history of Scripture and from it . . . to infer correctly the intentions of the authors of Scripture . . . Everyone will advance without danger of error . . . if they admit no principles for interpreting Scripture . . . save such as they find in Scripture itself.[2]

This program promised a universe of discourse transcending partisanship by adopting for Scripture-interpretation the universally accepted canons of natural science. For scholars, the prospect of getting beyond dogmatic particularity and disagreement to scientific universality and consensus was the value that outweighed whatever spiritual treasure accrued from treating Scripture differently from all other literature as a special language of divine truths. Having voted for scientific universality, the interpretation of Scripture became linked in the 19th century to the career of literary-historical interpretation at large. The analogy of the latter was decisive for the former.

The main conclusions of critics . . . rest upon reasonings the cogency of which cannot be denied without denying the ordinary principles by which history is judged and evidence estimated.
The character of a particular part of the OT cannot be decided by an *a priori* argument as regards what it *must* be; it can only be determined by an application of the canons of evidence and probability universally employed in historical or literary investigation.[3]

As it is often put: the Bible must be interpreted like any other ancient book.
   Western critics approach biblical literature with expectations formed from familiarity with western literature and literary criticism. Biblical narrative, history, legal writing, prophetic sermons, poems are judged by their presumed western counterparts. Order, progression, (con)sequentiality, regularity, consistency, coherence are the features of good western models of each of these genres. If flaws in these attributes occur they may signal corruption, tampering, or multiple authorship. Critical training of biblicists sharpens the perception of these attributes or the lack of them in the biblical texts, and accounts for the predominance of criticism based on such criteria in biblical scholarship. It is axiomatic that any other estimate of a literary piece follow upon a literary-historical analysis and depend on it. Before assessing the meaning of a prophetic sermon, one must give an account of its integrity—the criteria of this account having been drawn from elsewhere than prophetic literature.

One notes an increasing dissatisfaction with such a method of criticism; its standards are drawn from too narrow a range of literature and lack the support of extensive descriptions of biblical literature in its own terms. Despite the large amount of poetry in the Bible, the process and products of Hebrew poetic creativity aside from such structural matters as form, meter and parallelism have been slighted. (The application to biblical poetry of "canons universally employed in literary investigation" by earlier critics led to conclusions about meter and parallelism justifying wholesale rewriting of psalms; the enlarged horizon of post-Ugaritic scholarship makes that earlier criticism appear hopelessly parochial.) In the course of analyzing and describing the poetry and poetic devices of the Song of Songs, a scholarly poet has recently shown up the failures of modern scholarly commentary to the Song, due to a simple ignorance of what poetry is.[4] Since biblicists have so seldom produced systematic accounts of Hebrew rhetoric and storytelling, linguists, folklorists, comparativists and the like have ranged uninhibitedly up and down the Bible, often to the justified chagrin of biblicists.

We know so little about the principles of composition of the various genres of Hebrew literature that it behooves us to stay our hands until we open our ears. It is observed in the Midrash that "Scripture disregards chronological order"[5]; modern criticism has also noted that, and proceeds to rearrange text-material according to chronology. But if native Hebrew narrative (or editing) valued historical order less than we do, such a procedure only highlights the gap in values between us and them, without shedding light on their values. Standard critical procedure yields an analysis of the text that points up its tensions—according to history-oriented canons. The tension is resolved by separating the material into kernels and accretions whose combination allegedly produced the tension. But it is never demonstrated (it cannot be) that the tension was not there from the start, so that the tension-less reconstruction may be an answer to a modern critical, but no proven ancient, canon of composition. By such a procedure one can hardly be led to other principles of composition, compared to which the chronological might be subordinate (A corollary of the abovementioned midrashic observation, for example, is the legitimacy of inference from juxtaposition; i.e. propinquity is exegetically significant).[6]

As an alternative to both the foregoing, we propose a holistic interpretation, "emphasizing the organic or functional relation between parts and wholes" (Webster).[7] As the religious person approaches the text open to God's call, so must the interpreter come "all ears" to hear what the text is saying. He must subjugate his habits of thought and expression to the words before him and become actively passive—full of initiatives to heighten his receptivity. For an axiom, he has the working hypothesis that the text as he has it has been designed to convey a message, a meaning. For if it does have design and meaning, they will be discovered only by effort expended to justify such an assumption. Readiness to find evidence of design and significance is the exegete's analogue to openness to hear God's word on the part of the faithful reader.

How can such an approach be guarded against uncritical acceptance of things as they are, and against reading in ad hoc explanations or making fanciful connections? Here it appropriates something of the historical-analogical, namely, the inference from the text itself of principles of its interpretation. Being "all ears" means to lend a general attentiveness to the text given normally today only to poetry. One must be ready to find signifiers on several levels and of several types. Since one cannot know *a priori* where the clues lie, his attention must include vocabulary, grammatical forms, phonology, assonance. The following battery of questions is calculated to discover the pattern(s) of significance of a passage from inside it. (No mind is paid to overlapping.)

Is the unit which is delimited formally (by, say, opening and closing formulas)[8] shown to be a unit through its structure (a recognized pattern?), its content, its figures or its verbal devices?

How much interrelation and reference occurs among its parts?

How much repetition (if with variations, are they significant)?

How much irregularity occurs (in grammar, in length of lines etc.), and how much regularity?

In the event of non-sequentiality, is another ground of collocation evident (e.g., thematic, or verbal association)?

Are affective elements present besides the plain sense of sentences, such as alliteration, punning, or chiasm? To what do they call attention?[9]

How much ambiguity is present; what are its causes and effects?

Are elements which seem opaque illuminated by considering their placement (significance through juxtaposition)?

To what extent are themes, peculiarities or difficulties recurrent elsewhere? In identical or variant form? If not in the Bible, then outside it?

How far is one's perception of the main message of a unit corroborated by later readers (postbiblical literature, medieval commentaries); if there is a difference, why?

After submitting the text to such a battery and patiently pursuing all leads to significance, one may end up with intractable intrusions, anachronisms, opaque matter, which defy integration into a single (temporal, thematic) pattern. With respect to such matter, the working hypothesis will have failed; the alternatives of corruption, accident, or secondary, clumsy addition may be invoked. But these are last resorts, and there must always lurk in the back of one's mind the possibility that one has missed a point.

Was there a historical time in which the text was (or might have been) understood in accord with our holistic interpretation of it? To clarify this, we must put the same question to the theological and the historical-analogic methods. It seems that involved in the answer of each is a presupposition, a prejudice of a kind that casts doubt on the historical validity of any exegesis on the one hand, while, on the other, it justifies the (even contemporaneous) variety of interpretations of a text regarded as a cultural heritage.

Theological exegesis takes the text at face value—it is the inspired words of the prophet. Though the prophet spoke in particular circumstances, his message contains teaching for the godly of all ages, since the meaning of God's words is inexhaustible. The audience of the prophet caught his meaning according to the variety of their capacities, but even the prophet himself may not necessarily have plumbed the sense of what he spoke. Theological interpretation is ultimately uninterested in the historical question we posed above; its concern is to educe the timeless truths of the divine message. In all cases these truths are couched in the intellectual idiom of the exegete; if he is a midrashist, the prophet is made to speak the idiom and values of midrash; if an aristotelian, of Aristotle; if a kabbalist, of the Kabbala. The explicit intention of theological exegesis is to illuminate the text by the light of the best and deepest comprehension of divine matters known to the exegete. Theoretically, such a comprehension might have existed at any time; in the view of the exegete, it is not time-bound. That is the necessary implication of the theological prejudice concerning the inexhaustibility of God's word.

Historical-analogic exegesis aims at a perspective view of the biblical text: an original core having a meaning conditioned by time and place, with subsequent reworkings and additions—all portrayed as a process of development. As presently practiced, this method lacks empirically established criteria and therefore yields results too divergent to inspire confidence. That nevertheless it has been almost universally adopted as a criterion for scholarship in the field means that it answers some overriding need or prejudice. Two such may readily be identified. The triumphs of evolutionism in natural science have made it the hallmark of intellectual modernity. Over against the essentially medieval unconcern (and unawareness) of history, so characteristic of theological exegesis, current critical exegesis opposes its perspective, developmental view of the text as its chief qualification for intellectual respectibility in our time. Hence any proposal of literary development is better than none—better in that it demonstrates sophistication, that is, advance beyond medieval dogmatic prejudices and naivete.

A second need for the historical-analogic method arises from the situation of the Christian faith community which is its matrix. First, that community must justify its retention of the Old Testament alongside the New, and does so by showing that light is shed upon the New by viewing the Old as a series of steps leading up to it. The more fully this can be worked out, the greater the value set on the Old Testament. Second (though less articulated), that community, though buffeted by change and modernity, affirms the validity of its ancient Scripture in the present. This affirmation is accomplished by showing the biblical text itself incorporates a record of reinterpretation, adjustment to change and supplementation by later hands. Given the community's overriding need for validating constant reinterpretation, any proposal that roots that process in the biblical text itself will have a bias in its favor.

The validity of the historical outlook and the need of faith-communities to justify change is not impugned when one suggests that prejudices rooted in these underlie the academic encouragement of ever new and divergent analyses of literary development. Such prejudices make scholars tolerate the narrow, inadequately tested assumptions on which these analyses are based and the divergences that must undermine their claims to reflect the stages of textual development.

Our holistic interpretation seeks to reconstitute the perception of the text by an ideal reader living at a time when it had reached its present disposition. "Ideal reader" is a personified realization of the possibilities inherent in the text at that moment. In the case of Ezekiel, the context of densest significance for that ideal reader will have been the canonical book. As he read it the first time, each encounter with a fresh passage, a repetition, a variation on a phrase or theme will have affected him according to his growing experience of the book; on his second reading, these will have complexified as later elements now seemed foreshadowed, and as early elements resonated in later reminiscences. Our ideal reader will have been sensible of such resonances, echoes and allusions, and the holistic interpreter will attempt to reproduce his sensibilities. The ideal reader will also have been familiar with the literary, the historical, and the environmental allusions in the book; the exegete must resort to the rest of biblical literature (preferably, but not exclusively, to works that might have been known to the prophet), and, where relevant, to extrabiblical literature for such information. The ideal reader treats the book as full of significance (it offers a key to his people's destiny in the past and future); the interpreter will strain to discover this significance through the battery of questions listed above. Where he fails, he will consider, beside his own shortcomings, the possibility of faults or intrusions of various kinds in the text; in this he will use the early witnesses to the Hebrew, conscious of the limitations of such use. Evident compositeness of a literary unit will be duly noted, but not taken to release the interpreter from the obligation to see the interrelation of the components; for all he knows such interrelation as he may discover was already in the mind of whoever collocated these components, perhaps the prophet himself. Palpable accretions or intrusions, such as contradictions and anachronisms, the interpreter does not undertake, of course, to integrate into the surrounding material; but he will try to explain their presence and consider their (confusing) effect on the ideal reader (aided by the makeshifts of translators and early commentators).

In his quest for significance—necessarily, significance for him—the holistic interpreter partially resembles the theological exegete seeking timeless truth. In the historical controls he imposes on himself, he resembles partly the historical-analogic exegete. Resembling both, he compounds his risks; he must beware of reading into his texts private or modern significances on the one hand, and of overrating his historical-literary judgment on the other. What lures him into this double jeopardy? The chance that he may discover the cause of (and thus corroborate) the initial veneration of the Scriptures; that he may experience the editor-canonizer as a fellow intelligence, whose product became a classic not (perversely) in spite of its character but (deservedly) because of it. Ultimately, the holistic interpreter is animated by a respect for his cultural heritage that takes the form of a prejudice in favor of the ancient biblical author-editors and their transmitters. He requires more than a theoretical cause before discounting and disintegrating their products. He sees himself not so different from them as to be unable to appreciate what they did in terms at once native to them and meaningful to him. The holistic interpreter is prepared to risk failure in order to establish the claim of his cultural heritage on its heirs.[10]

* * * *

The following section contains an attempt to treat holistically one of the most baffling passages in the book of Ezekiel: the Jerusalem vision of chs 8-11. It is taken from a commentary in progress to the book, and is the last of a three-part treatment of these chapters; the first two parts are a translation and a textual-philological commentary. Predecessors from whom I have learnt, and with whom I carry on a (usually implicit) argument are J. Hermann (KAT, 1924), G.A. Cooke (ICC, 1937), G. Fohrer (HAT, 1955), W. Zimmerli (BKAT, 1955-65) and J.W. Wevers (NCB, 1969).

II. The structure and themes of Ezek 8-11

The diverse material of chs 8-11 is organized into a single visionary experience whose complexity indicates a considerable literary effort.

The opening and closing verses of the vision correspond, and form a frame for the whole:

(a)   8:1a date, location, audience
(b)   8:1b God's hand falls upon the prophet (start of vision)
(c)   8:2-3 A luminous human figure seizes the prophet; a wind transports him to Jerusalem in vision
(c') 11:22-24a the majesty is borne off eastward; the wind transports the prophet back to Chaldea in vision
(b') 11:24b the vision "lifts" off the prophet (ends)
(a') 11:25 the prophet tells what he saw to the exiles

The double agency in (c)—the luminous figure (the majesty) and the wind both involved in transporting the prophet—is confirmed in (c') where both recur, each going its own way. A hint of the troublesomeness of the majesty, as well as its integration in this vision, is thus given in the very framework.

In the course of the vision, the prophet is carried by a wind not only to and from Jerusalem (8:3b; 11:24), but within the temple precinct from the northern area where the first scene occurs to the east gate where the second takes place (11:1). This internal movement marks a major break in the continuity of the vision. The narrative elements grouped before it in the first scene (8:4—10:7) are—with the exceptions noted below—in an intelligible sequence; so too are those that follow in the second scene. But the latter scene seems out of sequence; after the general slaughter depicted in 9:6-8 how came twenty-five men to be at the east gate of the temple?

Allusions to the divine majesty and its bearers interrupt the flow of narrative in 8:2; 9:3 and 10:1, 3-5; the detailed description of the cherub vehicle in 10:8ff seems to replace it. The narrative is resumed in 10:18-19 with the flight of the cherubs, but halts again in vss 20-22 for repeated assertions of the identity of the cherubs with the creatures of ch. 1. If up to 10:7 these allusions are disconnected, in 10:18-19 (linked to 9:3; 10:4) and 11:22-23 they cohere, being a description of the gradual departure of the majesty from the doomed temple and city. Perplexing though they are, these allusions are too considerable a part of this vision to be disregarded in its interpretation; they are not a merely intrusive element.

But let us for the moment leave them aside and study the rest of the vision. It falls into two parts: A. 8:5—10:7: the abominations and their consequences and B. 11:1-21: the cabal and related matters.

A. in the main is reasonably well knit. It consists of 1. a climactic account of four (3 plus 1) abominations in the temple area (8:5-18), and 2. the slaughter of the sinners and the orders to burn the city (9:1-10:7). The particulars are in sequence; generally speaking the prophet moves along a north-south axis. Many features link 1. and 2. Not only is the border between them marked by an echo (8:18's *qara be'oznay qol gadol* in 9:1), but they share the expression of God's ruthlessness (8:18; 9:5, 10). The lawlessness mentioned in 8:17 at the end of 1. is enlarged upon in 9:9 at the end of 2. Indeed 8:17, where "filling the land (n.b. the extension of the horizon beyond the temple area) with lawlessness" caps the cultic abomination, forms a bridge to 2. in which social wrongdoing prevails, the doomed include the entire population of the city, and their offense is both city- and country-wide. The saying of the lawless at the end of 2., "YHWH has left the land; YHWH does not see" (9:9) virtually repeats in inverted form what the idolatrous elders said in 8:12.

The effect of the appearance of the man clothed in linen to report on his action in 9:11 is to suggest an unseen periphery to this vision, in which crucial events are occurring. Unity of place is thus preserved, owing to which the massacre of the city's inhabitants is not described.

The order to burn the city (10:2) is linked to what precedes through the man clothed in linen. It is linked to the majesty and the cherubs through the fiery coals drawn from among the cherubs. The theme of burning is abruptly broken off with the man's departure, nothing being said of how the order was executed. This has been needlessly thought to indicate that the original continuation has been lost; it may in fact be due to the desire to maintain unity of place throughout the vision. Notice of the cherub's handing over the fire to the man clothed in linen provides the point of linkage to the following long description of the cherub vehicle, which begins with the cherubs' hands (10:8).

B. 11:1-21, consists of 1. a scene of the cabal at the east gate (vss. 1-13) and 2. an assurance to the exiles that they will be restored to their land (14-21). At first glance 2. seems unrelated to 1. (However the revelation formula in vs 14 is no proof of that; cf. 21:6 where similarly God's response to a protest starting "Alas, O Lord" begins with the formula.) On reflection, it appears that in fact 2. serves as a reply to the prophet's cry, "Alas Lord YHWH are you putting an end to the remnant of Israel" with which 1. ends (vs 13). The exiles, says 2., shall be spared and regathered to their land; only the Jerusalemites (Judahites) will be annihilated. It is true that the responsive character of 2. is not explicit, and thus its relation to 1. less organic than that of A.2 (punishment) to A.1 (sin). Indeed it appears that originally independent entities have been juxtaposed in B in accord with the pattern of A. In both A and B the prophet is first shown wickedness, followed by punishment of death; he expostulates and receives a reply—in A, a justification of the punishment, in B an assurance of survivors (a happy ending to a dreadful vision). B appears to be a construct based on A with the aim of setting forth civil aspects of Jerusalem's guilt.

Other features promoted the connection of the two parts of B. Both open with a self-serving assertion of the Jerusalemites (vss. 3, 15b), followed by a command to prophesy God's angry reply. There is moreover a noteworthy assonance of *(h)syr . . . bśr* in vss, 3, 7, 11 (of 1.) with *hsyr . . . bśr* in vss. 18f. (of 2.).

As noted above, B.1 seems out of sequence; the general slaughter and burning reported in A.2 hardly leaves room for a *cabal* of twenty-five men at the east gate of the temple. One might suppose that in a vision temporal sequence need not be observed. But other features of B mark it as an echo or a(n inverted) correspondent rather than a sequel to A. (To be sure, B.1's location at the east gate links it to the eastward movement of the majesty in 10:19 (A.2), but that is a merely external connection; it facilitated the juncture of B to A, if it was not made for it.) Only here and in 8:16 (A.1) are groups of "(about) twenty-five men". In 11:6 *milletem ḥuṣoteha ḥalal* "you have filled its streets with slain" evokes *male'u hahaṣerot ḥalalim* "fill the courts with corpses" of 9:7. The accusation in B.1 is virtually identical with the ground given for God's irrevocable decree in 9:9 (A.2)—bloodshed and perversion of justice. Even more noteworthy are the connections between B.2 and A.1—the two extremes of the vision. Both refer to the abominable and loathsome practices of the Jerusalemites *(to'ebot, seqeṣ/siqquṣim)*. The ambiguous *leroḥoqa me'al miqdasi* (8:6) has an echo divided among 11:14-15: *raḥaqu me'al YHWH* and *miqdas me'at;* these expressions illuminate one another. In the opening scene God charges the Jerusalemites with being removed (alien-ated) from his sanctuary. It is therefore ironic that in the closing scene Jerusalemites should taunt the exiles with being removed from YHWH, and more so that God asserts he is a "small sanctuary" for the exiles while the Jerusalemites (amidst whom the sanctuary building stands) are destined for destruction. B.2 thus exhibits that resumption of opening themes or language which is characteristic in Ezek of closing passages. Whether its message of consolation is not out of place in a doom vision has been asked (but cf,chs. 14, 16, 17 and 20, each with some variety of consolation after dooms); due weight must be given, however, to the incidental nature of the consolation: what consoles the exiles is the prediction of Jerusalem's destruction. Whether this would have been regarded by the audience as a happy ending is itself a question.

The following overall pattern of thematic alternation appears in his vision:

A.1. cultic abominations, capped by social wrongdoing
A.2 punishment grounded on social wrongdoing
B.1 a *cabal* charged with social wrongdoing
B.2 preferment of exiles over Jerusalemites sunk in cultic abominations.

Such chiastic alternation, foreshadowed within A.1, suggests a deliberate design.

The majesty of God and its cherub vehicle have a prominent but not always clear role in this vision. From 10:18 on the sequence is clear: the majesty moves off the threshold of the House onto the cherubs; these take off, pausing at the east gate (vs 19), then bear the majesty away from the city to Mt Olives (11:22f.). Thus the majesty exits eastward in stages from temple and city.

Going backward from 10:18, through the description (vss. 8-17), we arrive at the obscure vss 10:1, 3-5. The cherubs are located to the right (south) of the house while the majesty is on the threshold. 10:4a repeats the movement of the majesty off the cherub (sing.) to the threshold already related in 9:3a (there the terms are *na'ala, 'elohe yisra'el*, here *wayyarom, YHWH*). The hardest passage is 9:3a where suddenly and in no context "the cherub (sing.) on which [the majesty] had been" is introduced, to say that the majesty left it for the threshold. Where was this cherub and what was the majesty's relation to it up to now? Why did it move off it to the threshold?

Let us trace the allusions to the majesty and cherub(s) from the start of the vision. The brilliant human figure in 8:2—evidently the majesty—is not expressly located (note that not it but the wind carries the prophet to and from Jerusalem), but it is plausible to say that it was in Babylonia. If it is identified with the majesty (k*ebod* '*elohe yisra'el*) waiting for the prophet somewhere in the temple area (vaguely "there") in vs 4, a certain leap must be postulated—tolerable perhaps in a vision—to bring the majesty from Babylonia to Jerusalem. Are the bearers of the majesty present in either verse? The language of 8:2 seems to exclude them; the phrase of 8:4 ("the majesty of the God of Israel") may (so in 1:28 and perhaps 3:23, see Comments there) or may not.

Is the majesty of ch 8 inside the sanctuary or outside; does it move about with the prophet? "There" in 8:4 is too vague for defining where the majesty was when Ezekiel arrived at the temple. That it is the subject of "he said to me" and "he brought me" in the following narrative does not prove it to be outside, since in 43:7; 44:2 the majesty speaks from inside the visionary temple of the future to the prophet. In 40:1-3 God "brings" the prophet in vision to "a high mountain" without actually accompanying him (throughout the book God "brings" objects everywhere without being "there" himself).

If we suppose the majesty of ch 8 to be outside the sanctuary and to include its bearers, the presence and exterior location of the cherubs in 10:1, 3, 18 etc. is accounted for. On the other hand, the subsequent movements of the majesty off the cherub on to the threshold and back again on to the cherubs (9:3a [10:4a]; 10:18) will be inane. If on the contrary we suppose that the majesty of ch 8 is inside the sanctuary, the external cherubs of 10:3 etc. are not accounted for, but the outward movement of 9:3a to the threshold (for so it will then be) will then be of a piece with its continuation in 10:18, and significant: the divine presence is departing from the temple. The cherub (singular) from which the majesty moved to the threshold (9:3a [10:4a]) will be the statuary in the holy of holies "where [the majesty] has been" ever since the temple was inaugurated (cf I Kings 8:10f and Weinfeld, *Deuteronomy* 204f.).

Neither supposition, then, accomodates all the data or resolves the ambiguities. Is the text, therefore, to be judged in disarray, the result of inorganic layering? Some disarray must be allowed, especially in ch. 10; but the allusions to the majesty and its bearers are too rooted in the vision to be explained away. If they are excised, much that does make sense is lost (e.g. the conterpoint between God's departure and human "removal" from the sanctuary [*or from him*] referred to in 8:6 and 11:15).

The difficulty seems related to the paradoxical notion shared by all ancient religions that the deity is at once localized in its temple and "in heaven" (or ubiquitous). The image in the pagan temple is literally the seat and residence of the deity; through their images, Marduk dwells in his temple in Babylon and Sin in Haran. Analogously, the cherub statues in Jerusalem's holy of holies (like their antecedents in the tabernacle) were the throne on which YHWH sat, shrouded in darkness. At the same time the pagan god dwells in heaven or on the mountain of the gods, and moves freely about the universe (for the paradoxical notions concerning the ancient Near Eastern gods see *Biblical Archaeologist Reader* I. 152-4, 159, 164, 169-71). Similarly YHWH dwells in heaven, his majesty covers the heavens and fills the earth, and he rides the clouds or a cherub on his travels. Haran puts it well:

We must emphasize the fact that although the cherubs of the ark-cover and the ark symbolize a throne and a footstool respectively, the Bible *does not* bind the deity to them or for a moment suppose that he is located (as it were) only there . . . God's chief place is conceived to be in heaven and there too is the place of his throne. His heavenly throne is supported by living cherubs; as a reflection of those heavenly cherubs the Israelites fashion cherub statues in the holy of holies of the tabernacle. The throne behind its curtain is only a miniature and a replica of the celestial throne: the heavenly cherubs are "living creatures" as Ezek calls them . . . creatures of reality and will; the cherubs on the ark are metal figures. The heavenly cherubs are huge, those of P occupy a space on the two ends of a plate two-and-a-half cubits square. Yet P's metal cherubs serve also as a seat—God appears upon them and talks from between them to Moses (Exod 25:22); upon them he manifests himself in a cloud (Lev 16:2) ("Ark and Cherubs" [Hebrew], *Eretz Israel* 5 (1958) 88f.)

All this applies equally to the cherubs of the Jerusalem temple; in its light the contradictions of our vision, while not resolved, are at least understandable.

The luminous figure—the majesty—appears at the start of the vision, not because otherwise the prophet cannot be transported (for it is the wind that actually bears him to and fro), but to focus attention on its presence: this vision will convey something about the majesty. When the prophet arrives at the temple area, "the majesty of the God of Israel" is "there" waiting for him; it is ubiquitous and not bound by the law of contradiction. The narrative has to establish its presence in the temple area; whether with or without its bearers, inside the temple or outside is of no consequence and so not noted. Only 9:3's notice of the movement of the majesty off the cherub forces upon us the awareness that it had previously been located on it; and since the only meaningful direction of motion to the threshold is from inside outward, we gather that the cherub here refers to the statuary in the inner sanctum, and the majesty—to the permanent divine presence within it. This outward movement occurs just before the order to slay the population of Jerusalem is given, suggesting that it signifies God's withdrawal of his protecting presence from the city.

Next, just before the order to burn the city is given, mention is made of the (apparently empty) throne above the cherubs (10:1); this awkwardly placed notice seems to anticipate and be related to the departure of the majesty from the threshold and its alighting upon the cherubs in vs 18. If so, these cherubs must be outside the temple; these must be real celestial cherubs (among which alone fiery coals [vs 2] are to be found), and indeed 10:3 expressly places them to the south (away from the abomination-side) of the temple. How and when they came to be in the court south of the temple is less important to the narrator than following the movements of the cloud that screened the majesty (in an obscure passage, 10:3b-4, in part related to I Kings 8:10f.). However, 10:5 gains some point if the noise of the cherubs' wings alludes to their arrival in flight on the scene coincidentally with the movement of the majesty to the threshold, mentioned in vs 4; as the inner majesty began its departure, the celestial throne vehicle arrived to receive it.

The vision's unity of location dictated that the theme of the burning of the city be broken off with the departure of the man dressed in linen to execute his orders (vs 7). A detailed description of the cherubs follows, beginning (vs 8) with their just-mentioned hands (vs 7), and ending with their movement in unison—to which the account of their taking off is juxtaposed (17-19). The placement of this static interruption of the flow of events is at a juncture—the incendiary has gone off to his terrible business; the majesty must now start on the next stage of its departure. The structure of the description must now be examined.

The items of this description are similar to (but not identical with) those of the creatures of ch. 1; the similarity increases when the isolated notices of 8:2, 10:1, 5 are taken into account. The reference to ch 1 is underlined by inverse order of the items listed in our vision—excepting the hands and the motion in unison whose location here is determined by their links with the adjacent narrative.

our vision	*verse in ch 1*
8:2 luminous human figure	27
10:1 throne	26
10:5 sound of wings	24
(10:8 hands	8)

10:9-13 wheels	15-18
10:14 faces	10
(10:16-17 motion in unison	19-21)

The use of inversion to signal literary reference was first observed by M. Seidel ("Citations from Psalms in Isaiah," *Sinai* 5616 [1956] 149ff.) and elaborated by R. Weiss (*Bet Miqra,* year 7 (5622 [1962] 46ff.; note examples from Ezek listed there p. 49 [8:12—9:9; 11:3—7—11]), though neither alludes to this striking example (observed however by Abarbanel).

The reason for the detailed description, so far as is hinted in the text, is the realization expressed in 10:20, when the prophet saw the entire apparatus rise in flight: "They were the creatures I saw beneath the God of Israel at the Chebar river; I now realized they were cherubs." The creatures at Chebar were so different from the traditional portrayal of cherubs—viz. from the cherub statues in the temple—that the prophet could not at that time identify them; hence the use of the neutral *ḥayyot* "living beings" throughout ch 1. (For one thing, the statues were two, the creatures four.) In the temple vision, the bearers of the majesty appeared again, this time in propinquity to the cherub statues. For the threeway identification, the prophet repeats the gist of ch 1's description, replacing *ḥayyot* by *kᵉrubim;* at the sight of the apparatus in flight—the very circumstance in which he first beheld it—he notes his realization of its identity. (The artificial distinction between the singular "cherub" for the statues (9:3; 10:4) and plural "cherubs" for the real ones (on *kᵉrub* in 10:2 see Comments) may be due to the difference in their number; singular is a pair (statues), plural is two pair (real).

The marked disorder in the gender of pronominal elements referring to the *ḥayyot* gives way to regularity in the case of the cherubs, for unlike the former, the grammatical and real gender of the latter agree. Other differences between the two descriptions are hard to explain: the use in 10 of *rum* (qal and nifʿal) for *hinnaśe* "rise" of ch 1; the face of a cherub replacing that of a bull; the reference to the wheels as *galgal.* If in addition there are also substantial changes (see comments to vss 12, 14), the repetition of the entire description is easier to account for; that of ch 10 will be the record of a variation on the experience of ch 1 scrupulously distinguished from it in terminology, despite its essential identity. Most recent critics regard the description of ch 10 as secondary, some conjecturing a tendentious reason for it (Halperin, *VT* 26 [1976], 9 ff; Houk, *JBL* 90 [1971] 42-54 includes the description in the supposed reworking of the entire chapter from a purification to a punishment scene). This touches on a larger issue concerning the interpretation of the entire vision.

158   The Divine Helmsman: Lou H. Silberman Festschrift

Complex, in some parts disjointed and lacking sequentiality, the vision
is treated by recent commentators either as a patchwork of additions laid
upon an original kernel or as a compilation of separate entities. Fohrer
finds four pieces (temple abominations, burning and abandonment, evil
leaders, promise to exiles); the description of the cherubs is an
"elaborating gloss to 1:1-28a". Zimmerli retains an essence of 8:1—10:7;
the allusions to the cherubs are secondary (through the majesty's coming
in full panoply to Jerusalem as it came to Babylon in ch 1, Ezekiel's
"school" rationalized the paradox of its being in Jerusalem as well as in
heaven); so too is all of 11:1-21. Such analyses aim at "restoring" a form
of text free from the tensions of the present one; their diversity—
reflecting different tolerances of tension—does not inspire confidence in
the criteria underlying them.

The working assumption underlying our attempt to interpret the text
without eliminating the tensions is that the present composition is an
intentional product. That assumption has to an extent been justified by the
evidences of design and interconnection of parts that have been found.
Enough tensions remain to render plausible the guess that not all the
elements of this vision were from the first united (e.g. one might conjecture that the evil *cabal* at the start of ch 11 belonged to a different, parallel
vision). But they have been put together with some art; whoever did so
must be supposed to have recognized the incompatibility of those elements upon which the modern critic bases his analysis, yet what was
conveyed by the composition as a whole overrode considerations of
consistency and total coherence. Since this is a report of a visionary, not a
real, experience, perhaps some incoherence was not felt as a fatal
objection to the combination of these parts.

What is the message conveyed by this complex vision?

After receving the anouncement of "the end" in ch 7, due to the social
and religious wrongdoing of the people, and with occasional echoes of the
Flood story ("the end is coming," "the land is filled . . . with lawlessness" vss. 6, 23; cf. Gen 6:13), the prophet is made witness in a vision to
the corrupt practices of the Judahites (described again in Flood story
terms, 8:17; 9:9) and is shown their destruction (with *sht* used in 9:2, 6, 8,
cf Gen 6:13, 17). In earlier prophecy, visions occur (e.g. 1 Kings 22:17-
22; Amos 7:1-9; 8:13; 9:1; Isa. 6) and at least in the case of Elijah, transportation by the wind (1 Kings 18:12; 2 Kings 2:1ff., 16); Ezek is the only
prophet to have experienced visionary transportation, here and twice
again (ch. 37; 43). Eye-witnessing, so agreeable to the vivid realism of this
prophet's imagery, here serves theodicy: the prophet sees with his own

eyes the depravity of the people and hears judgment pronounced with the culprits in his presence.

The motive of the two constitutive elements of the vision is provided by the twofold assertion of the culprits, "YHWH does not see us; YHWH has left the land" (8:12; 9:9). By way of confuting the first part, God takes the prophet on a tour of the temple area, showing him the various abominations practiced there, and checking on the prophet's observation by asking him at each site, "Do you see, human being?" The prophet knows that God has seen all, including the clandestine rites of the elders who believe him blind to them. As for the second part of their assertion, it turns out to be ironically prophetic: God had in fact not left the land when the people believed he had, but now their behavior brought it about; the prophet witnesses the divine presence departing from temple and city. This is the first example in the book of oracles built upon, perhaps occasioned by, sayings of the people that had reached the prophet. The second part of our passage consists primarily of oracular responses to two popular sayings (11:3, 15); see Greenberg, *Bet Miqra* 50 (5732 [1972]) 273-278.

No temple was destroyed—so was the common belief in the ancient Near East—except its god had abandoned it, whether reluctantly under coercion of a higher decree ("Lamentation over the destruction of Ur," ANET 455ff., ". . . over the destruction of Ur and Sumer," 617d), or in anger because of the offenses of the worshipers (Cyrus inscription, ANET 315c). The mother of Nabonidus accounts for the desolation of Haran and its temple by the Manda hordes (ibid., 311b) thus: "in the 16th year of Nabopalassar, king of Babylon, when Sin, the king of all gods, became angry with his city and his temple, and went up to heaven, and the city and the people in it became desolate" (ANET 560d). In our vision, this commonplace is expressed by the intertwining of the stages of the majesty's departure with scenes of the people's wrongdoing. When, on the other hand, the gods were reconciled and their temples rebuilt, they returned and took up their abode among their worshipers again (see the above cited texts). Accordingly, when the prophet is shown a vision of the future, rebuilt temple, he sees also the return of the majesty to the holy of holies, expressly corresponding to our vision of its departure (43:4ff., 9).

The midrash perceived the gradual nature of God's exit from temple and city in this vision as bespeaking his patient hope that the disaster might be avoided. It augments the few stages of our text into ten by a mosaic of other prophetic passages, and draws out the last stage for years. The gist of it counts these stages: (1) from one of the Ark cherubs to the other (Ezek 9:3, hence the singular "cherub"); (2) from that to the temple's threshold (10:4); (3) from there to the cherubs (vs. 18); (4) from there to the east gate (vs 19); (5) thence to the court (vs 4[!]); (6) thence to the altar (Amos 9:1); (7) thence to the roof (of the temple, Prov 21:9[!]; (8) thence to the (temple) wall (Amos 7:7); (9) thence to the city (Micah 6:0[!]); (10) thence to Mt Olives (Ezek 11:23). R. Jonathan said: For three and a half years the Presence tarried on Mt Olives, proclaiming thrice daily, 'Return, O you backsliding children' (Jer 3:22). When it saw they would not repent, it flew away saying, 'I will go back to my (heavenly) abode till they realize their guilt; in their distress they will seek me and beg for my favor' (Hos 5:15) (Pesikta de-Rab Kahana 13:11 [Mandelbaum 234-5]; trans. Braude 261-2). Note the accord between the last sentence and the citation from the mother of Nabonidus adduced above.

The prophet is guided through the northern area of the temple from one cultic abomination to the next. The stress on north (8:3, 5 [twice], 14) may have a symbolic meaning: we recall the Ugaritic notion that the seat of the gods was in the north. The coming of the executioners from the north may be connected with the location of the temple sins there, or is it also a reflection of the common notion (Jer 1:14, etc.) that misfortune comes from the north (see Sarna, EM, s.v. ṣpwn)? The concentration of pagan rites and their simultaneous performance by groups oblivious of each other lends a certain unreality to the scene. It appears as a montage of whatever pagan rites ever were conducted at the Jerusalem temple rather than a representation of what occurred there in the summer of the sixth year of Jehoiachin's exile. (T. Gaster with bold invention reconstructed an elaborate pagan harvest rite out of elements in chs 7-9 JBL 60 [1941] 289-310), resumed in Myth, Legend, and Custom in the OT [New York & Evanston: Harper & Row, 1969] 607-615; Albright, Archaeology and the Religion of Israel [Baltimore, 1946] 165-8 largely rejected Gaster's suggestions.) Scholars have generally accepted the data of ch 8 as giving a true picture of the state of Judahite religion contemporary with Ezekiel, but their contrast with the data of Jeremiah and Lamentations whose authors were actually in Jerusalem at the time of the fall, points to an opposite conclusion. Only a visionary and an audience at a remove from the reality of Jerusalem, and suffering the exile threatened for breach of covenant might have accepted and understood at once the point of such a fantasy: to collect and display vividly the notorious instances of cultic pollution of the sanctuary, so as to bring home the aweful realization that its sanctity had been hopelessly injured, and its doom irrevocably sealed. In the Introduction it is argued that the public pagan rites of ch 8 belong historically to the age of Manasseh; the secret cults of vss 10-12 are another story, and may have been practiced in Ezekiel's time. A certain veracity is given to the account by the naming of Jaazaniah—evidently a prominent man of the times; report of his practice might have reached Ezekiel through letter—a form of communication between Judah and the exiles testified to by Jer 29.

While the pagan rites are never referred to again, the social wrongs denounced here recur in the parable of Judah's rapacious kings (ch 19) and the rebuke of its evil leaders in ch 21. Both Jeremiah and Lamentations give concurring testimony: in the former, Jehoiakim is blamed for having spilled innocent blood and pursuing illegal gain (Jer 22:17; cf 2:34); in the latter, priest and prophet are denounced for having shed innocent blood (Lam 4:13). The Book of Kings says nothing of the kind about the last kings of Judah; however, since it does not allude as a rule to social wrongs (Manasseh's "filling Jerusalem with innocent blood from one end to the other" [2 Kings 21:16] is a notable exception), its silence is inconclusive. The socio-political turmoil of Judah's last years may well have generated violence; the notorious case of the royal murder of the prophet Uriah (Jer 26:20f.) may have sufficed for the blanket accusation of Jer 2:30. We do not have the data to say what the state of civic morality was in Judah at this time, and whether the biblical accusations are sober or exaggerated for the sake of theodicy.

Six years before the fall of Jerusalem, the prophet wrote the city off—he "saw" its population massacred and its buildings condemned to flames. Some years after the fall, with the same assurance, he saw a vision of his nation's resurrection and the restoration of its temple (chs 37; 40ff.). Prophetic vision represented future events as accomplished; when they occurred, they appeared as but the fulfillment of prophecy—the effect intended (2:5). God's management of history was thus demonstrated.

The visionary destruction is a glimpse, rare in prophecy, of the "upper storey" of events (cf. e.g., 1 Kings 22:19-23). Human agents would eventually execute judgment on Jerusalem and Judah, but they would only be translating a prior heavenly into an earthly reality. Basically, the enemy is God; the Babylonian army is but a later projection of his celestial executioners. The latter, incidentally, further enhance Ezekiel's picture of the divine realm as containing a variety of supramundane beings.

This anticipation in vision of the destruction of Jerusalem had an afterlife. Lam 4:6 avers that Sodom's destruction at the hand of God was preferable to Jerusalem's at the hand of men; Sodom was spared vengeance, rapine and pillage, and the humiliation of being vaunted over by a conqueror. From that angle, the visionary destruction depicted here, of a temple and a city forsaken by their God, snatches triumph away from the

Babylonians. This is spelled out in postbiblical literature. According to the Apocalypse of Baruch (2 [Syrian] Baruch), the invading Babylonians were preceded by angels who destroyed Jerusalem's walls and temple "lest the enemy should boast and say, 'We have overthrown the wall of Zion, and we have burnt the place of the mighty God . . . A voice was heard from the interior of the temple, after the wall had fallen, saying: 'Enter ye enemies and come ye adversaries; for he who kept the house has forsaken it' '' (chs 6-8). The midrashic version conditions Jerusalem's fall upon the (unbiblical) departure of its resident prophet: "As soon as Jeremiah left Jerusalem, an angel descended from heaven and placing his feet on Jerusalem's walls, breached them. He cried, 'Let the foes come and enter a house whose owner has abandoned it . . . a vineyard . . . whose watchman has deserted it—so you may not boast and say that you conquered it! A conquered city you have conquered, a slain people you have slain'' (*Pesiqta Rabbati* 26 [Buber 131]).

As he beholds the sentence of death being executed in this vision, the prophet twice cries out on behalf of the condemned people (9:8; 11:13). These are the only instances of Ezekiel's attempt to intercede for his people, and they may have to do with his (visionary) presence amidst the slain. The otherwise striking omission of intercession from the book (on the prophetic duty of intercession, see now the insightful studies of Y. Muffs, *Molad* 35/6 [5735-1975]; *Eretz Israel* 14 [Ginsberg Festschrift], Jerusalem, 1978, 48-54 [both in Hebrew]) is perhaps connected with its unconditional message of doom; compare how God repeatedly thwarts Jeremiah's attempts at intercession (Jer 7:16; 14:7-15:4).

The Jerusalemites' arrogation to themselves of all the exiles' property (11:14f.) since the latter have been removed from YHWH is not reflected elsewhere (the similarity to the issue of Josh 22:24ff. has been remarked), but that is no reason to suspect its existence. The issue is treated here because of the centrality to this vision of questions of YHWH's nearness and distance. The divine answer to the Jerusalemites is given to the exiles: YHWH is, to be sure, diminished in presence among the exiles ("a small sanctuary"), yet they will be the ones who will return and purge the land of the abominations set up in it by its present doomed occupants. Doubts have been expressed about the location of this passage, since its message of consolation seems out of place, and it is very like the post-fall passages 33:23-29 and 36:24-28.

The claim of the Jerusalemites did indeed survive the fall, but to assimilate our passage to 33:23-29 is to miss the difference in historical circumstances reflected in these passages. Our passage adverts to "the inhabitants of Jerusalem", 33:24 and 27 to "the inhabitants of these ruins . . . those who are in the open country . . . in fastnesses and caves"; the former is from before the fall, the latter from after it. The first part of the Jerusalemites' sayings differs significantly: in our passage they haughtily thrust the exiles away from YHWH, in 33:24 they pathetically base their claim on their numbers—relative to Abraham who was but one yet inherited the land. Such a ground bespeaks the fewness of the claimants and reflects the decimated remnant of Judah in post-fall times. Our passage then belongs to a pre-fall situation.

There is a consolatory side to the divine answer, but its main burden is to reject the claim of the Jerusalemites; promise of restoration is necessary to show that the present homelanders will be supplanted; promise of removing the exiles' heart of stone is incidental to the angry assertion that they will remove the defiling abominations left by the punished present occupants. One cannot rule out the possibility that such consolatory messages incidental to dooms belonged from the first with the dooms. The similarity of 11:17-20 to 36:24-28 is however suspicious, the more so since in vs 17 the 2nd pers appears, ineptly here but correctly in ch 36. Some contamination with ch 36 seems to have occured; whether all of 11:17-20 originally belonged here, whether particularly ch 36's singular doctrine of the compulsory observance of the law, may well be doubted.

These four chapters offer a panorama of the crimes of the Jerusalemites and the divine intervention to punish them, featuring the two planes of events, the aweful preview of the execution of God's wrath prior to his abandoning temple and city, and, finally, the rejection of the Jerusalemites' claims to the land in favor of the exiles. In course, three popular sayings are exposed as wrath-provoking delusions. The various materials that have been fitted into the framework of the vision have been so disposed that the statement of the main theme (sin and punishment) is followed by an echo (not necessarily sequential or contemporaneous) analogous in structure and content. An auxiliary theme (abandonment) runs through the whole from beginning to end. Material within the vision as well as its narrative framework is arranged in successive "envelopes" so that first corresponds to last, second to next-to-last, and so forth. An integrating design is clearly evidenced.

NOTES

[1] J. Levie, S. J., *The Bible, Word of God in Words of Men* (Eng. trans. from French by S. H. Treman), New York: Kenedy, n.d. (imprimatur, 1961) 130f.

[2] The Elwes translation (reprinted New York: Dover, 1951) 99, adjusted to Wirzubski's (Hebrew, Jerusalem: Magnes, 1961) 79.

[3] S. R. Driver, *An Introduction to the Literature of the Old Testament*, 9th ed. (Edinburgh: Clark, 1913) vii f., x. On the "omnicompetence of analogy" for criticism, see the citation from Tröltsch in G. von Rad, *Old Testament Theology*, vol. I, (Eng. trans. from German by D. M. G. Stalker; Edinburgh and London: Oliver and Boyd, 1962) 107, fn. 3.

[4] M. Falk, *The Song of Songs: a verse translation with exposition*, Stanford University dissertation, 1976; see especially 133ff. on the *wasf*.

[5] Mechilta to Exod. 15:9, "The enemy said"; see comments of J. Goldin, *The Song at the Sea* (New Haven and London: Yale 1971) 174ff.

[6] Sifre, Numbers to 25:1; see W. Bacher, *Die exegetische Terminologie der jüdischen Traditionsliteratur*, 2 vols (Leipzig 1899, 1905; reprinted Darmstadt: Wissenschaftliche Buchgesellschaft, 1965), I, 133; II, 143.

[7] Many have followed a similar method in studies of individual pieces of biblical literature, without much effect on modern Bible commentators. I have been most instructed by M. Weiss, who describes and illustrates his "Total-Interpretation" in SVT 22 (Congress Volume Uppsala, Leiden: Brill, 1972) 88-112 (see p 90, fn 1 for earlier items) and in his book *Hammiqra kid^{e}muto*[2] (Jerusalem: Bialik, 1967). A recent contribution full of interest is Alan M. Cooper, *Biblical Poetics: a Linguistic Approach*, Yale University dissertation, 1976.

[8] This characteristic of Ezekiel is, of course, not shared by all other prophetic books.

[9] Although commentators are increasingly alert to the presence of such elements, they are notably remiss in interpreting them; a lesson in the interpretation of alliteration and chiasm is the luminous study of the Tower of Babel story in J. P. Fokkelman, *Narrative Art in Genesis: specimens of stylistic and structural analysis* (Amsterdam: Van Gorcum, Assen, 1975).

[10] An important appeal for serious consideration of the exegetical and theological significance of the canonized form of biblical literature—heightened by awareness of its probable antecedent stages—is made by B. S. Childs, in "The Exegetical Significance of Canon for the Study of the Old Testament," *Congress Volume: Göttingen 1977* (SVT, xxix, Leiden: Brill, 1978) 66-80.

CHARTING THE WAY OF THE HELMSMAN ON THE HIGH SEAS
STRUCTURALISM AND BIBLICAL STUDIES

DANIEL PATTE

VANDERBILT UNIVERSITY, NASHVILLE, TN 37240

I. MIDRASH AND STRUCTURALISM

If you wish to know Him . . . learn the Haggadah

A parable by Pascal. Louis Marin proposes a detailed analysis: several dimensions of the text are elucidated. Lou H. Silberman responds by telling a story, *Puss in Boots:* the multi-faceted richness of Pascal's parable is displayed.[1] The sophisticated analytical commentary merely describes the facets; the telling of a comparable story renders the glitter of Pascal's story.

The specialist in midrashic studies and the structuralist scholar, despite their different approaches, share a fundamental insight: the meaning of a story cannot be posited anymore than the glitter of a jewel can be. It is an effect, a fleeting effect unveiling a mysterious reality,[2] an effect resulting from the interrelation of the several textual facets and of the light in which they are perceived. Expressing this effect in a formula (*e.g.*, a dogma) which is supposed to represent *the* meaning of the story might satisfy the common sense's eagerness for ordered knowledge, but occults the mystery. Perceiving meaning as an entity pictured in the story might permit its appropriation, but involves confusing the live glitter of a jewel with the still shine captured on one of its photographs.[3] Thus both the midrashic scholar and the structuralist are aware of the delusory fascination for making a fossil-like image out of a story's meaning.

Middoth and Structuralism

The midrash resists this temptation by multiplying the stories so as to reflect kaleidoscopically the biblical text's mystery. Indeed, this is an adequate (and possibly the only feasible) way to appropriate the textual meaning effect as effect. Yet, do the new stories properly reflect the

165

biblical text's effect or do they distort it, or even eclipse it? Are the middoth[4]—possibly influenced by hellenistic rhetoric—sufficient as a safeguard against this risk?

Structuralism as an analytical tool cannot directly contribute to the appropriation of the textual meaning-effect as the midrash does, yet it promises to provide controls for the hermeneutical process.

First, the structuralist study of a text, because it views the text as a meaning producing network of relations, excludes any possibility to perceive its meaning as monolithic or as an aggregate of meaning entities. Even if in its infancy, structuralism cannot reach other results, this negative effect of an analysis is to be treasured. By dispelling the illusion of meaning as entity, it establishes a fundamental condition of possibility for an actual hermeneutical appropriation of the text. As such structural analysis is always deeply threatening. Yet its ironic challenge of any "serious" knowledge is also liberating. One can then appreciate the wisdom of what might otherwise appear to be a childish story-telling—is it not childish to tell *Puss in Boots* in response to a learned paper? A midrashic interpretation (of one type or another) becomes a live possibility.

More constructively, structuralist research attempts to establish *middoth*-like hermeneutical rules. Some of these—the semiotic rules or structures—apply to the interpretation of any text, as the early rabbinic *middoth* applied to the interpretation of any biblical text. In addition, the structural analysis of a given text insofar as it describes the conditions of possibility of its textual meaning-effect also defines the conditions of possibility of the proper hermeneutics of this text—*i.e.*, the structural "rules" allowing the interpreter to determine which other stories and discourses properly reflect the text. Structural exegesis clearly promises such ultimate results, as our research indicates,[5] yet they can only be reached about a given narrative after a detailed analysis showing the textual network of relations through which its meaning-effect is produced. At the present stage of structuralist research only some aspects of this network can be systematically studied. Furthermore, the very scope of this network still needs to be described: the present essay is intended as a contribution toward a description of the structural network in *narratives* (as contrasted with other types of texts).

The Need for A Linguistic-based Approach

So as to dispel the illusion that a narrative is a monolithic meaning entity, literary studies emphasize the multiplicity of its potential meanings. Several readings of a given text are possible and eventually valid. This common experience can be understood as resulting from a twofold phenomenon: a) the relationship text-reader is constantly changing, each time involving a different hermeneutical "circle"; b) the text can be read at several different levels and thus one can distinguish among various levels of meaning. Structuralism also recognizes this distinction although it is now viewed as referring to two broad categories of structural relations: a) the relations which are characteristic of the *process* of communication, author-text-reader; b) the relations which are found in the text as *system of significations*.[6] Both types of relations simultaneously participate in the overall meaning-effect of the text: both belong to a single network of structural relations and thus interact with each other. Yet by distinguishing them we imply that two broad dimensions of the meaning-effect have different (although interrelated) conditions of possibility.

This first distinction already challenges the common sense's understanding of meaning as entity. Yet the deconstruction of the meaning effect of the text, which also is a quest for hermeneutical rules, needs to be carried further.

The categories of rhetorical criticism (to which the middoth are related) are most helpful in dealing with certain aspects of the text as process but cannot adequately account for other aspects of the process of communication and for the text as product. Following Lévi-Strauss' and Barthes' pioneering works, structuralist research is characterized as an attempt to study literature and other cultural manifestations as instances of the phenomenon of communication. In brief, structuralism is an attempt to apply, after the necessary transpositions, various linguistic theories to the study of cultural manifestations. It is also termed *semiotics* since these linguistic theories are often centered on the nature, role, and function of "signs".

The Structuralist Technical Vocabulary as Reflection of the Text's Mystery

There is no need to belabor the potential fruitfulness of using the results of contemporary linguistic research for the study of another instance of communication such as discourses and texts. The study of language led to the identification of linguistic elements (*e.g.*, phonemes, semes, signs) and their relations. In the same way, structuralist and semiotic research involves the identification of relations among intratextual and extratextual elements. In this analytical process, a microscopic view of the text is substituted for the macroscopic view of the common sense's perception which does not apprehend these elements as discrete although interrelated entities.[7] Thus these elements and relations need to be expressed in a technical vocabulary which, unfortunately, has to be different from the technical vocabulary used in other types of literary studies: the elements and relations considered in structuralist studies do not directly correspond to the traditional literary categories because they are defined in terms of linguistic models.

Non-structural literary studies consider the relations among meaningful elements—*i.e.,* meaning entities such as characters, parts of a plot, symbols. Such studies effectively challenge the common sense's view of the text as having a monolithic meaning. Yet, in most instances, they still presuppose that the meaning of a text is the combination of discrete meaning entities which either are added to each other or modify each other. Thus it is still possible to envision the appropriation of the meaning of a text as the compilation of the meaning data found in the text.

Following contemporary linguistic theories, structuralism presupposes that meaning is a relational effect: *i.e.,* the effect produced by the relations among various elements which in and of themselves do not have meaning, but are merely the poles between which the sparks of meaning flash. Each element identified by structuralism can thus be viewed as polarized and even as having a meaning-potential—the potential of participating in a variety of meaning-effects through its relation with other elements. Yet in and of themselves structural elements are meaningless not because of a "lack of meaning" but rather because of a "surplus of meaning": they have so many potential denotations and connotations that they would be hopelessly ambiguous without the selecting process performed by the network of relations. As such, structural elements do not correspond to the meaning-centered elements considered in non-structuralist literary studies. In fact, from a structuralist perspective, these meaningful units are, by definition, an effect produced by a network of relations: they are complex units which need to be deconstructed in order to show what their structural elements are. The need for a technical vocabulary to describe these elements is clear. Structuralism also considers the relations among complex units which more or less correspond in scope to the units studied in non-structuralist studies, yet it does so in order to determine the meaning-effect produced by the interaction of these units. The use of a structuralist technical vocabulary for the description of these units is essential to make clear that they are not viewed as meaning entities, but as complex structural elements which have merely a potential to produce certain types of meaning-effects through their relations with similar units.

The structuralist technical vocabulary, far from being a gratuitous jargon, constantly manifests that meaning is a mysterious relational happening and prevents the return to the false security of fossil-like images of meaning. The structuralist game-like multiplication of technical vocabulary joins the midrashic childish multiplication of stories in the kaleidoscopic reflection of the text's mystery, while attempting to establish hermeneutical rules—the conditions of possibility of certain meaning-effects. Conversely, this multiplication of technical vocabulary must befit its purpose and thus it must be limited by it, in the same way that the midrashic multiplication of stories cannot be allowed to run wild (as it did in later periods when the original *middoth* were no longer strictly respected). By describing in the following pages the various dimensions of the meaning-effect which, in my view, need to be accounted for in a narrative, I would like to help circumscribe the areas for which a technical vocabulary is necessary. I will attempt to chart what too often appears as a *tohû-wa-bohû* on the basis of the collective research of the scholars who participated in the "Consultation on Structuralism and Exegesis" focused on studies of Genesis 2 and 3 (held in the context of the national meeting of the Society of Biblical Literature, New Orleans, November 1978).[8]

II. CHARTING THE STRUCTURALIST *TOHU-WA-BOHU*

One Text, Several Structures

The meaning-effect of a narrative can be viewed as produced by a complex structural network which needs to be deconstructed so that its mechanism might be elucidated. It can be viewed as a series of structures which govern the organization of corresponding systems (either static or dynamic systems). These structures are superimposed upon each other and interwoven so as to form a network. This is to say that the same textual material simultaneously participates in several systems organized by corresponding structures. Consequently, in most instances, a given textual feature participates—either as an element or as a component of an element—in several systems in which it is set in relation with various other textual features. The analogy of a handwoven blanket might be helpful here: a brown thread might at once participate to the warp of the blanket (that is to the system "fabric produced by the structure of the loom" in which it is opposed to the woof), to the system of colored threads used by the weaver (as such the brown thread is contrasted with the other colored threads), to a part of the design (*e.g.*, a system of iconic forms, in which the thread participates as an element of a given form that is contrasted with other iconic forms). Thus one cannot speak of *the* single structure of a text, but rather of the plurality of its structures. A text must be viewed as the superimposition and interweaving of several textual systems each governed by a specific structure.

This theoretical remark helps to understand why various structural analyses of the same text have often quite different results . . . a puzzling fact for the readers of structuralist work not involved in structuralist research. Each structural analysis needs to limit itself to the study of one or a few textual systems. Consequently, structural analyses considering different textual systems break up the textual material in different elements and elucidate different structures. This situation led to a bewildering multiplication of theories and methods. Yet the growing interaction among scholars involved in semiotic and structuralist research progressively brings about the recognition of the place and role of each structure in a complex structural network.

Two Types of Structures, Five Types of Structuralist Research

In the plurality of structures we must first distinguish two types of structures which govern the organization of the various textual systems: a) *universal structures* which characterize narratives as part of the universal phenomenon of communication: these structures are rules which govern the interrelation of variable elements; b) *structures which characterize each specific narrative* and/or each specific use of this narrative in a communication process: these structures are often themselves a system of significations (*e.g.*, a system of values or of symbols).

This first distinction helps to understand the differences among five broad types of structuralist research.

1) Certain studies aim at elucidating the structures which characterize a given text (or a given use of a text) by examining the text (or the use of that text) in and of itself. Implicitly or explicitly such studies presuppose that the organization of the text in textual systems can be elucidated on the exclusive basis of what is found in the text . . . and thus without accounting for universal structures. The proponents of this approach have strong reservations vis-à-vis the deductive methodologies and the structural exegeses which propose to analyze a text on the basis of a semiotic theory. They suspect these methodologies of projecting on the text something foreign to it . . . as if their own approach was free of presuppositions! In fact, these exegetes read the text with pre-

understandings about the nature of the relevant textual systems and of the pertinent textual features. Indeed they hold implicit semiotic and structuralist theories about the nature of a meaningful text which would need to be examined. I anticipate that such an examination will show that most of these studies are dealing with specific textual systems and with structures which have indeed a place in the structural network that theoretical semiotic research strives to describe. Such studies often provide significant insight on the text, yet their methodological weakness does not allow one to assess what dimension(s) of the meaning-effect is thus disclosed.

2) At the other extreme, we find almost pure theoretical research—usually termed semiotic research—aimed at establishing the universal structures. It aims at establishing what is characteristic of a narrative *qua* narrative. While this research is still in process, significant results have now been reached by considering narrative as a specific instance of the phenomenon of communication. Since both language and narrative belong to the same phenomenon, one can expect that they have similar characteristics. The first decisive result of this research was to point out that the universal characteristics of both language and narrative are rules (or *structures*) which govern the relation among their respective elements and not specific elements. For instance, since each specific language is characterized by a specific set of phonemes, no given set of phonemes can be characteristic of the universal phenomenon of language, yet the rules which govern the organization of phonemes in various phonetic systems have been shown to be universal.[9] Similarly, when considering narratives, we can say in a first approximation that characters are variable (a narrative remains a narrative whether it is about cowboys and Indians, knights and squires, etc.) while certain rules governing their relations are constant. Thus the research is aimed at showing the rules or structures which are universal. In so doing, one also identifies the type of textual features which are set in relations, and thus what are the textual systems (as I termed them above) that characterize narrative *qua* narrative. This research is by nature quite abstract and leads to different (although not necessarily contradictory) results according to the linguistic theory (or more generally the theory about the phenomenon of communication) upon which it is based—we shall come back to this issue below. This theoretical research needs to be complemented by inductive analyses of texts and verified by deductive analyses.

3) Inductive analyses study specific texts in order to discover the universal rules or structures which govern the organization of meaningful

texts. Such analyses are very disappointing for the exegetes: they do not reveal anything about the meaning of the text under study (or, if they do, it is only by accident). Yet they are necessary in order to develop further the semiotic theories.

4) Deductive analyses of texts are used in order to verify if a structuralist theory (previously proposed either on the basis of theoretical research or of inductive analyses) is valid or not. The text and its meaning-effect are not the focus of the study which aims rather at establishing a semiotic theory. But once it is established, this theory becomes the basis upon which methods of structural exegesis can be developed.

5) Various kinds of structural exegeses are aimed at the study of specific textual systems and how they contribute to the overall meaning effect of a given text. This type of study—at last!—helps elucidate various dimensions of the meaning-effect of the text, as the first type discussed above also does, but this time, with a more rigorous methodology, that is with an awareness of the place of the specific textual system under study in the overall meaning effect of the text.

As long as one is not aware of the differences among these five broad types of structuralist research, one cannot but be bewildered by such a diversity. And yet each type contributes in its own way to the structuralist project: the first and the fifth study the characteristics of specific texts in order to elucidate various dimensions of their meaning-effects. The other types of study are parts of a methodological research aimed at providing sound semiotic and structuralist theoretical basis for structural exegetical methods.

Two Diverging Semiotic Theories: Two Complementary Types of Structural Exegesis

The universal structures command the attention of the structural exegetes in that they permit them to identify the textual systems which participate in the meaning-effect of a specific text. The difficulty is that at the present stage of the research there is apparently very little agreement among scholars regarding these structures. Each school, if not each individual author, has developed its own model for these structures, together with its own technical vocabulary. An international semiotic congress is a methodological Tower of Babel. Yet the general semiotic theories recently published clarify the situation by integrating numerous partial theories. Furthermore, they show that beyond the diversity of technical vocabulary and details, the main divergence in the perception of

these structures results from two different conceptions of the phenomenon of communication. Two recently published works are representative:
the book by U. Eco, *A Theory of Semiotics*[10] and the encyclopedic
dictionary by A. J. Greimas and J. Courtès, *Sémiotique. Dictionnaire
Raisonné de la Théorie du Langage.*[11]

Both these works acknowledge that the phenomenon of communication
involves two types of components: a) processes of communication and b)
systems of significations. Both theories attempt to account for these two
dimensions of the phenomenon, yet in opposite ways.

Eco takes the most fundamental structure of the phenomenon of
communication, to be "the elementary structure of communication"[12]
that is a characteristic of the process which can be represented as
follows[13]:

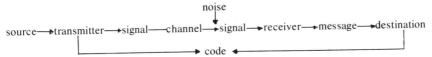

While recognizing the need to use different approaches for the study of
the two components, Eco subordinates the study of signification systems
to that of the communication processes because the latter always
presuppose the former.[14] From this perspective one identifies the various
elements of the phenomenon in terms of their function in the communication process. The codes as systems of significations as well as the different
types of signals, channels, transmitters, receivers, are classified in terms
of the various types of communication processes in which they participate.

Thus despite the fact that Eco studies separately on the one hand the
codes as systems of significations, and on the other hand the communication process (sign production), he defines a code as a "communicational
framework" or rule which interrelates "signals", "notions" and "behavioral responses", that is, as the structure which interrelates items
from various systems (systems of signals, of notions, of behavioral
responses). For him these systems and their own organization "deserve
theoretical attention only when it is inserted within a significant or
communicational framework (the code)."[15] Thus he studies the "sign
function" because "properly speaking, there are not signs, but only
sign-functions".[16] Despite Eco's well balanced approach (which integrates results of research on signification systems), it remains that the
focus on the system of communication and its structure leads him to
underestimate the role of the structure of the other systems. Thus rather

than focusing upon the study of signs as part of a system of signs, he proposes a typology of signs classified in terms of their respective function.[17]

The validity and fruitfulness of this first type of general semiotic theory is clear. When transposed to the study of texts, it proposes models for the formal identification of features of the text in terms of their effect upon the reader and for the structure of the hermeneutical process. The fact that this theory deals with the communication process as a whole is both its strength—it has the potential to elucidate the meaning-effect as a whole—and its weakness—especially when applied to texts. The difficulty is that the verification of such models necessarily involves the effect of the communication act upon the addressee, since these models include theories about "the general possibility of coding and decoding" and about the process, or labor, "required in order to produce and *interpret* signs, messages or texts."[18] While one can eventually envision such a verification in the communication of certain aspects of simple messages (for instance, in the fact that they bring about some behavioral responses) it is impossible to study adequately the effect of the communication upon the addressee's vision of life or ideology. This problem is especially acute when dealing with complex texts or discourses. In most instances one must rely on the evidence found in the encoded message (as is clear in Eco's argument).

Without denying the fundamental importance of the structure of communication, another semiotic and structuralist tradition focuses its research upon the systems of significations. This type of research—best represented by A. J. Greimas' work—studies the systems of significations as manifested in the encoded messages, such as texts, without presupposing a model for the structure of the communication process. In this approach the provisory results of both theoretical elaborations and inductive analyses can be refined progressively and verified by means of deductive analyses. In the case of texts, various textual systems, their respective structures and their interaction are gradually identified. As such this research has a much more modest goal than the preceding one: it aims merely at establishing conditions of possibility of the communication process. It is not in a position to say anything about the structure of the communication process. Yet this type of research contributes indirectly to its study by progressively circumscribing the field of the possible theories about the structure of the communication process.[19] Accordingly, Eco carefully took into account the results of the research on the systems of significations available at the time of his writing (between 1967 and 1974). While it is the best theory of the communication process available, certain of its aspects need to be revised in light of new results of the research on signification systems. In brief, as Greimas saw, the structures of the communication process must be defined on the basis of an understanding of the structures of the signification systems, and not the other way around.

The present state of structural exegesis reflects this twofold theoretical research. Certain methods aim at studying various features of the text as part of the communication process, while others aim at studying specific textual systems of signification. The former methods promise more striking exegetical results (dealing as they are with the meaning-effect as a whole) but are methodologically weaker (the theories upon which they are based cannot be really tested); by contrast the latter methods aim at more modest results (the characteristics of a few aspects of the meaning-effect) but have a stronger methodological base (the models upon which they are based *can* be verified, even though further verifications and refinements are always necessary).

From the preceding discussion it appears that these two types of structural exegesis are complementary and not exclusive of each other: they deal with different dimensions of the meaning-effect of the text. Yet, at present, it is difficult to understand clearly their relation. As we progress in our charting of the various methods of structural exegesis we shall suggest how their interdependence might be envisioned.

At this point it might be useful to represent in a table the broad categories of structuralist research we have identified so far:

Study of	Signification Systems	Communication Process
through structural exegesis	Signification systems of a given text as specific investments of universal structures	Communication process (or system) as specific investment of universal structures
semiotic research	Universal structures characteristic of signification systems	Universal structures characteristic of communication process

As this table shows, both types of structural exegesis study specific characteristics of a text or of its communication viewed as the investments of universal structures manifested either in the signification systems of the text or in the specific process of communication to which the text participates. In the following pages we shall not directly deal with the universal structures, yet we need to keep in mind that to each signification system and to each dimension of the communication process correspond universal structures which govern their organization. Implicitly or explicitly each specific structural exegetical method presupposes an understanding (or better, a model) of these universal structures. My own attempt to show the interrelation between these methods is based upon my ongoing semiotic research aimed at elucidating the structural network in narrative.

III. METHODS FOR THE STRUCTURAL EXEGESIS OF TEXTUAL SIGNIFICATION SYSTEMS

When considering a narrative text such as Genesis 2 and 3 as an encoded message whose meaning effect is produced in part by the interrelation of its elements within the message itself, we must first acknowledge that the textual "stuff" (as Hjelmslev designates it) can be broken up in any number of elements interrelated in a variety of ways so as to form different systems. The question is: which among these elements and systems are pertinent, *i.e.*, actually participate in the production of the specific meaning effect of the text? The structuralist exegetes respond: those systems which are organized by universal structures, that is by relational rules which can be found in any narrative. At first, such a view is surprising: is this not excluding what might be the most original component of a text's meaning-effect? Yet one needs to keep in mind that the specificity of a text's meaning-effect can only be perceived by comparison with a similar meaning-effect. Thus, only those elements and signification systems which can be contrasted with comparable elements and systems in other texts truly participate in the meaning-effect. In order to avoid any misunderstanding, let me emphasize that the above statement is aimed at discriminating among various ways of breaking up the text in elements and systems and not among meaningful and meaningless parts of the text. This view does presuppose that the entire text participates in the production of the meaning-effect: not a single letter should be discounted!

First one needs to distinguish between the signification systems of the expression and of the content of the narrative. The signification systems of the expression include linguistic systems of signs, and various systems of stylistic features (*e.g.*, phonetic or graphic features which characterize the poetic or prosaic expression of the text). Structural exegesis focused on signification systems has not developed methods at that level—possibly because of the awareness that the significance of such analyses would depend upon their contribution to an understanding of the text as part of the process of communication. At any rate, methods of structural exegesis for the study of signification systems are almost exclusively focused upon the narrative content.

In the narrative content of the encoded message one needs to distinguish between two types of signification systems: the syntagmatic and the paradigmatic systems.

Structural Exegesis of the Syntagmatic Systems

The plot of a narrative—*e.g.*, the narrative development from the barren and empty earth to the posting of the cherubim to the east of the garden of Eden in Genesis 2 and 3—is a complex syntagmatic system in that it is composed of several syntagmatic sub-systems that I will simply list[20] with an illustration from Genesis 2 and 3:

(1) The basic narrative syntagmatic unit is the *transformation:* an Object is transmitted to a Receiver, who is therefore transformed from a state of lack (not having the Object) to a state of lack fulfilled (having the Object). Transformations are usually manifested by the verbs of the category of "doing," although they can also be expressed in nominal forms. Two examples shall suffice here. When the woman gave the fruit of the tree to her man (Gen 3:6) "man" is the Receiver and "the fruit", the Object. Then their eyes were opened (Gen 3:7): either "their eyes" is the Receiver, and "openness" the Object, or "man and woman" is the Receiver and "opened eyes" is the Object (the choice among these two possible interpretations is dictated by the interrelation among transformations). Thus the plot can be viewed as a *system of transformations*. It has been suggested that this system was structured by a main transformation: the plot being the passage from an initial situation of lack to a concluding situation in which the lack is fulfilled through the intermediary of secondary transformations. According to this model, in Genesis 2 and 3 the initial situation of lack is that there is no man to till the earth, Gen. 2:5-6; this lack is overcome in Gen 3:22-24.[21] Yet, this model is not valid because narratives often continue to unfold after the initial lack is liquidated. It is clear that the plot emphasizes certain transformations, yet the plot as a system of transformations is not structured by a transformation.

Rather, the transformations are first organized in various syntagmatic units which are themselves interrelated so as to form the plot.

(2) A transformation is part of a larger syntagmatic unit, which I term *narrative program,* characterized by the actantial model proposed by Greimas:

$$\text{Sender} \longrightarrow \text{Object} \longrightarrow \text{Receiver}$$
$$\uparrow$$
$$\text{Helper} \longrightarrow \text{Subject} \longrightarrow \text{Opponent}$$

In other words a transformation takes place only when there is a Subject who is willing to do it (the volition is established by the Sender) and able to do it (*i.e.,* who has adequate Helpers to overcome any eventual Opponent). Through their participation in programs, transformations are organized in various clusters.

a) *They are organized in pairs of opposed transformations.* Thus the transformations of the programs of the hero and the villain in folktales are often opposed (one giving something, the other taking it away; one giving an Object to somebody, the other giving it to somebody else; etc. . . .) The textual manifestation is often more complex. The same personage might play both the roles of Subject and of Opponent; and the opposed transformations might be expressed in conditional or hypothetical statements. Yet in each narrative one finds such oppositions. In Genesis 2 and 3 we identified nineteen such pairs of opposed transformations[22], among them:

3:16e—man (domination→woman) *vs* 3:17b—Adam (listening→woman)

(the Objects "domination" and "listening" are opposed as "domination *vs* a form of "submission".)

3:16b—Yahweh Elohim (labor pain→woman) *vs.* 3:6e—woman (pleasing fruit→woman).

These oppositions play a special role in the production of the meaning effect of the text by marking certain transformations as particularly significant because of the very fact that opposite transformations are manifested: accordingly, they are termed "pertinent transformations." They appear to have at least a twofold function.

First, they participate in the unfolding of the narrative development in the form of *action sequences*[23] according to the model "action *vs.* counter action." Thus in Genesis 2 and 3, Robert Culley identifies six action sequences. It is enough to mention four of these here. Two of the sequences are of the type "wrong/wrong punished": the man and the woman eating the fruit and being punished (2:16-17; 3:1-6, 9-13, 16-19). The "wrong" itself involves a succession of transformations, namely a prohibition and a violation of this prohibition. Similarly the serpent does wrong (3:1-5) and is punished (3:14-15). Two other sequences belong to the type "difficulty/difficulty removed". The characteristic acquired by man through eating the fruit poses a difficulty or problem for Yahweh Elohim, which is resolved by the expulsion from the garden (3:22-24). Similarly the sequence concerning the creation of the woman (2:18-25), which resolves the problem or difficulty expressed in Yahweh Elohim's statement: it is not good that the man be alone.[24] By participating in interwoven action sequences, these pairs of transformations also show the narrative development to be polemical in nature: they establish a principal and a polemical axis along which the textual elements are gathered.

This participation of the pairs of opposed transformations in the narrative development is certainly not their only role: some of these pairs are indeed established by the introduction of textual elements which do not contribute to the unfolding of the plot. For instance, one of the effects of introducing the excursus about the river(s), 2:10-14, is to oppose the watering of the garden by the river (v. 10) to the watering of the earth by the "mist" (*ed* v. 6)—in this case the same Object "water" is attributed to two different Receivers, "garden" and earth".[25] This observation and other theoretical reasons led us to conclude that the pairs of opposed transformations form a *system of pertinent transformations which is closely associated with the symbolic system of the text.* Each pertinent transformation (a syntagmatic unit) is, so to speak, the center of a magnetic field around which textual elements are gathered together whether or not they contribute to the narrative development.

b) *The transformations are also organized so as to form chain-like series* in order to describe a complex action process. For instance, the creation of the woman in Gen. 2:21-22 involves a series of successive transformations. When they are defined in terms of the actions, these chain-like series form what is termed by Greimas *narrative trajectories.* When considering the actual organization of narratives, the uninterrupted chain-like series of transformations form *elementary narratives* (often, a part of the story of one or another personage). The plot as a system of transformations appears as a system of elementary narratives. A study of the interrelation of the elementary narrative shows that they can be grouped in *narrative levels* according to the way in which they are interrelated. The elementary narratives which *converge* with each other (that is, which contribute to the narrative development through cause/ effect and action/counteraction relationships) belong to the same level. In Genesis 2 and 3, we find two such narrative levels: Genesis 2:4b-9, and 15; Genesis 2:16-3:21. The narrative development continues to unfold from one to the other but not as the result of a cause and effect, or action and counteraction relationship. Rather, the narrative moves forward on the basis of a character's recognition or attribution of a certain "value" (or meaning) to the preceding narrative development. The new narrative development which proceeds from this interpretation can be viewed as *diverging* from the preceding narrative development. In the present case, Yahweh Elohim's command is not a direct response to any of the preceding transformations. Rather, it presupposes the attribution of a certain value to the preceding narrative development: the man and the Garden together with its content should be in a specific relationship. In 2:18 we find a second interpretation of the situation by Yahweh. It is focused, this time, on the loneliness of man. The serpent's intervention in 3:1-7 presupposes another and conflicting interpretation of the relationship between man and Garden which converges, according to the category action/counteraction, with Yahweh's. Such a diverging narrative development, often marked by cognitive verbs or by certain types of direct discourses, signals a shift from one narrative level to another[26].

Syntagmatic and Paradigmatic Systems

The importance of this identification of the narrative levels according to the principles briefly outlined above[27] resides in the fact that it allows the exegete to identify the broad outline of the organization of a text's symbolic and semantic systems. The second narrative level is characterized by the fact that it presupposes certain values related to evaluations of the preceding narrative development. Consequently, the symbols found in this part of the text are held together by semantic connotations which are different from those found in the first narrative level. In other words, a study of this syntagmatic system (the system of elementary narratives) prepares the study of the paradigmatic system (the symbolic system, the codes, the semantic universe) of the text.

The other syntagmatic systems—the system of pertinent transformations, of the narrative trajectories, and of the action sequences— correspond themselves to paradigmatic systems. Their identification prepares a detailed study of the symbolic and semantic dimensions of the text. Yet, they are valuable in themselves. A comparison of texts at this level (for instance, in order to establish genres or sub-genres) is quite appropriate: because of the correspondence between syntagmatic and paradigmatic systems, explicitly or implicitly, they take into account essential characteristics of the symbolic and semantic organization of these texts.[28]

Structural Exegesis of the Paradigmatic Systems

Among the studies of textual signification systems, those focused on the paradigmatic systems reach exegetical results which have the most significant implications for a hermeneutic of the text and thus also for theology. The mere descriptions of the codes, of the symbolic system, of the semantic connotations of each symbol, and of characteristics of the text's semantic universe invite a comparison with contemporary codes, symbolic systems and semantic universes.

The study of the paradigmatic systems of the text is often performed independently from the study of the syntagmatic systems (whether they are juxtaposed or not to such studies). In such a case, models usually derived from Lévi-Strauss' research on myths are used in order to identify the symbolic and semantic oppositions as well as the codes. By contrast the members of the Society of Biblical Literature seminar attempt, in various ways, to relate the study of the paradigmatic systems to that of syntagmatic systems (as well as to that of features of the communication process). For, indeed, there is a great number of semantic oppositions and categories which can be identified in each text. The question is to know what are the oppositions and categories which truly characterize the text—i.e., the pertinent oppositions and categories. More or less elaborated theories about the correspondence between the syntagmatic and paradigmatic systems are used as a methodological tool to guide this choice. For instance, in Genesis 2 and 3, T. Boomershine[29] identifies five codes—an alimentary, an animal, a sexual, a geographical and a life/death code—after having performed a syntagmatic analysis in terms of the actantial model. Jobling, while identifying similar features, focuses his analysis on semantic oppositions such as inside/outside and on the role of semantic categories (such as life and death, knowledge, man and his helpers) on the basis of a narrative analysis in terms of a refined Proppian method[30]. Similarly Parker and Patte[31] propose an analysis of paradigmatic systems on the basis of a study of the text's syntagmatic organization (especially, of its narrative levels and system of pertinent transformations). For this purpose they use a detailed model of the relationship between the syntagmatic systems of pertinent transformations and the symbolic and semantic systems.[32] They endeavor to elucidate the semantic universe of Genesis 2 and 3 which involves two isotopies (or set of deep values): the one concerning the specific connotations that the "power to create" has in this text, and the other concerning the text's view of human existence as related to various aspects of the world, of the divine and of human experience. For Parker and Patte, such an analysis displays the general semantic framework undergirding both the narrative and symbolic organizations of the text and, consequently, prepares the detailed study of the symbolism.

Since each of these studies deals with paradigmatic systems of deep values presupposed by the text, one is tempted to think that they deal with a single signification system. In fact, the codes, the symbolic system (and its semantic categories) and the semantic universe (and its isotopies) are three distinct, albeit interrelated, systems of deep values.

The codes are cultural systems which characterize a text as one expression among many of a given culture. In the analogy of a hand-woven blanket proposed above, the codes would correspond to the system of colored threads. It includes a limited number of colored threads and certain constraints defining how they can be associated and con-trasted. It is available to all the weavers belonging to the same culture (or sub-culture). This system is manifested in each hand-woven blanket of the culture. Similarly, codes are systems of deep values which form one of the semantic framework of texts in a given culture.

The symbolic system (and its semantic categories) is characteristic of a given text. It corresponds to the system of iconic forms of a hand-woven blanket. The deep values that it manifests are complex semantic units[33], which form the semantic framework directly undergirding the narrative development. As such, the deep values of the symbolic system can be relatively easy to express as the author's anthropology, cosmology, theology or epistemology. In other words, they can be expressed in discursive forms which involve the presentation of values in the context of a (narrative or logical) development.

The semantic universe is also characteristic of a given text, but at a deeper level. The deep values which form it are the semantic framework undergirding the symbolic system (and thus, indirectly, the narrative development). They are self-evident truths which characterize the overall gaze (regard) of the author[34] (and of the readers insofar as they submit to the text). They are the semantic framework without which nothing in the text makes sense. They are the semantic universe inside which the author thinks, speaks, and acts (to be contrasted with the symbolic system that the author dominates, transforms and creates, at least to a certain extent).

These deep values are the "meaning horizon" of the text.[35] As such they are not the central values manifested by the text's symbolism. They are peripheral although foundational. They are not that upon which the text is focused although they are what focuses the text, its *visée*.[36] Because of their self-evidence, they belong to the category of the revealed, of the transcendent. They characterize the author's very faith, that we contrast with the many possible expressions of this faith in symbolic or theological discourses or acts.

The differences among these three types of semantic systems appear clearly when comparing the essays by Boomershine, Jobling, and Parker and Patte. There is no doubt that they are closely interrelated. But the laws governing their complex interactions have not yet been fully established. In order to understand this phenomenon we will need to take into account features of the communication process. At the present stage of the research, analyses of the signification systems provide nevertheless a number of criteria allowing the exegetes to verify the validity of hermeneutical discourses. The organization of the symbolic and semantic systems defines the field of the possible hermeneutical discourses which should be based upon symbolic and semantic systems prolonging (and thus compatible with) those of the text.[37] Furthermore, the description of the symbolic and semantic systems of a text is in itself an invitation to compare them with the systems of our own discourses. Such comparisons are themselves hermeneutical discourses brought about, and controlled, by the exegesis.

IV. METHODS FOR THE STRUCTURAL EXEGESIS FOCUSED UPON THE COMMUNICATION PROCESS

The hermeneutical rules which are derived from the exegesis of the textual signification systems are primarily negative criteria. Exegeses focused upon the communication process as manifested in the text promise to offer more specific hermeneutical rules. Such analyses should permit one to elucidate the precise target toward which is directed the meaning-effect of the text. Is the text aimed at communicating information to be used by the addresses in their own discourse? Is it aimed at manipulating the addressees so as to make them do something *(faire faire)*, or so as to make them believe *(faire croire)*? In such cases how does the text affect the addressees' systems of values (either their symbolic system or their semantic universe)?

A general answer given to this last question by certain exegetes affirms that the text affects the addressees by inviting them to identify themselves with specific characters at one or the other stage of the narrative development. Following a method termed "rhetorical criticism"[38] these exegetes, among whom T. Boomershine,[39] study the syntagmatic organization of the narrative a) in terms of the "variations in narrative points of view" (what are the narrative components which are presented from the perspective of an observer, or rather from the perspective of a character as an inside view); b) in terms of "norms of judgment" (the "criteria of right and wrong which are the implied basis for the narrator's attitudes toward the characters and their actions"); c) in terms of the "dynamics of distance in the characterizations" (that is, "the degree of sympathy or alienation, involvement or detachment which occurs in the various relationships in the narrative between the narrator and his audience and between the audience and the characters of the story"); d) and in terms of the "establishment and reversal of expectations" which characterize the plot.

This exegetical method leads to important conclusions prescribing certain hermeneutics of the text.[40] Yet as is clear from the above criteria, the analysis involves many judgments that the exegete must make upon very few formal textual evidences. Boomershine attempts to remedy this weakness by complementing this exegesis with a study of certain textual signification systems (the narrative syntagmatic system of actantial functions and the paradigmatic system of codes). While Boomershine's methodological research needs further development, it is most appropriate, in view of the obvious relationships which exist between the rhetorical criteria and the signification systems discussed above.

H. White[41] sees that such a promising exegetical method cannot be established as long as it is not based upon a sound theory about literary communication processes. His article is almost exclusively theoretical rather than being exegetical. This represents well the state of the research aimed at establishing a structuralist exegetical method focused on the communication process. What is at stake here is the identification of enunciative markers, that is of textual features reflecting the communication process to which the text partipates (or participated). Following Searle,[42] Austin[43] and primarily Benveniste,[44] White emphasizes the role of the deictics (the pronouns, I, you, etc., the demonstratives, this and that, and the time markers) and, consequently, the role of the alternance of direct and third person discourses as means of recognizing the narrator/narratee relationship.

While this type of methodological research has long stagnated we can expect it to progress rapidly now. The exegetical paper by H. White as well as the responses by G. Phillips, B. Kovacs, R. Detweiler and J. D. Crossan[45] present promising elements of method. The structural categories established for the study of textual signification systems help, in my view, to conceive models of the universal structures which characterize the communication process, even though these structures are quite different from those of the signification systems.[46] Here we must be content to list some of the issues which need to be resolved.

In the case of narrative, the primary meaning-effect is aesthetic rather than informational. In other words, a narrative has for effect either the transformation or the reinforcement of the symbolic and semantic systems of the addresses. A large part of this effect results from the distance (harmony or disharmony) between the text's symbolic and semantic systems from those of the addressees. In the case of disharmony, it can be either a conflict of semantic universes (or semantic horizons) or a conflict of symbolic systems (within the same narrative universe), or again a conflict regarding cultural codes, or several of these combined. The question is to know if there are textual markers which would allow the exegetes to identify what type of aesthetic effect characterizes the text. The interrelation of the various components of the semantic system needs to be studied anew. The analysis of the signification systems aims at showing how the various semantic components form an overall system. In the present case, we need to study the semantic, symbolic and narrative connectives which articulate the different components. Why are the connectives manifested in the text? Furthermore, the enunciative markers (such as deictics, and the shift from direct to indirect discourse), which are found in the syntagmatic organization of the text, do not necessarily correspond to the narrative, symbolic and semantic organizations of the signification systems. What is the significance of discrepancies? of absence of discrepancies? For instance, White's analysis[47] of Genesis 2 and 3 in terms of markers of the enunciation and in terms of the types of subjectivity manifested by the form of the discourses reveals an enunciative organization which is part of the time consistent with the organization of the symbolic and semantic systems, and, at other times, at odd with it. Furthermore, one has to wonder whether or not the distance between the text's symbolic systems from those of the addressees corresponds to tensions found in the text. More specifically, would it correspond to the tension between modes of subjectivity which is revealed by the study of the modes of discourses as proposed by White? Answers to these questions and others of the same type might help progress toward a methodology which would allow the exegetes to identify the type of a text's aesthetic effect as well as the parts of the symbolic and semantic systems which are particularly significant for the communication process. In this way the exegesis would define more specifically what the proper hermeneutics of a given text are.

V. STRUCTURALISM AND HERMENEUTIC

Structuralist research, an ongoing quest for hermeneutical rules: the text's shallow self-evidence becomes a multi-dimensional mystery. An exegesis of the text's symbolic and semantic organization: the text is allowed to define the field of its valid hermeneutics. An exegesis of the dynamics of the communication process inscribed in the text: the text's aesthetic power will, hopefully, be released on the targets it sets for itself in the addressees' experience. New stories are generated out of the addressees' experience submitted to the impact of the text's meaning-effect. The text's mystery is reflected in the new discourses.

Such is the ultimate goal that the members of the Society of Biblical Literature seminar pursue through their structural exegetical research. Much needs to be done to establish a complete exegetical method which would allow the hermeneuts to proceed to a "theopoetic" prolonging the biblical text and respecting its mystery.

Theopoetic. Throughout his career Amos Wilder made a plea for theopoetic.[48] It is appropriate to refer to him in conclusion of this essay. It is to him that the structural exegetical research of American scholars owes its characteristic concern for hermeneutic[49] conceived as deeply rooted in the creative imagination and as finding a privileged form of expression in story-telling. No wonder, then, that the midrashic scholar finds himself at home in structuralist research.[50] Structural exegetical research is, at least to a certain extent, rediscovering the midrashic way of making theology: haggadah, theopoetic.

NOTES

[1]This exchange took place in the context of a conference at Vanderbilt University in 1975. Its proceedings have been published in *Semiology and Parables*, D. Patte editor (Pittsburgh: Pickwick press, 1976). For Louis Marin's paper and Lou H. Silberman's response, see 189-219; 236-241.

[2]"If thou wishest to know Him at whose word the world came into being, then learn the Haggadah, for through it thou shalt know the Holy One, praised be He," Sifre to Deut. XI, 22 quoted by J. Theodor in *Jewish Encyclopedia*, New York and London: Funk and Wagnalls Company, 1906, Vol. VIII article "Midrash Haggadah." "Three things are too wonderful for me; four I do not understand . . . the way of a ship on the high seas . . ." Proverbs 30:18-19.

[3]John Jones, in his forthcoming Vanderbilt Ph.D. dissertation, expresses the same point in the following comment on H. Frei, *The Eclipse of Biblical Narrative* (New Haven: Yale University Press, 1974): "Whether taken as historical reportage, allegory or myth, the text has been consistently read to mean something beyond itself: historical event, moral lesson, cultural context, authorial intent . . . Such a reading (Frei holds) misses the way in which the story is the meaning, or alternatively, that the meaning emerges from the story form, rather than being merely illustrated by it."

[4]The hermeneutical rules used in early rabbinic judaism: cf. H. L. Strack, *Introduction to the Talmud and Midrash* (Philadelphia: Jewish Publication of America, 1931) 93-98 and 284-85 (notes). Here, I refer primarily to the rules for haggadic interpretation. On the relationship of these rules with hellenistic rhetorical rules, cf. S. Lieberman, *Hellenism in Jewish Palestine* (New York: Jewish Theological Seminary of America, 1950) 46-82; and D. Daube, "Rabbinic Methods of Interpretation and Hellenistic Rhetoric," *HUCA* 22, 1949, 251-60; and D. Patte, *Early Jewish Hermeneutic in Palestine*, Missoula: Scholars Press, 1975, pp. 109-115.

[5]Cf. Daniel and Aline Patte, *Structural Exegesis: From Theory to Practice* (Philadelphia: Fortress Press, 1978) 61-112.

[6]On the distinction between "process of communication" and "system of significations", see U. Eco, *A Theory of Semiotics* (Bloomington, London: Indiana University Press, 1976) 8-9.

[7]Cf. Daniel and Aline Patte, *Structural Exegesis: From Theory to Practice* 1-10.

[8]The proceedings of this consultation will be published in a special issue of *Semeia*, Fall 1979.

[9]As Professor W. von Raffler Engel pointed out in a communication in the seminar of the Structuralist Research Group at Vanderbilt University, referring to the work of scholars such as Roman Jakobson.

[10]U. Eco, *A Theory of Semiotics*

[11]A. J. Greimas and J. Courtès, *Sémiotique: Dictionnaire Raisonné de la Théorie du Language* (Paris: Hachette, 1979). English translation forthcoming.

[12]U. Eco, *op. cit.*, 32; cf. also 316.

[13]*Ibid.*, 33.

[14]Ibid., 9.

[15]Ibid., 38.

[16]Ibid., 49.

[17]For a much simplified model of such a typology, see E. Leach, *Culture and Communication* (Cambridge: Cambridge University Press, 1976) 9-16.

[18]U. Eco, *op. cit.* 152 [italics mine].

[19]The constant temptation for the scholars involved in this research is to extrapolate either general theories about the communication process or understanding of the overall meaning-effect of a text out of the strictly limited results of their research. Once more, the conclusions should not exceed the premises.

[20]For a complete theoretical presentation of this model, see Daniel Patte and Aline Patte, *Structural Exegesis. From Theory to Practice*, chapter II.

[21]As noted by David Jobling, Judson Parker and Daniel Patte: D. Jobling, "A Structural Analysis of Genesis 2:4b-3:24" and J. Parker and D. Patte, "Structural Exegesis of Genesis 2 and 3." *SBL 1978 Seminar Papers* Volume 1, Paul Achtemeier, ed., (Missoula: Scholars Press, 1978) 62-70 and 141-160.

[22]Cf. J. Parker and D. Patte, *op. cit.*, 145-148.

[23]Cf. Robert Culley, "Action Sequences in Genesis 2-3," *Seminar Papers*, Volume 1, 51-60.

[24]Cf. Robert Culley, *op. cit.*, 54-56.

[25]This phenomenon is not limited to texts which are the product of a redactional activity. It is found in one form or another in quite different types of narrative.

[26]In Genesis 2 and 3 a second shift is found in Genesis 3:22 (which presupposes an interpretation of the value of the narrative development from 2:16 to 3:21).

[27]For a detailed explanation of these principles, see Daniel and Aline Patte, *Structural Exegesis. From Theory to Practice*, chapters II and III.

[28]This is examplified by Culley's works. Cf. Robert Culley, *op. cit.*, 51-60 and *Studies in the Structure of Hebrew Narrative, Semeia Supplements* (Philadelphia: Fortress Press and Missoula: Scholars Press, 1976).

[29]Thomas E. Boomershine, "Structure and Narrative Rhetoric in Genesis 2-3," *Seminar Papers*, Volume 1, 31-49.

[30]David Jobling, *op. cit.*, 61-69. See also his use of this method (as combined with semantic analysis) as applied to other Old Testament texts; David Jobling, *The Sense of Biblical Narrative. Three Structural Analyses of the Old Testament* (Sheffield: Journal for the Study of the Old Testament, 1978).

[31]J. Parker and D. Patte, *op. cit.*, 141-159.

[32]D. and A. Patte, *Structural Exegesis. From Theory to Practice*, chapter II.

[33]They are mythemes which combine two types of semantic features, the functions and states. D. and A. Patte, *Structural Exegesis*, 16-22.

[34]We borrow this metaphor from Michel Foucault, *The Birth of the Clinic* (New York: Vintage Books, 1975).

[35]We borrow this metaphor from H.-G. Gadamer, *Truth and Method* (New York: Seabury Press, 1975).

[36]Greimas uses the metaphor "visée du monde" to make clear that a semantic universe is a dynamic, and not static, reality. Cf. Greimas and Courtès. *Dictionnaire*, 127.

[37]D. and A. Patte, *Structural Exegesis*, chapter IV. Furthermore, the description of the symbolic and semantic systems of a text is in itself an invitation to compare them with the systems of our own discourses. Such comparisons are themselves hermeneutical discourses brought about, and controlled, by the exegesis.

[38]See the collective book, *Rhetorical Criticism: Essays in Horror of James Muilenburg*, Jared S. Jackson and Martin Kessler, editors. (Pittsburgh: Pickwick Press, 1974).

[39]Cf. T. Boomershine, *op. cit.*, 31-38. The following description of the criteria for rhetorical criticism are taken from Boomershine's essay.

[40]In addition to the essays mentioned above, see T. Boomershine, *Mark the Storyteller: A Rhetorical Critical Investigation of Mark's Passion and Resurrection Narrative*, (Union Theological Seminary dissertation, Ann Arbor, Michigan, microfilm, 1974). R. Tannehill, *The Sword of His Mouth*, (Philadelphia: Fortress Press, 1975) uses a similar method on other types of Gospel texts. The two basic methodological books upon which this exegetical method is based are Wayne Booth, *The Rhetoric of Fiction* (Chicago, 1961) and Edward Corbett, ed., *Rhetorical Analyses of Literary Works* (New York, 1969).

[41]Hugh White, "Direct and Third Person Discourse in the Narrative of the 'Fall'," *SBL 1978 Seminars Papers*, Volume 1, Paul Achtemeier, ed. (Missoula: Scholars Press) 121-140.

[42]J. Searle, *Speech Acts* (Cambridge: University Press, 1970).

[43]J. Austin, *How to do Things with Words*, 2nd edition (Cambridge, Massachusetts: Harvard University Press, 1975).

[44]E. Benveniste, *Problèmes de Linguistique générale* (Paris: Gallimard, 1966).

[45]All these papers will be published in a forthcoming issue of *Semeia*.

[46]C. Snelling, in his response to be published by *Semeia*, showed that the models for the various stages of the development of logical reasoning—derived from Piaget's work—are also most helpful in understanding the relationship among these various structural levels.

[47]Cf. White's forthcoming article in *Semeia*.

[48]Amos N. Wilder, *Theopoetic. Theology and the Religious Imagination*, (Philadelphia: Fortress Press, 1976).

[49]This debt was acknowledged by the dedication of two special issues of *Semeia* to Amos Wilder. *Semeia* Volumes 12 and 13 (fall 1978) entitled "The Poetics of Faith. Essays offered to Amos Niven Wilder." Volume 12 has for subtitle "Rhetoric, Eschatology and Ethics in the New Testament," and Volume 13 "Imagination, Rhetoric and the Disclosures of Faith." The hermeneutical concern of D. Via is expressed in the title of his book: D. Via, *Kerygma and Comedy in the New Testament: A Structuralist Approach to Hermeneutic* (Philadelphia: Fortress Press, 1975). Hermeneutic is the main preoccupation of J. D. Crossan: cf.

especially J. D. Crossan, *The Dark Interval: Toward a Theology of Story* (Niles, Illinois: Argus Communications, 1975); and *Raid on the Articulate. Comic Eschatology in Jesus and Borges* (New York, London: Harper and Row, 1976). A chapter is devoted to hermeneutic in D. Patte, *What is Structural Exegesis?* (Chapter I) and in D. and A. Patte, *Structural Exegesis From Theory to Practice* (Chapter IV). The same concern is clear in McKnight's work—E. McKnight, *Meaning in Texts. The Historical Shaping of a Narrative Hermeneutics* (Philadelphia: Fortress Press, 1978)—, as well as in Detweiler's publication—R. Detweiler, *Story, Sign and Self. Phenomenology and Structuralism as Literary-Critical Methods, Semeia Supplements,* (Philadelphia: Fortress Press and Missoula: Scholars Press, 1978).

[50]Cf. L. H. Silberman, "Between Chaos and Creation: A Survival Myth", *Journal: Central Conference of American Rabbis,* Summer 1977, 107-119 and his forthcoming book on the midrash.

NEW HEARTS AND THE OLD COVENANT: ON SOME POSSIBILITIES OF A FRATERNAL JEWISH-CHRISTIAN READING OF THE JEWISH BIBLE TODAY

EMIL L. FACKENHEIM

UNIVERSITY OF TORONTO, TORONTO, CANADA M5S1A1

1.

IN 1936 Martin Buber published a classic essay, "The Man of Today and the Jewish Bible."[1] In this he made some assertions which we should like here to use as hermeneutical principles. First, the Jewish Bible, though composed of many books, is nevertheless *one* Book because of its "basic theme," the "encounter of a people with the Nameless One." Second, generation after generation must wrestle with this book, although they do not by any means always do so in a spirit of "obedience" and a "willingness to listen," but often with "annoyance" and even "outrage." Third, decay takes place only when, as with modern man, all sense of commitment to the Book has vanished. We wish to follow these assertions, here used as guiding principles, with only three qualifications necessitated by the events that have occurred since the essay was written. First, we look at the world of today, and find that we can no longer speak of "modern man" but rather, in this context, only of modern Jews and Christians. Second, shortly after Buber's essay was written, an unprecedented event threatened and widely succeeded in dividing Jew and Christian, by murdering the one and tempting the other to become a bystander, accomplice or even active participant in the crime. Third, this event has created a new moral and religious necessity to do everything possible to bridge the ancient gulf between the two alienated brothers. But any such attempt depends in large measure on the ability of Jews and Christians to read the Book together.

2.

In this essay we shall not consider the One Book but only one chapter of one book of the One Book and, moreover, shall confine ourselves still further to only two passages which, in the JPS version, read as follows:

> Thus saith the Lord:
> A voice is heard in Ramah,
> Lamentation and bitter weeping,

191

Rachel weeping for her children;
She refuseth to be comforted for her children,
Because they are not.

Thus saith the Lord:
Refrain thy voice from weeping,
And thine eyes from tears;
For thy work shall be rewarded, saith the Lord;
And they shall come back from the land of the enemy.
And there is hope for thy future, saith the Lord;
And thy children shall return to their own border.
(Jeremiah 31:15-17)

Behold, the days come, saith the Lord, that I will make
a new covenant with the house of Israel, and with the house of Judah;
not according to the covenant that I made with their fathers in the
day that I took them
by the hand to bring them out of the land of Egypt;
forasmuch as they broke My covenant, although I was a
lord over them, saith the Lord. But this is the covenant that I will make with the house of Israel after
those days, saith the Lord, I will put My Law into
their inward parts, and in their hearts will I write
it; and I will be their God, and they shall be My
people; and they shall teach no more every man his
neighbour, and every man his brother, saying: 'Know
the Lord'; for they shall all know Me, from the least
of them, unto the greatest of them, saith the Lord;
for I will forgive their iniquity, and their sin will
I remember no more.
(Jeremiah 31:31-34)

The importance of the second above passage for the Christian reader is obvious: the very name 'New Testament' derives from it (See Heb. 8:8 ff.; 10:16-17). Since the importance of the first above passage for the Jewish reader is not so obvious, we shall furnish an illustration. A third century Midrash reads as follows:

The night is divided into three watches, and in each watch sits the Holy One, blessed be He, and roars like a lion: 'Woe unto Me who have destroyed My house and burned My temple and sent My children into exile among the Gentiles!' (Bab. Talmud, Berakhot 3a)

God Himself, as it were, weeps for His children. He weeps not for symbolic children in a symbolic exile but rather for actual children in an actual exile. He weeps as would a flesh-and-blood father or mother. He weeps as Rachel does.

Gershom Scholem has noted that it took nearly a thousand years for this Midrash to find liturgical expression.[2] If God wakes up at midnight, shall *we* not wake with Him? And if He weeps for us and our children, shall we too not weep, not so much with Him as *for* Him?[3] And shall this divine-human community of waking and weeping not be the turning point, the beginning of the redemption? *Tikkun Hatzot*—the liturgical "midnight watch"—was thus divided into two parts. To be sure, the second—*Tikkun Leah*—consists of prayers expressing the hope for redemption. These prayers, however, would be fleshless, bloodless and vapid unless they were preceded by *Tikkun Rachel*—the mourning for the flesh-and-blood children in exile, suffering and unredeemed. This writer has heard of one man in his own city who observes *Tikkun Hatzot* to this day.

Must Jews and Christians, then, give different weight to the two Jeremiah passages which are our text? Perhaps this is inevitable. But let it be remembered that the two passages—part of the same chapter!—belong to the one Book. Neither passage may be denigrated, belittled, overlooked.

The most obvious way of reaching this hermeneutical goal lies in objective scholarship, opposed as it is to all bias. The Biblical scholar may be dubious about Buber's "One Book" thesis. He is committed, however, to a "value-free" stance in which no part of the Book is denigrated—or exalted—at the expense of others. Hence a venture in Biblical scholarship can be shared by participants who are Jews, Christians and those who are neither.

Let us test this commitment to a value-free stance with an example. The Anchor Bible is a respected work of Biblical scholarship. Its contributors include Christians and Jews. Its translations are accompanied by a maximum of philological notes and—presumably because of a suspicion of value judgments—by a minimum of interpretive comments. Yet John Bright, the author of the Jeremiah volume, writes as follows about Jer. 31:31 ff.:

This passage represents . . . the high point of his theology. It is certainly one of the profoundest and most moving passages in the entire Bible.[4]

Of the Rachel passage Bright has nothing to say.

Whether or not assertions concerning "high points in theology" are value judgments is too large and deep a question for this brief essay and will therefore be dealt with only marginally below. But there is surely little doubt on the score about judgments concerning "profundity." And all doubt vanishes when a text is described as "most moving." We ask: most moving *for whom?* We might answer our question by resorting to a complicated philosophical discourse. However, far more telling in the present context is the simple and indisputable fact that, at least ever since the institution of *Tikkun Hatzot,* at least all Jews observing the rite have been moved far more deeply by the Rachel passage; and they have surely found themselves unable to pass on to the "new covenant" passage *except through* the Rachel passage. And what was true through the ages of a small group of observant Jews is true today of all Jews who remember—how can they forget?—what happened to the children of Rachel at Auschwitz and Ravensbruck.

4.

Remarks by scholars about "moving passages" and "high points in theology" could be dismissed as mere lapses from the standards of value-free objectivity. Yet it is not merely the frequency of such "lapses" in the writings of Biblical scholars that gives us pause and raises questions, vis-à-vis the One Book, about the nature of objectivity itself. For one thing, no scholar, however committed to impartial justice to all parts of the One Book, can give equal attention to every segment within it: selectivity is inevitable. For another—and this is more serious still—, the scholar's task extends beyond such external matters as dating the texts to an attempt to understand them, and it is a notorious and possibly inevitable fact that one scholar's understanding differs from another. Thirdly, to these difficulties which apply to all texts must be added the difficulty concerning *this* text: the scholar, if he is Jewish or Christian, is heir to a tradition which regards it as revealed. (One might say in passing that a scholar who *qua* scholar denied the revealed status of this Book would surely be as little objective as one who *qua* scholar affirmed it, and that it is by no means obvious that this Book's claim to revealed status can even be suspended by resort to purely objective standards.) These difficulties cause the possibility to come into view that a truly *objective* selectivity from the texts and understanding of them, as well as an equally objective stance toward one's own tradition, cannot be found in the texts *alone*—confronted, as it were, nakedly—, but must lie at least in part in objective *standards brought to* the texts.

Let us test this view of scholarly objectivity by summarizing and comparing two interpretations of Jer 31:31 ff., both of which, consciously or unconsciously, express and illustrate it.

Interpretation A:
This passage is the "climax" of Jeremiah's prophecies of salvation, for the new covenant is not a mere renewal of the old. Its essence lies in the "tranformation" of the "duty to obey" the "covenantal law" as the "expression of an alien will" into a "need to obey felt by the heart itself," with the result that the law loses its "heterogeneous character."[5]

Interpretation B:
This passage represents the resolution of a "tension" between the "moral demand that sets limits to the working of God" and the "religious demand that subjects all to divine control." The "eschatological" resolution will render man "incapable of sinning."[6]

We make four observations:

(a) Neither interpreter *finds* his categories *in* the text, which does not know of an "alien" will or a "heterogeneous" law any more than of a "tension" between a "moral" and a "religious" demand. Consciously or unconsciously, these categories are *brought to* the text.

(b) The categories used by both interpreters are recognizably Kantian.

(c) Despite this fact, the two interpretations not only differ; if pressed, they are incompatible. For the first interpreter the new covenant *may* become (if it is not *already*) a *reality,* so that the old covenant may become (if it is not already) *de facto* superseded. (If further proof of this is needed, this first interpreter supplies it in full.)[6a] For the second interpreter, the new covenant is an *ideal* which as such can be approximated but *never* be real, so that the old covenant as a *reality* is not and *cannot be* superseded.

(d) The author of the first interpretation is a Christian, that of the second, a Jew.

These four observations, taken together, pose a question. Shall we argue that the two interpreters have arrived at their respective categories on purely objective-philosophical grounds, so that it is only by dint of a happy coincidence, as it were, that the conclusions reached by them conform to their respective religious commitments? Or shall we argue that happy coincidences such as these are past reasonable belief, that on the contrary the choice of categories of interpretation is somehow dependent on a prior religious commitment? To be sure, it would be wayward to accuse serious scholars of what might be called philosophically-disguised propaganda—the deliberate use (or abuse) of whatever philosophical categories fit a predetermined religious case. But it is not wayward to suggest that there is at work, in both these cases and possibly inevitably, a pre-reflective understanding of the text which, to put it cautiously, somehow enters into the choice of interpretative categories once reflection comes on the scene. If such is our answer to the question, it follows that the highest degree of self-critical acumen, and hence possible objectivity, is reached only once the pre-reflective understanding of the text—in the one case Christian, in the other, Jewish—is brought to full self-consciousness.

Such is in fact part and parcel of the most sophisticated contemporary hermeneutical theory.[7] This latter argues that the modern interpreter cannot stand either above or over against history but is as much immersed in *his* history as is the text itself in *its own*. It pursues this doctrine ruthlessly with the insistence that the highest objectivity attainable for the interpreter is the rise above his own "bias" in the recognition of it, and that he can reach none higher. This radicalism has one virtue that excels all others: it induces humility toward interpreters of different ages and other traditions. Above all, it induces humility toward the text itself.

5.

This sophisticated modern theory has a certain resemblance to much pre-modern, pre-critical, "old-fashioned" hermeneutical theory, both Christian and Jewish. Thus much Christian thought holds that a sacred text, to be understood, must be read in the spirit in which it was written, and that is the Holy Spirit at work in the history of the church (See e.g. Thomas À Kempis). On its part, much traditional Jewish teaching has it that "everything is in the Torah" (*Pirke Abot* V 25), that this is found when the Torah that is "written" is read in the light of the Torah that is "oral," and that this latter is alive in an unbroken tradition of learned and pious interpreters. However, whatever the persisting merits of this "old-fashioned" hermeneutics—and they are considerable—it is clear at once that it cannot lead to the Jewish-Christian dialogue which, as was hinted at the outset, is a contemporary imperative. To return to our texts, there is no need for examples or proofs to show that for the "old-fashioned" Christian hermeneutic the "new covenant" of Jer 31:31 ff. is a present, at least in principle accomplished fact in the Church of the Christ, that the spiritual children of Rachel have returned from their spiritual exile, and that their mother has long since heeded the divine bidding to refrain from weeping and tears. As for her physical children in their physical exile, they are at best an embarrassment and at worst an anachromism.[8]

Less obvious is the case of the "old-fashioned" Jewish hermeneutics if only because, unlike the Christian, it is required to take both texts on their

own terms and not from a purportedly higher point of view. Rashi
(1040-1105), the most popular of medieval Jewish commentators, simply
omits any comment on Jer 31:31 ff. *ad locum,* although he does comment
briefly—and innocuously—on the passage elsewhere.[9] Kimchi (1160?-
1235?), one of the most sophisticated, does offer a comment which,
however, includes the following sentence:

He [i.e., Jeremiah] does not say that they will all be equal in wisdom, for *this is not
possible.* . . . , but to "know Him" means to fear Him and follow in His ways.
(Italics added)

Kimchi's words are as telling as Rashi's silence. Both contain a hidden
apologetic, and this is anti-Christian. This element is present even when
(as e.g. in one Midrash) a new covenant superseding the old is openly
acknowledged—but firmly projected into the world-to-come.[10]
    On the "old-fashioned" basis, then—or at least on it alone—, it is
clearly impossible for Jews and Christians to read our texts together. The
revealed authorities which inspire their respective reading are incompatible and mutually exclusive. There can be no "dialogue."

6.

A "modern" hermeneutic is more promising for three main reasons.
First, it must accept the methods of modern scholarship and can quarrel
with specific results on no extraneous grounds and for no ulterior motives.
Second, it cannot base a religious commitment—if such there is—on a
revealed authority but must, on the contrary, view any acceptance of a
revelation and its authority as resting on a logically prior religious
commitment.[11] Third, it must bring to the fullest possible critical consciousness a "bias" on the interpreter's own part which is by no means
confined to his unconscious or pre-conscious bond with a religious
tradition (to say nothing of a free, fully-conscious religious commitment
listed separately as our second point), but rather encompasses the full
length and breadth of his historical situatedness as a whole. (With the
last-named factor we resume contact with the contemporary hermeneutics to which reference has already been made.) It is obvious that, each in
its own way, all three factors encourage what Franz Rosenzweig terms an
"unfanatical" dialogical openness.
    Of the first above factor nothing more need be said in the present
context. Concerning the second and the third, the most thought-
provoking question is which is the more fundamental in our time. At one

time, much theologizing would lay most of the emphasis on the second if it did not ignore the third altogether. The events of our time, however, have caused our historical situatedness to loom so large as to render suspect any faith-commitment which is divorced from it. Indeed, even prior to these events hard-headed critics (of which Marxists are only the most vocal, and far from the most profound) have always viewed all commitments made in an historical vacuum with a well-warranted skepticism.

We may illustrate the need for such skepticism by considering two recent interpretations of our texts by two respected scholars. In a work published in 1963 Samuel Sandmel understands Jer 31:31 ff. as pointing to a "transition from the old Hebrew religion to Judaism." The "old Hebrew religion"—the covenant shared by a flesh-and-blood people in a land and a state—did in fact end, and "was inexorably bound to end in doom" when "the Babylonians had invaded and captured and destroyed." For the "Judaism" to follow—a "new worship" based on "inner conviction" and for that reason possible "outside Palestine"—"exile" was "no longer . . . a climactic catastrophe" but merely a "significant incident."[12] Such is this Jewish author's view of the new covenant. Of Rachel and her children he has nothing to say.

A good deal is said on this latter subject by S. R. Hopper, the "expositor" of the Book of Jeremiah in the respected *Interpreter's Bible*. However, the exile of the children, hardly mentioned, becomes at once transformed into "the abyss of emptiness within." And throughout the entire ensuing discourse it seems legitimate to resort to Yeats, Hölderlin, Francis Thompson and Heidegger for significant symbols of exile and return from exile. Only one thing seems totally ruled out: a confrontation with *non*-symbolic, *actual* exile, and the promise of a physical return from it. Thus it comes as no surprise that, whereas Sandmel's account of Jer 31:31 ff. spiritualizes the flesh-and-blood people, Hopper's account does away with it. (Indeed, having recourse to Heidegger, he does not hesitate to suggest that the old covenant was not with God but only with a "god"—and that this god is "passing.") Jer 31:31 ff. is the "gospel before the Gospel," superseded once the Gospel itself comes on the scene.[13] In short, Sandmel spiritualizes the flesh-and-blood children of Rachel. Hopper spiritualizes them away.

That both these expositions are shot through with commitments to a faith is surely obvious, and would be admitted by both at least in a moment of encounter. However, their conflict in faith would seem less significant than the bias which they share: both fail to confront Rachel's children in their actual exile, and neither brings to consciousness the bias which produces this failure. At one time any Marxist critic might have disposed of the faith of both writers as part of the ideological superstructure of a bourgeois existence that dwells in safety. However, such a criticism, in any case shallow and less than fair, has shown itself in our time as shot through with exactly the same bias as the would-be objects of its criticism. For no Marxist thinker that this writer knows of has as yet shown signs—any more than these two works, both written many years after it happened—of having confronted what was done to the utterly non-symbolic, physical children of Rachel during the Nazi Holocaust.

7.

According to a reliable witness at the Nuremberg trials, this is what took place at Auschwitz in the summer of 1944:

Witness: . . . women carrying children were [always] sent with them to the crematorium. The children were then torn from their parents outside the crematorium and sent to the gas chambers separately. When the extermination of the Jews in the gas chambers was at its height, orders were issued that children were to be thrown straight into the crematorium furnaces, or into the pit near the crematorium, without being gassed first.

Smirnov (Soviet prosecutor): How am I to understand this? Did they throw them in the fire alive, or did they kill them first?

Witness: They threw them in alive. Their screams could be heard at the camp. It is difficult to say how many children were destroyed in this way.

Smirnov: Why did they do this?

Witness: It's very difficult to say. We don't know whether they wanted to economize on gas, or if it was because there was not enough room in the gas chambers.[14]

This is a report about Rachel's children. A Ravensbrück witness supplies the missing report about Rachel herself:

In 1942, the medical services of the Revier were required to perform abortions on all pregnant women. If a child happened to be born alive, it would be smothered or drowned in a bucket, in front of the mother. Given a new-born child's natural resistance to drowning, a baby's agony might last for twenty or thirty minutes. . . .[15]

It is not possible for Rachel today to refrain her voice from weeping, or her eyes from tears. It is not possible for God's prophet or God himself today to bid her do so or, if doing this bidding, to be obeyed. Jews today cannot obey such a bidding. Neither can Christians. For, as Irving Greenberg has written,

Judaism and Christianity do not merely tell of God's love for man, but stand or fall on their fundamental claim that the human being is . . . of ultimate and absolute value. ("He who saves one life is as if he saved the whole world"—Bab. Talmud, Sanhedrin 37a; "God so loved the world that He gave His only begotten son"—John 3:16.) It is the contradiction of this intrinsic value and the reality of human suffering that validates the absolute centrality and necessity of redemption, of the Messianic hope . . . The Holocaust poses the most radical counter-testimony to both Judaism and Christianity . . . The cruelty and the killing raise the question whether even those who believe after such an event dare talk about God who loves and cares without making a mockery of those who suffered.[16]

Christians today cannot pass over or beyond Rachel's tears. That Jews cannot do so has already found liturgical expression. It took a thousand years for the Midrash in which God weeps for His exiled children to find liturgical expression. One generation after Auschwitz and Ravensbrück there already exists a portion in a Yom Kippur liturgy which begins with Jer 31:14—Rachel weeping and refusing to be comforted—and climaxes with the question: "How can Your presence abide in a world where murder rules?"[17]

8.

Then how can either Jewish or Christian readers proceed from the "Rachel" passage to the "new covenant" passage, the one in hope, the other with a faith in an (at least in principle) accomplished fact? It is tempting to overlook, belittle, denigrate this text, but this is not possible. Indeed, a new necessity exists for Jews and Christians to read it together. However, an "ugly, broad ditch" has erupted between the weeping Rachel and the good news of the new heart, and we "cannot get across" it, "however often and however earnestly . . . [we may try] to take the leap."[18] Lessing (whose celebrated statement we quote) had in mind nothing more serious than a theological problem.[18a]("How can the acceptance of contingent historical truths be the source of my eternal salvation?") For this reason, he could hope for a theological solution which would "help him over" his ditch. *Our* ditch has erupted, however, not because of a theological "problem" but because of a human predicament without precedent. A theological "solution" of *this* predicament could consist only of some such assertion as that the burning and drowning children were a necessary part of the old covenant, or—"a reminder of the sufferings of the Christ"[18a]—reenacted and overcome in the new. But such assertions are not "solutions" of a "problem" but rather a "mockery of those who suffered." What may or may not have been once a "high point in theology" has become a human impossibility.

Our ugly, broad ditch, then, remains. And we, who are at one side of it and must attempt to, yet cannot, reach the other have reached the point at which, as Buber said a generation ago, we must continue to occupy ourselves with the text but can no longer do so in "obedience," or a "willingness to listen," but only with "annoyance" and even "outrage."

9.

It would be both thoughtless and un-Biblical to be annoyed-in-general or outraged-in-general. Instead, we are required to focus all attention on the unique scandal that, today, haunts us and gives us no peace. In this century (but prior to the kingdom of darkness) a great Christian thinker, Rudolf Otto, was able to write that even Job himself finds peace. This occurs when at length he surrenders to the numinous divine Presence, and so complete is the peace that when finally children are restored to him they are a mere "extra payment thrown in after quittance has already been rendered."[19] In the previous century Sören Kierkegaard, a still greater (and far more Biblical) Christian thinker had considered this "payment" neither "extra" nor indeed a "payment" but had rather perceived it as an essential gift of divine grace, so that, if Job is "blessed," this is solely because he has "received everything double."[20] Otto writes as he does because he considers the Christ as the "solution" of "that most mystical of all problems of the old covenant, the problem of the guiltless suffering of the righteous."

The thirty-eighth chapter of Job is the prophecy of Golgotha. But on Golgotha the solution of the problem, already adumbrated in Job, is repeated and surpassed.[21]

On his part, Kierkegaard writes as he does because he is not concerned with "problems" to be "solved" (as they are for Otto) in a process of religious "evolution" but rather with a human predicament which is not just Job's but his own as well. Hence he writes:

Did Job lose his case? Yes, eternally: for he can appeal to no higher court than that which judged him. Did Job gain his case? Yes, eternally . . . for the fact that he loses his case *before God*.[22]

But does Job receive *everything* double? A. S. Peake notices that "while his possessions are doubled, it is a fine trait that the number of children is the same as before"—a fine trait at least "for us" who believe that "no lost child can be replaced."[23] It seems that even Kierkegaard (who speaks of Job's restored gifts indiscriminately as "everything"), though more Biblical than Otto, is not Biblical enough.

But then, is the Bible itself, as it were, Biblical enough? Joseph and Benjamin are irreplaceable children of Rachel. Other irreplaceable children in the Bible include Isaac, Jacob, Rebeccah, Leah and Rachel herself. Isaac is Abraham's "son," his "only son," whom he "loves." (Gen. 22:2) But what is true of such as these is not true, so it seems, of the children of Job. What of children such as these? Writing in Budapest in 1943, Rabbi Yissachar Shlomo Teichthal, a leading Hasid of the Munkacher Rebbe, had the boldness to write the following words:

Now if we shall rise and ascend to Zion, we can yet reconstruct the souls of the people Israel who were murdered sanctifying the divine Name since, owing to their sacrifice, we were stimulated to return to our ancestral inheritance . . . Thus *we bring about their rebirth* . . . (Italics added)[24]

Like Job, Rabbi Teichthal did not seek an illegitimate refuge from his present anguish in the hereafter. But unlike Job he was exposed to so unprecedented an extremity that he could not (like Job according to Otto) carry out a mystical surrender; nor (like Job according to Kierkegaard) find himself blessed by receiving what Job had received. Presumably he did not or could not know of the children of Auschwitz and Ravensbrück. But what he did know was enough. And his knowledge forced him into the desperate faith that the return from exile of the children who had survived would restore to life the countless and nameless ones who had been brutally murdered. But whereas the return came to pass, this desperate faith—the hope for the End and the determination to help bring it about—did not.

Our "annoyance" with and "outrage" at the text—the stern refusal of Rachel to be comforted—is focused, then, on one single fact. This fact haunts, or ought to haunt, the religious consciousness of Jews and Christians alike. To Job sons and daughters are restored; but they are not the same sons and daughters. Children of Rachel have returned from exile; but they are not the same children.[25]

10. *Postscript*

Simha Holzberg is an orthodox Jew and a Hasid. He fought in the Warsaw Ghetto Uprising. He survived, made his way to Israel, and prospered. Holzberg, in short, was fortunate. But he was also haunted and without peace, rushing from school to school, kibbutz to kibbutz, synagogue to synagogue, always urging Jews to do more, to mourn more deeply, to remember more prfoundly. It was not enough. It could not have been enough. Then came the Six Day War, and with it its widows and orphans. Then he made the deepest commitment of his life. He became the adoptive father of orphans, vowing to care for them until they were married.

Holzberg has remained a man of anguish. The great Wound is not healed nor can it be healed. The unprecedented extremity is not "overcome" or reduced to a "problem" about to be "solved" or already solved. However, this Israeli Jew has ceased to be haunted and has even found a measure of peace. When last heard of by this writer, he was already the adoptive grandfather of more than a hundred grandchildren.

NOTES

[1]*Werke* (Heidelberg: Lambert Schneider, 1964), vol. 2, 849 ff.

[2]*On The Kabbalah and Its Symbolism* (New York: Schocken, 1965), 146.

[3]See ibib. 149: "In observing . . . [*Tikkun Rachel*], men 'participate in the suffering of the *Shekhinah*' and bewail not their own afflictions, but the one affliction that really counts in the world, namely, the exile of the *Shekhinah*."

[4]John Bright, *Jeremiah* (New York: Doubleday, 1965) 287. See also the amazingly similar comments in the *Cambridge Bible Commentary:* E. W. Nicholson gives only factual material about the Rachel passage but writes of Jer 31:31 ff. as follows: "This short passage is one of the most important in the Book of Jeremiah. Indeed it represents one of the deepest insights in the entire prophetic literature in the Old Testament" (Jeremiah 26-52 [Cambridge University Press] 70).

[5]Arthur Weiser, *Das Buch des Propheten Jeremiah* (Göttingen: Vandenhoeck & Ruprecht, 1952) 293 ff.

[6]Yehezkel Kaufmann, *The Religion of Israel* (Chicago: University of Chicago Press, 1960) 75.

[6a]Weiser's commentary on Jer 31:31 concludes as follows: "According to Luke 22:20 and 1 Cor 11:25 Jesus, in instituting holy communion, understands Jeremiah's promise of the new covenant as fulfilled in his own person . . ."

[7]We have in mind especially, though not exclusively, the work of H. G. Gadamer.

[8]See e.g. Calvin on Jer 31:31 ff.: "He says that the covenant which he will make will not be such as he had made with their fathers. Here he clearly distinguishes the new covenant from the Law. The contrast ought to be born in mind; for no one of the Jews thought it possible that God would add anything better to the Law. For though they regarded the Law almost as nothing, yet we know that hypocrites pretended with great ardour of zeal that they were so devoted to the Law that they thought that heaven and earth could sooner be blended together than any change should be made in the Law . . ." (*Commentaries on the Prophet Jeremiah and Lamentations* [Edinburgh, 1854] 128).

[9]On Lev. 26:9 Rashi writes: ". . . and will establish My covenant with you": a new covenant not like the first covenant which you broke, but a new covenant which will not be broken, as it is written in Jer 31:31 ff . . ."

[10]See e.g. *Tanh.B.*, Yitro 38b: "God said to Israel, 'On this day I have given you the Law, and individuals toil at it, but in the world to come I will teach it to all Israel, and they will not forget it."

[11]See my treatment of this issue elsewhere, e.g. *Quest For Past and Future* (Boston: Beacon, 1970), ch. 8.

[12]Samuel Sandmel, *The Hebrew Scriptures* (New York: Knopf, 1963) 147 ff.

[13]*The Interpreter's Bible* (New York-Nashville: Abingdon, 1956) vol. 5, 1031 ff.

[14]Quoted by Irving Greenberg, "Cloud of Smoke, Pillar of Fire: Judaism, Christianity, and Modernity after the Holocaust" in *Auschwitz: Beginning of a New Era*, E. Fleischner, ed. (New York: Ktav, 1977) 9 ff.

[15]G. Tillion, *Ravensbrück* (New York: Anchor, 1975) 77.

[16]Greenberg, ibid. 9-11.

[17]*Gate of Repentance* (London: Union of Liberal and Progressive Synagogues, 1973) 297 ff.

[18]*Lessing's Theological Writings,* H. Chalmers, ed. (London: Adam and Charles Black, 1956) 51-56.

[18a]Common charity prevents me from naming the Christian theologian who made this statement.

[19]Rudolf Otto, *The Idea of the Holy* (Oxford University Press, 1950) 77 ff.

[20]S. Kierkegaard, *Repetition* (Princeton University Press, 1946) 132.

[21]Otto, ibid., 172 ff.

[22]Kierkegaard, ibid. 133

[23]A. S. Peake, *Job* (Edinburgh: T. C. & E. Clark, 1904) 346. The "fine trait" perceived by Peake is not perceived by the *Anchor Bible* commentator and translator who—alone, it seems, and on dubious philological evidence—renders Job 42:13 "He had twice (?) seven sons and three daughters" and proceeds to comment: "In any case, the number of daughters remains the same. A larger number of girls would have been a burden rather than a boon . . . The pagan Arabs used to bury unwanted daughters at birth for fear that the family would be impoverished by feeding them or later disgraced by their conduct . . . ." (M. H. Pope, *Job* [New York: Doubleday, 1965] 289, 291) Why the behavior of some pagan Arabs should be the key to the understanding of a crucial Biblical passage Pope does not say. We should mention that Rash, *ad loc.* too—one may perhaps say disappointingly—asserts that the number of Job's sons is doubled. However, he at least spares us comparisons between Job and "pagan Arabs."

[24]Quoted by P. Schindler, *Responses of Hassidic Leaders and Hassidim during the Holocaust in Europe, 1939-45* (Ann Arbor: University Microfilms, 1972) 102 ff.

[25]Astoundingly, the nineteenth century "Malbim" *ad locum* (Meir Loeb Ben Yechiel Michael) attributes to the rabbis the view that Job is given back the *same* children. He relies on the seventeenth century commentator Shmuel Edels (the "MaHa RShA") who in turn bases himself upon Bab. Talmud Baba Bathra f.15ff. However, this Talmudic passage gives no stronger encouragement to this interpretation than the failure to include among its citations from the Book of Job the passage (1:19) in which the death of Job's children is reported.

WHEN HISTORY STOPS: APOCALYPTICISM AND MYSTICISM IN JUDAISM AND CHRISTIANITY

CHRIS HAUER, JR.

WESTMINSTER COLLEGE, FULTON, MISSOURI 65251

THE era of the late Roman Republic and the early Empire was a fertile period for the development of esoteric religious phenomena. Such mystical movements as Neoplatonism, Gnosticism and Hermeticism spring readily to mind. Further, many of the burgeoning mystery cults practiced vigils, disciplines, and ritual actions calculated to induce a sense of the holy. Some direct apperception of holiness, or a ritual simulation thereof, seems to have been the goal of mystery initiation.[1]

The eastern Mediterranean area, the heartland of Judaism and early Christianity, was the point of origin, or the point of transmission to the Roman world, for most of these movements. The cultural penetration of even the Jewish homeland by Hellenism is a truism of modern scholarship no longer requiring detailed documentation. Under these circumstances it is not surprising to discover esoteric religious phenomena flourishing among Jews and early Christians, whether Jewish or otherwise. Nor is it surprising that the Jewish and Christian expressions of esotericism shared things in common with their pagan counterparts. Clearly, a doctrine of special creation is not necessary.

However, distinctive cultural groups tend to express even ubiquitous phenomena in a distinctive way. So the diverse and widespread manifestation of religious esotericism in the world about does not alone supply an adequate account for the flourishing of Jewish and Christian esotericism in the forms expressed by the two then still closely related religious communities.[2]

Apocalypticism, a visionary and highly symbolic form of religious expression and perception, had flourished in Judaism since the second prechristian century, and in Christianity from its inception. Whatever its extrajudaic and non-prophetic components, apocalypticism and the literature embodying it seems to represent to some measure a linear development out of prophecy.[3] It is, notoriously, a literature of perceived adversity. Lou Silberman summarized its thrust in the abstract to his Schweitzer centennial lecture, "The movement from human stasis to human action following divine intervention—however it is described— implies not the end but the renewal of history . . . The intent of this paper is to demonstrate that apocalyptic hope rather than being a- or antihistorical is, at its heart, the hope for a return to history, suspended by the absence of one of the actors, not God but the community of man."[4]

The first century of the Christian era and the early decades of the second also supply the earliest evidence of Jewish mysticism in a form that appears to be continuous with later kabbalism. This does not necessarily mean that Jewish mysticism originated during the first century AD. It is simply that some of the earliest documentary evidence issues from this period.[5]

Kabbalism assumed two basic forms, determined by its principal object of contemplation, in both instances of biblical origin. The divine chariot of Ezekiel's visions (Ezek 1:1-28 *et passim*) provides the governing symbol for *merkabah* ("Chariot") mysticism. The *merkabah* circles also were fascinated by the *hekhaloth* ("palaces") to be perceived on each cosmic level as the adept made his passage upward through the seven heavens. Thus, *merkabah* and *hekhaloth* become practical synonymns for the same school of mystical speculation. The unmediated light of the first day of creation (Gen 1:1-5) supplies the governing symbol for the second form of kabbalism, *bereshith* ("creation") mysticism.[6] The early origin of these two forms is witnessed by the injunction of Mishnah Ḥagigah 2:1, that one is not to give an exposition of "the Story of Creation before two, nor the Chariot before one alone, unless he is a Sage that understands of his own knowledge."[7]

Related mystical currents seem to have been running in the early Christian community as well. Indeed, some of the earliest datable allusions to the kabbalistic motifs noted above are found in Christian sources. St. Paul's famous and perhaps autobiographical observations about the man who was caught up into the third heaven (2 Cor 12:2-4) echoes the *merkabah* interest in the passages through the levels of heaven.[8] The prologue of the gospel of John (1:1-18) associates the Logos with the light of the first day of creation, and light symbolism remains a continuing theme throughout the book. A connection with early *bereshith* mysticism seems to be a natural inference from the combination of light and the P account of creation.

Some sort of connection between apocalypticism and kabbalism has been widely supposed because of features that they share in common.

Gershom Scholem enumerated among these (1) descriptions of the structure and the inhabitants of the hidden world (heaven, garden of Eden, Gehennom, angels, etc.), and especially the Throne of Glory and its Occupant, (2) anonymnity and a pseudepigraphic approach, and (3) asceticism.[9]

Several possible connections come readily to mind. It has been noted that some Jewish and Christian mystical symbolism was taken from the Bible. The main stream of Pharisaic/Rabbinic Judaism and of Christianity accepted at least one apocalyptic book (Daniel) as scripture. Fringe and sectarian movements probably recognized more extensive canons, including additional apocalyptic works. The New Testament canon of catholic Christianity ultimately contained a Christian apocalypse and a number of smaller scattered apocalyptic units. So the Bible and other common traditions constitute a possible connection.

Further, apocalyptic material purports to be visionary in nature. It embodies dreams and visions, information confided by supernatural visitants, auditions, and transports through ethereal realms. All of these experiences fall into the esoteric region of apperception associated with mysticism. That is, the same sort of sensitivity is presupposed for either the role of apocalyptic seer, or that of mystical adept.[10]

This is not to say that apocalyptic seers or inspired apocalyptic interpreters of earlier writings were mystics in the formal sense, or that later mysticism grew out of the experiences of the apocalyptic seers.[11] On the former score, the evidence is ambiguous. The latter on existing evidence is no more than a plausible conjecture. On one occasion, Daniel told his three companions to "seek mercy of the God of heaven concerning this mystery," apparently through earnest prayer. In due course, Daniel received a night vision detailing the meaning of Nebuchadnezzar's secret dream (Dan 2:18-19). On another occasion, Daniel fasted to gain a vision (Dan 10:2). The dream vision of chapter seven and the vision of chapter eight in Daniel may be spontaneous. But Gabriel appeared to him in chapter nine only after a long and intense prayer (9:1-27). Here one discovers Daniel was also a student of scripture, at least of Jeremiah (9:2,24). More enigmatic are the words of the Christian seer in Revelation 1:10, "I was in the spirit on the Lord's day. . ." This is ordinarily taken to refer to a trance state, but whether the trance was induced by spiritual discipline or was spontaneous is not obvious. Fasting, prayer, and certain postures and bodily motions are witnessed as part of the discipline of later kabbalism.[12] The one thing that does seem clear is that chemical stimulation played little or no part in Jewish and early Christian esoteric experiences.[13]

Finally, some apocalyptic visions may be of literary rather than ecstatic origin.[14] One must note, however, that the mere fact that the contents and symbolism of a particular vision are heavily dependent upon a vision reported in earlier literature does not necessarily mean that the later report was only a prosaic and/or tendentious literary product. That the contents of visions and other esoteric states are strongly conditioned by cultural expectations is surely a well-founded generalization of anthropology and the history of religions.

Yet another connection may arise from the very nature of apocalyptic literature itself, seen against the historical conditions that called it forth, and the frustrated hopes that it may have subsequently engendered. John Gager applied Festinger's concept of "cognitive dissonance" to this disappointment in the early Christian community.[15] "Cognitive dissonance" denotes a strongly perceived disjunction between conditions as they are in the world, and conditions as they should be according to community belief and teaching. Unresolved, cognitive dissonance threatens both collective and individual psyches with intolerable tensions, threatens the very existence of the community. Gager, following Festinger's theory, applied the concept to early Christianity facing apocalyptic disappointment. But apocalyptic itself responds to cognitive dissonance at an earlier stage. It announces that God will intervene to break the oppressive power which immobilizes the community so that history, meaningful sequence in human events, may be restored. Israel will be freed from the Roman yoke, or in the Christian ambience, the Messiah who was taken away will return in great glory.

The apocalyptic promise could draw on a stock of historic credibility in the first century AD. The deliverance promised in Daniel and related literature had in fact taken place, though not precisely in the form anticipated by Daniel, and indeed in a form the Daniel circles probably did not approve. But as the first century wore on, the apocalyptic promise must have appeared more and more like the disease of which it purported to be the cure. The first Jewish war of national liberation against Rome ended in catastrophe. In Christian circles, the parousia was long delayed. Gager argued that the early Church overcame cognitive dissonance through vigorous evangelistic activity, a sort of concretizing of the bandwagon fallacy. But Judaism was in no position to deal with cognitive dissonance in such a fashion, given the problematic position it occupied in the aftermath of war. Yet there was a similarity of outcomes in both Judaism and Christianity regarding apocalyptic concerns. This would suggest some—if not total—common structure of resolution.[16]

The earliest evidence of organized mystical activity in Rabbinic circles dates from the aftermath of the events of AD 70, a time of intense cognitive dissonance for Judaism.[17] This date is less crucial for Christianity, and indeed the Pauline evidence precedes it. But already in Paul's time some communities were exhibiting symptoms of cognitive dissonance.[18] This order of things, first apocalypticism, then explicit mysticism, may reflect nothing more than the fortunes of literary transmission. But it is possible that the development of mysticism in Jewish and early Christian (still essentially Jewish) circles was a response to the failure of apocalyptic hopes. Inner, personal religious experience is the final redoubt of piety, and mysticism constitutes the more sophisticated extension of direct religious experience. Faith may endure extensive external disappointment so long as it receives continued confirmation from this quarter. A direct personal foretaste of deliverance in the form of mystical experience, including perhaps a reliving of some of the apocalyptic visions, could assuage a great deal of doubt and rekindle hope in the midst of adversity.[19] First century Jewish and Christian mysticism would, in these terms, constitute *an internalization of apocalyptic.*[20]

What conditions would have to be satisfied for this possibility to be more than mere speculation? Ideally there would be direct evidence, documented testimony from someone that their ventures into mysticism had enabled them to overcome, or at least to live with, apocalyptic disappointment. Wanting this ideal confirmation, one might state *the conditions that would be likely to obtain were such a situation the case,* and then ascertain *whether any identifiable communities or circles of the appropriate epoch actually exhibit these conditions.* Such a list of conditions would include some combination of at least the following:

1. Evidence of active mystical involvement by at least a leadership elite.

2. Persistence of apocalyptic hopes and imagery in the language of the group.

3. Some means for permitting a larger "lay" circle of non-mystics to share the insight of the adepts.

The import of these conditions may be clarified by noting the circumstances presupposed by other possible outcomes. For example, the turn to mysticism might result in the displacement of apocalyptic hopes by the inner mystical fulfillment. Something like this seems to have happened in gnostic Christianity.[21]

Alternatively, apocalyptic symbolism might be reinterpreted to the point that it lost its historical and political import and came to be understood as representing some other state of affairs (perhaps a "spiritual" one) in human experience. Various theories of "realized eschatology" advanced by New Testament interpreters may serve as examples.[22] Certain Rabbinic adaptations to the loss of the temple point in a similar direction. If prayer and good deeds are the true sacrifices, then the messianic restoration of the cultus is not such an urgent matter.[23]

Two identifiable circles in early Rabbinic Judaism and early Christianity satisfy the conditions noted above to such an extent as to justify further examination, the circle of Rabbi Akiva and the Johannine circle.

The involvement of the Akivan circle in mystical activity can be considered well established. The renowned account of the fate of Akiva and his colleagues when they "gazed into paradise" (B Ḥagigah 14b) is among the best-known data of early kabbalism. The same unit of tradition documents Akiva's superior esoteric wisdom.[24] Akiva seemed to be carrying on the kabbalistic tradition of the school of Rabbi Yohanan ben Zakkai.[25] He presumably passed it on through his pupil, that legendary mystic, Rabbi Simeon ben Yochai.

Akiva seemed to deviate, however, from the opposition to military messianism which characterized Rabbi Yoḥanan's immediate circle.[26] Akiva's great modern biographer, Louis Finkelstein, doubted that Akiva played an active role in the Second War with Rome, let alone that he was its intellectual instigator. But that Akiva recognized Simeon ben Kokhba as the Messiah and publicly endorsed his messianic claims Finkelstein took to be established beyond doubt.[27] The apocalyptic skepticism expressed by Rabbi Joḥanan ben Torta in the wry observation, "Akiva, grass will grow from your jaw and still the son of David will not have come," seems more typical of Rabbinic attitudes than Akiva's apocalyptic activism, limited though it may have been. One may note Akiva's active interest in the early reconstruction of the Temple (B Mak 24b) and the enigmatic saying attributed to him by M Aboth 3:17 as additional indicators of apocalyptic interest.

Was there some connection between Akiva's mysticism and his identification of Simeon ben Kokhba as the messiah? It was an esoteric vision which led Nathan of Gaza to identify Sabbatai Ṣevi as the messiah.[28] But historical analogy is risky enough even when it does not involve arguing backwards through a millennium and a half. One may note a precedent closer to hand in a Jewish or at least quasi-Jewish source. The transfiguration account in the synoptic gospels should almost certainly be understood as a messianic confirmation vision.[29] But there is no evidence in Akiva's case and so the matter is best left as an interesting speculation.

But if the combination of mysticism and apocalypticism in the Akivan circle be taken as pointing to the internalization of apocalyptic, how was this insight shared with a larger circle involving non-mystics? The devoted observance of Torah, and particularly the observance of the Sabbath may be understood as an anticipation of the messianic era, even the world to come. Thus the non-adepts could participate with the observant mystics in the foretaste of bliss afforded by Torah piety.[30]

The circle which produced the Gospel of John supplies in early Christianity an example of mystical interests coupled with allusions to apocalyptic motifs.[31] Though the geographic locus of the Johannine school is not essential to the argument of this paper, it is interesting to note that some recent scholarship would make the Johannine and Akivan circles chronological and even geographic neighbors, even if the final production of the Gospel took place outside the Jewish homeland, in Ephesus or elsewhere.[32]

The question concerning the Gospel of John has not been whether mysticism is involved, but what kind. Gnosticism, proto-Gnosticism, proto-Hermeticism and Neoplatonism (Philonism?) have all been advanced.[33] I have suggested above that the Gospel is related to early *bereshith* mysticism. The prologue should be read as a meditative kabbalistic midrash on Genesis 1:1-4, especially verses 3-4. The highly influential logos terminology of the prologue does not carry over into the body of the Gospel. However, the logos theme establishes that life, glory and light are borne into the created order by the very wisdom and creative-recreative purpose of God. And the closely related themes of life, glory and light *are* carried over into the rest of the Gospel. The light which shines in the darkness and cannot be overcome is, of course, that unmediated light of the first day of creation, the object of the evangelist's meditation and the central symbol of *bereshith* kabbalism. The mystical themes of the participation of the Son in the Father and of the faithful in the Son are elaborated throughout the Gospel. John's sacramentalism is also taken, and properly so, as an aspect of his mysticism.[34] We shall return to this theme momentarily.

The Fourth Gospel also advances notions associated with apocalypticism, including the parousia (or, in Rabbinic terms, the messianic era), resurrection and judgement.[35] The occurrences in chapter 6 are particularly interesting since they intertwine the apocalyptic motif with sacramentalism. The symbolism of the Christian sacraments of baptism (death and resurrection) and eucharist (messianic banquet) points explicitly toward the eschaton. And in its sacramentalism, the Johannine circle satisfies the third condition established above, namely a practice which would permit non-mystics to share and participate in the insight of the adepts. Gager even suggested that the Revelation of John may have been utilized as a dramatic and liturgical instrument for "the attainment of millennial bliss through myth."[36] Gager's view has not been universally applauded,[37] but it is if nothing else provocative enough to justify further consideration. Cornfeld's reading of archaeological findings relating to Christian holy sites, some of which he holds to be dated earlier than 70 AD, reinforces the notion that ritual-sacramental activities played a larger part in Jewish Christianity than is sometimes supposed. He notes a reference in Eusebius to mysteries celebrated at "sacred and mystic grottoes" (Bethlehem, particularly). He also points to evidence of ritual activity at other early Christian holy sites.[38] It goes beyond the purview of the present study, but these data may suggest that the combination of mysticism and apocalypticism, or perhaps more precisely, the relatively muted apocalypticism reflected in the synoptic Gospels, goes back to an early period in the history of Christian tradition, perhaps to Jesus himself.[39] Such a state of affairs would lend credence to Marvin Harris' anthropological reconstruction of the secret of the peaceful messiah.[40] At any rate, these considerations do nothing to weaken the picture of the Johannine circle as one in which mysticism, apocalypticism and sacramental practice stood in a symbiotic relationship. They rather suggest a highly favorable environment.

The intertwining of mystical and eschatological concerns in the Akivan and Johannine circles renders at least plausible a process of internalizing apocalyptic such as here proposed. At a time when history was arrested and the hope offered by traditional apocalypticism was becoming jaded, the respective communities would be sustained by anticipatory participation in the future deliverance through mystical, halakic and/or liturgical means. But was the posture of these communities, as Lou Silberman suggests, one of resignation to timeless suspension until God acted?[41]

This is a question which is raised both by anthropological and by historical data. The anthropological data arise from studies of the "cargo cults" of the south Pacific.[42] These cults, derived at least in part from Christian apocalypticism among people who perceive themselves as oppressed and deprived, and informed by visionary prophets, suggest by their behavior that even those in a state of relative helplessness will do what they can to help restart history, even if it is only to build bamboo control towers and radar antennae to guide ghostly aircraft to their destination.

The historical datum arises from the Lurianic kabbalah of the 16th and 17th centuries, which supposed that sufficiently powerful mystical exercises might perform the great *tikkun,* the great act of spiritual healing, and hasten the dawn of the messianic age.[43]

Is there anything in first century teaching to indicate that such a key was thought to be available? The earliest datable inkling again comes from St. Paul with his argument in Romans 11, that the failure of the majority in Israel to recognize Jesus as the Messiah is in fact providential since it permits time for more Gentiles to enter the kingdom. The implication is that if a majority of Israel recognized the messiah, the parousia would come much sooner. That is, cosmic history responds to human action. Similarly, both Tannaitic and Amoraic authorities asserted that either a genuine repentance by Israel, or the perfect keeping of one or two sabbaths would bring in the messianic kingdom.[44] These dicta are not, on the face of the matter, mystical, though they are in a sense mildly apocalyptic. But the historic connection between Torah piety and mysticism in Judaism should cause one to walk softly. As in the case of messianic confirmation visions, the judicious verdict is to reserve judgement. Neither the Johannine materials nor the traditions of the Akivan circle contain obvious evidence.

What, then, may one finally conclude? One may make the Maimonidean argument[45] that the hypothesis of this paper, that the mysticism of the Akivan and Johannine circles represents an internalization of apocalyptic thought, has been warranted as a plausible if not finally proven hypothesis. Two further provocative possibilities have been advanced, namely the questions of messianic confirmation visions and of a possible "mystic key" to advance the dawn of the messianic era. A programmatic proposal to interpreters of Rabbinic and early Christian materials, to test the hypothesis of apocalyptic internalization against both more intensive and extensive bodies of data, and to pursue the two provocative questions further, is certainly in order. Especially should students of early Christianity be alert to the possibility that early Christian mysticism is at least as likely to be continuous with kabbalism as with Hellenistic mystical models, though in due course it became thoroughly Hellenized.

NOTES

[1]Cf. H. R. Willoughby, *Pagan Regeneration, A Study of Mystery Initiations in the Graeco-Roman World* (Chicago: The University of Chicago Press, 1929).

[2]J. Danielou (*The Theology of Jewish Christianity* [Philadelphia: Westminster Press, 1964]) noted that "Christianity remained until the middle of the second century a Judaic religion" (9). His basically theological analysis revealed a vital if secondary Jewish influence on Christianity into the fourth century (10). The world view of Jewish Christianity he took to be largely apocalyptic (4, 204; cf 173-204 for his discussion of apocalyptic).

[3]P. D. Hanson, *The Dawn of Apocalyptic* (Philadelphia: Fortress Press, 1975) 7-9, 29-31. Cf. also D. S. Russell, *The Method and Message of Jewish Apocalyptic* (OTL; London: SCM Press, 1964) 88-100. M. E. Stone, by way of contrast, argues that it may be deceptive to see an exclusively prophetic origin for apocalyptic. He takes the Qumran manuscripts of the Enoch literature to point toward a 3rd century BC origin for "sacred science and speculative ascent experiences" in Israel. The circles pursuing this type of inquiry are not, on his view, represented in the canonical literature ("The Book of Enoch and Judaism," *CBQ* 40 [1978] 488-491).

[4]L. H. Silberman, "Apocalyptic Revisited: Reflections on the Thought of Albert Schweitzer," *JAAR* 44 (1976) 489. The remainder of the article, of course, develops the thesis (490-501). Cf also L. H. Silberman, "The Human Deed in a Time of Despair: The Ethics of Apocalyptic," *Essays in Old Testament Ethics,* ed. J. L. Crenshaw and J. T. Willis (New York: KTAV, 1974) 196, 198-200. On the theme of apocalyptic and history, see further: Russell, *Method and Message* 217-234; H. H. Rowley, *The Relevance of Apocalyptic* (rev ed; New York: Harper, nd) 150-178; W. Schmithals, *The Apocalyptic Movement* (Nashville: Abingdon, 1975) 33, 40. G. I. Davies has argued that apocalyptic is in fact a way of reading and understanding history ("Apocalyptic and Historiography," *JSOT* 5 [1978] 15-28). J. J. Collins noted that while historical reviews are not a constant feature of Jewish apocalyptic, those which occur show a clear apocalyptic interest in history ("Psuedonymnity, Historical Reviews and the Genre of the Revelation of John," *CBQ* 39 [1977] 333).

It is doubly appropriate to cite Lou Silberman's essays in this context. They constituted the catalyst which turned a four year old note to myself ("Kabbalism as internalization of apocalyptic," it said) into an active research project.

[5]Cf. Stone, "Enoch," 491, for a 3rd century BC origin of esoteric speculations and experiences (n 3, above).

[6]G. G. Scholem, *Major Trends in Jewish Mysticism* (New York: Schocken, 1961) 20, 40-79 (esp 41-43); *Kabbalah* (New York: Quadrangle, 1974) 1-14; I. Epstein, *Judaism* (London: Penguin, 1959) 223-226. I recognize a possible anachronism in the use of the term "kabbalism" in reference to this early period. However, it *is* the standard term for Jewish mysticism. The mystical phenomena

with which we are concerned here are continuous with later Jewish mysticism. I wish to emphasize this continuity.

[7]The gemara on this passage contains some of the most interesting information on mystical lore in the rabbinic literature, as will be noted at specific points below. Cf. B. Ḥag 11b-16a.

[8]G. G. Scholem, *Jewish Gnosticism, Merkabah Mysticism and Talmudic Tradition* (New York: The Jewish Theological Seminary of America, 1965) 17-19.

[9]Scholem, *Major Trends* 43, 72; *Kabbalah* 10-17; "Kabbalah," *Encyclopedia Judaica* 10 (Jerusalem; Keter Publishing House, Ltd, 1972) 498. Scholem asserted elsewhere that the (later) *merkabah* writings always contained apocalyptic chapters (*The Messianic Idea in Judaism* [New York: Schocken, 1971] 7. Perhaps the earliest recorded "Throne Vision" outside the canon is that found in 1 Enoch 14; 1-25; cf. R. H. Charles, *Apocrypha and Pseudepigrapha of the Old Testament in English* 2 (Oxford: Oxford University Press, 1913) 196-198. See Stone, "Enoch," 491. The theme of seven heavens is also found in 4 Esdras 7:81-87 ("seven ways;" Charles 2, 588), T Levi 2:6-3:8 (Charles 2, 304-306), and 2 Enoch 3-22 (where there turn out to be ten heavens; Charles 2, 432-443). There is a somewhat garbled account of five heavens in 3 Baruch 2:1-11:9 (Charles 2, 534-540). Cf. also B Ḥag 12b, 14b. The Ascension of Isaiah gives an account of seven heavens, perhaps in Christian guise; cf. Rowley, *Relevance* 110-111; Russell, *Method and Message* 66, 158-173. Stone adds the "Angelic Liturgy" from Qumran to the literature that should be considered in this connection ("Enoch," 488). Cf. also J. J. Collins, "Jewish Apocalyptic Against Its Hellenistic Near Eastern Environment," *BASOR* 220 (1975) 27-36, especially 31, on the role of apocalypticists as *maskilim*.

[10]Russell, *Method and Message* 28, 107-118, 158-177.

[11]I would reserve the terms "mysticism" for disciplined exercises aimed at gaining profound religious experience (direct apperception of holiness), and "mystic" for the practitioners of the art. The adjective "mystical" may, I take it, be used in a broader sense to cover random or spontaneous experiences as well. Mysticism, like religious experience generally, encompasses a continuum of forms ranging from intellectual enlightenment to devotional ecstacy.

[12]Scholem summarized the account of Hai ben Sherira, head of a Babylonian academy c. 100 AD. The adept fasted, put his head between his knees, and whispered hymns and songs (*Major Trends* 49). The much earlier Talmudic account noted that Rabbi Joḥanan ben Zakkai wrapped himself in his *tallith* before the beginning of a *merkabah* exposition (B Ḥag 14b).

[13]This can be asserted with considerable confidence despite J. M. Allegro's efforts to show otherwise (*The Sacred Mushroom and the Cross* [Garden City, NY: Doubleday, 1970]). The nearest thing to a documented use of chemical stimulants in the major sources of lore is 4 Esdras 14:39, when Ezra drank a cup of water the color of fire and was inspired to dictate 94 books to his five scribes. Of these, 24 are presumably the Jewish Scriptures and the other 70 the apocalyptic corpus (Russell, *Method and Message* 87). See 4 Esdras 14:1-48 for the complete

account (Charles 2, 620-624). The scroll eaten by Ezekiel was surely a symbol for the prophetic internalization of the divine word (Ezek 2:8-3:3). Ezekiel's account almost certainly inspired the similar experience of the seer, John (Rev 10:8-11).

The one possible exception can be put down to serendipity. S. H. Steckoll, Z. Goffer, H. Nathan and M. Haas report that the extensive staining of bones found in the Qumran cemetery was due to long-term ingestion of a brew steeped from madder root which contained alizarin ("Red Stained Human Bones from Qumran," *Israel Journal of Medical Science* 7 [1971] 1219-1223). P. Bar Adon reported that bones found in the cemetery of the Qumran sect installation at 'En el-Ghuweir were similarly stained ("Another Settlement of the Judean Desert Sect at 'En el-Ghuweir on the Shores of the Dead Sea," *BASOR* 227 [1977] 16-17. Steckoll, *et al*, attributed the use of the brew to a belief in the magic properties of madder root. However, alizarin, a quinone, probably has antimalarial properties, which may account for belief in its efficacy in a malarial region. Quinones are also believed to cause hallucinations in some individuals. Thus the use of this medicine or charm in the highly apocalyptic Qumran sect may have had the unintentional side effect of producing visionary experiences among its members. (Though the interpretation here is the responsibility of the author, I wish to express appreciation to my colleague, J. W. Page [anthropology], for clarification on several points in this note.)

[14]G. W. Buchanan, in a printed paper presented before the seminar on comparative midrash at the 1978 annual meeting of the Society of Biblical Literature, held that apocalyptic visions were in fact of a literary nature. The apocalypticists, he argued, had the OT text before them. The things they "heard" or "saw" were really *midrashim* on the text. Apocalyptic inspiration would thus be a sort of interpretative imagination ("The Word of God and the Apocalyptic Vision," *Seminar Papers, SBL* 14 [Missoula, MT: Scholars Press, 1978] 183-192).

[15]J. G. Gager, *Kingdom and Community, The Social World of Early Christianity* (Englewood Cliffs, NJ: Prentice-Hall, Inc., 1975) 39-49.

[16]C. K. Barrett has argued for a sort of ambivalent parallelism between Judaism and Christianity in their post-70 AD development. Alternatives to the failure of apocalyptic hopes were among the topics he explored (*The Gospel of John and Judaism* [Philadelphia: Fortress Press, 1975] 66-69). Elliott Aronson has offered an extended explanation and numerous illustrations of applications of the theory of cognitive dissonance (*The Social Animal* [San Francisco: W. H. Freeman and Company, 1972] 89-139). He remarked, "The theory of cognitive dissonance does not picture man as a rational animal, rather it pictures man as a rationalizing animal" (94). He noted that a great deal of dissonance reducing behavior is "irrational" and "maladaptive," preventing the learning of important facts or the finding of real solutions to problems (98). Gager's account seems to propose an irrational resolution, the bandwagon fallacy. But Aronson also observed that rational (adaptive?) behavior was possible (99, 138-139). The resolution adopted by Rabbinic Judaism and New Testament Christianity should, on a track record of 1,900 years' survival, be regarded as in large measure "adaptive."

[17]Cf. B Ḥag, which mentions Rabbi Joḥanan ben Zakkai in connection with a "chariot" exposition.

[18]1 Thess 4:13-18; 2 Thess 2:1-12. Cf. also 2 Tim 2:17-18.

[19]William James long ago observed, "Mystical states, when well developed, usually are, and have the right to be, absolutely authoritative over the individuals to whom they come . . . They break down the authority of the non-mystical or rationalistic consciousness, based on the understanding and the senses alone." (*The Varieties of Religious Experience* [New York: Collier Books 1961] 331). He was, in this study, describing a powerful antidote for cognitive dissonance.

[20]Silberman may have anticipated this proposal when he wrote of the apocalyptist, ". . . *within the more limited sphere of individual response*" (emphasis added) holding his ground and performing the deed that transforms the meaningless into the meaningful in the midst of external meaninglessness ("Ethics of Apocalyptic," 200). It is basically enlarging on this notion to suggest that the internalization of apocalyptic through mysticism opens to a larger circle what the apocalyptic seer achieved at the level of individual response. The prolongation of the "suspension of history" ("Apocalyptic Revisited," 489) produced the dissonance which made this, or some other, remedy essential.

A. Schweitzer had earlier approached the articulation of this idea with his conception of Paul's "Christ mysticism" (*The Mysticism of Paul the Apostle* [New York: Seabury Press, 1968]). He wrote, "This whole mystical doctrine of the world as in process of transformation is nothing other than the eschatological concept of redemption looked at from within" (112). Paul's mystical and sacramental doctrines were, he said, built up completely out of eschatological ideas, with no Hellenistic components (334). However, the disjunction between "Christ mysticism" and "God mysticism" (3-13), the lack of any notion of general continuity between apocalypticism and mysticism, and the neglect of Jewish mysticism, in Schweitzer's work, inhibit its direct application to the issue at hand. Of course, Scholem's monumental contribution lay more than a decade in the future when Schweitzer issued his work on Paul in 1931.

[21]James M. Robinson, *et al, The Nag Hammadi Library* (San Francisco: Harper and Row, 1977) 1-6, 9-10; R. M. Grant, *Gnosticism and Early Christianity* (New York: Columbia University Press, 1966) 27-38.

[22]C. H. Dodd gave the classic and perhaps also the definitive statement of this view (*The Parables of the Kingdom* [New York: Charles Scribner's Sons, 1961] 159-165).

[23]ARN 4; Midr Pass on 5:4; P Ber 4b; George Foot Moore, *Judaism In the First Centuries of the Christian Era, the Age of the Tannaim* 2 (Cambridge: Harvard University Press, 1958) 217-219.

[24]Scholem, *Jewish Gnosticism*, 14-19; L. Jacobs, *Jewish Mystical Testimonies* (New York: Schocken Books, 1977) 21-25; J. Bowman *The Fourth Gospel and the Jews* (PTM 8; Pittsburgh, PA: Pickwick Press, 1975) 21.

[25]B. Ḥag 14b contains a story of Rabbi Joḥanan ben Zakkai and Rabbi Eliezer ben Arak sharing *merkabah* exposition.

[26]See the account of Rabbi Joḥanan ben Zakkai's escape during the siege of Jerusalem and his accomodation with Vespasian (ARN 4). Cf. Moore 2, 114-116. But note also Aboth 2:3, where Rabban Gamliel expresses well-advised skepticism about the virtue of getting involved with the (Roman) government.

[27]L. Finkelstein, *Akiba, Scholar, Saint and Martyr* (New York: Atheneum, 1975) 269. Finkelstein cited B Sanh 97b, Lam Rab 2:2, and P Ta'an 4.7, 68d as the pivotal references. Rabbi Johanan ben Torta's rejoinder is transmitted in the last of these. Cf. also L. Ginzberg, "Akiba ben Joseph," *The Jewish Encyclopedia* 1 (New York: Funk and Wagnalls, 1906) 305; Moore 1, 89; Moore 2, 116, 345. Harry Freedman, *et al,* made Akiva enthusiastic about the revolt, but merely says that he apparently recognized Bar Kochba ("Akiva," EJ 2, 490).

[28]G. G. Scholem, *Sabbatai Ṣevi, the Mystical Messiah* (Bollingen 93; Princeton: Princeton University Press, 1973) 204-205.

[29]Mark 9:2-8; Matt 17:1-8; Luke 9:28-36.

[30]A. J. Heschel, *The Sabbath, Its Meaning for Modern Man* (New York: Farrar, Strauss and Young, 1951) 8, 19, 52, 73-76, 79-83. Is it significant in this connection that the martyrdom of Akiva was attributed to his defiance of the postwar edict against teaching Torah, not his support of the war itself (Finkelstein, *Akiba* 272-277; Ginzberg, "Akiba," JE 1, 305; B Ber 61b)?

[31]R. E. Brown, *The Gospel According to John* I-XII (AB 29; Garden City, NY: Doubleday, 1966) cxv-cxxi; C. K. Barrett, *The Gospel According to John* (London: SPCK, 1960) 26, 57-58, 71-74; Barrett, *John and Judaism*, 73-74; Schweitzer, *Paul*, 352-372.

[32]Barrett, *John and Judaism,* 38-39; Barrett, *Gospel According to John,* 105-114; Brown, *Gospel of John,* lxxx-civ.

[33]R. Bultmann is, of recent exegetes, most frequently associated with the notion that important aspects of Johannine thought go back to some sort of gnostic or proto-gnostic roots (*The Gospel of John* [Philadelphia: Westminster Press, 1971] 23-31). C. H. Dodd seemed to split the difference between an early Hermeticism and a Philonic Platonism (*The Interpretation of the Fourth Gospel* [Cambridge: Cambridge University Press, 1960] 10-73, 263-285). W. D. Davies seemed to favor a sort of proto-Hermeticism (*Invitation to the New Testament* [Garden City, NY: Anchor Books, 1969] 398-408).

[34]Schweitzer in fact spoke directly of "sacramental mysticism" in John (*Paul,* 359-364).

[35]A list of passages setting forth traditional eschatological notions in the Fourth Gospel would include 5:27-29, 6:38-40, 44, 54, 12:48, 14:3 and 21:22, among others. Barrett notes that "In John alone is the transliterated form of the Hebrew or Aramaic *mashiaḥ, meshiḥa,* used" (*Gospel According to John* 59; cf. also 56-58). Cf. Brown, *Gospel of John* cxv-cxxi. Bultmann was inclined to assign such passages to an editorial hand (*Gospel of John* 219, 261-262, 345).

[36]Gager, 49-57. This observation does not necessarily imply a connection between the circle of the Apocalypse and that of the Gospel.

[37]Cf. E. Fiorenza, "Composition and Structure of the Book of Revelation," *CBQ* 39 (1977) 354-355.

[38]G. Cornfeld, *Archaeology of the Bible: Book by Book* (New York: Harper and Row, 1976) 269, 271, 279-281, 291, 306-308.

[39]Schweitzer asserted that Jesus' own preaching contained "Christ mysticism" as a "mystery" (*Paul* 105), or in a form appropriate to the time the Messiah was walking on earth in human form (*Paul* 109). Brown observed, "Within Jesus' own message there was a tension between realized and final eschatology" (*Gospel of John* cxix). One could suspect that the request of Jesus' disciples, "Lord, teach us to pray, as John taught his disciples" (Luke 11:1), was a request for instruction in mystical prayer. The apocalypticism of the Baptist circle, at least as portrayed in the Gospels, is hardly in doubt (Mark 1:1-8, Matt 3:1-12, Luke 3:1-18; cf. Matt 11:2-6, Luke 7:18-23). Fasting was also practiced in the Baptist circle (Mark 2:18, Luke 5:33). Jesus and his circle were not noted for fasting (Matt 11:19, Luke 5:33; but cf. Matt 6:16-18). The synoptic references to Jesus' own practice of prayer may suggest a mystic discipline. He prayed intensely, sometimes alone (Mark 1:35, 6:46, Matt 14:23). He prayed all night before selecting the Twelve (Luke 6:12-13). Luke also reports that when Jesus took his disciples to the mount of transfiguration, it was to pray (9:28-29; cf. Matt 17:1-2, Mk 9:2-3). The Synoptic Apocalypse is a notably modest example of the genre (Mark 13:5-7, Matt 24:4-36, Luke 21:8-36). A particular reticence is expressed in Mark 13:32-14:36. If this apocalyptic restraint reflects the attitude of Jesus, it would support the notion advanced here.

[40]*Cows, Pigs, Wars and Witches* (New York: Vintage Books, 1975) 179-203. One may grant that Harris is not an authority in Biblical history, and recognize that his reconstruction is not radically different from that of some Biblical exegetes (see his extensive acknowledgements, pp 274-275). Still, by coming at the matter with a fresh perspective he states the case in a particularly trenchant manner. The same may be said of his treatment of non-Christian Jewish messianism (155-175). I would diverge from his reconstruction largely in urging that Jesus and his circle, like that of Rabbi Johanan ben Zakkai, were most probably advocating a "peaceful," though not non-apocalyptic, messianism prior to 70 AD. See n 39 above.

[41]"Apocalyptic Revisited," 500; "Ethics of Apocalyptic," 199.

[42]P. M. Worsley, "Cargo Cults," *Scientific American* 200 (1959) 171-173. Cf. Harris, 133-152.

[43]Scholem, *Sabbatai Ṣevi* 27-66; "Redemption Through Sin," *The Messianic Idea* 78-141 (cf. "The Holiness of Sin," *Commentary* 51 [1971] 41-70).

[44]B. Yoma 86b, B Sabb 118b, J Taʾan 64a.

[45]I allude to the methodological side of the RAMBAM's discussion of the preferability of his doctrine of creation over Aristotle's doctrine of an eternal universe (*Guide for the Perplexed* 2 [Chicago: University of Chicago Press, 1963] 284-359).

CAUSATION AND CHOICE IN THE PHILOSOPHY OF IBN DAUD

NORBERT SAMUELSON

TEMPLE UNIVERSITY, PHILADELPHIA, PENNSYLVANIA 19122

Introduction

THE subject matter of this paper is Abraham ibn Daud's account of the nature of and relationship between causes and choice in human events. Most scholars would claim that the subject matter is free will and determinism. However, the two issues are not the same (see Samuelson:2-3) and ibn Daud only discusses the former. For ibn Daud the subject matter is the following: "Are the actions of man necessary or does he have choice over them?" (1b14) The central discussion of this topic is given in Part 2, Principle 6, chapter 2 of *The Exalted Faith* (henceforth to be referred to as "EF"). However, this discussion cannot be looked at entirely independent of the entire body of EF since this topic is the central issue of the book. Every other topic discussed serves ibn Daud only as premises and background for this discussion. In his own words, "We presented this book for the sake of and because of the subject matter of this chapter." (201a14-15)

As ibn Daud introduces this chapter he tells us that his general discussion of the role of causation and choice in human actions presupposes the following discussions: A proof that God gives to this universe the best possible moral ordering; an account of the sources and causes of good and evil; an explanation of how it is possible for there to be unrealized potentialities; an account of how divine providence operates. (210a12-15) In fact the issue of unrealized potentiality is an account of the nature of contingency in contrast to what is either necessary or impossible.

A more accurate listing of the general topics subsumed under the subject matter of the chapter would be the following: The ordering of things in the universe (201b1-205a9); the nature of human choice (205a9-208a14); the nature of divine providence (208a15-208b11). His ordering of things is based directly on his introduction to Part 2 of EF, which in fact is a

223

summary of the relevant positions stated and definitions noted in Part 1, which consists of three chapters in which the basic terms of his sciences are defined (essence and accident in chapter 1, matter and form in chapter 2, and motion in chapter 3), the nature of motion is explained (viz., that a material entity is not infinite and has no infinite power in chapter 4, and that all motion is both from and to a mover in chapter 5), and his principles of Psychology (the nature and powers of the soul in chapter 6, and that the rational power is not material in chapter 7). The most important thesis of this first section of EF is stated in the eighth chapter, viz., that the heavens are rational entities that move by rational will. In other words, the principles of Psychology also are the principles through which God governs the universe as a whole. The nature and actions of God are the subject matter of the first four principles of Part 2 of EF. The first principle is that God is a necessary being. The second principle is that God is one. The third principle and the first chapter of the sixth principle deal with divine attributes. The former argues that divine attributes are either negative or relations. The latter argues that divine attributes are to be understood as equivocal terms. The fourth principle is an account of divine actions which in fact is a demonstration of the existence of angels (chapters 1 and 2) and a detailed account of the hierarchy of entities in the universe that was presented first in the introduction to this second part of the book. Only the fifth principle has no direct bearing on the subject matter of Principle 6, chapter 2. The stated subject matter of the fifth principle is the nature of prophecy, but in fact this topic is the subject matter only of the first chapter which constitutes one step in a general discussion of the origins and transmission of an authentic religious tradition in order to demonstrate that the Torah is as valid a source for truth as is true science or correct use of human reason. This discussion serves as a basis for the discussion in Part 3 that deals with the relation between ethics and religious duties.

Our focus in this paper will be solely on what ibn Daud argues about human events in Part 2, Principle 6, chapter 2 of EF. While our discussion presupposes familiarity with the whole of the book, in the interest of confining the length of this paper references to other sections of EF will be given sparingly. (However, even though it is not the subject matter of this paper, it should be noted that not everything that ibn Daud says in this chapter is consistent or coherent with what he argued earlier.) Furthermore, the only other philosophic work to which ibn Daud refers as a source for this discussion is Saadia's *Book of Beliefs and Opinions*. (Although ibn Daud cites no specific references, clearly the pertinent section of Saadia's work is Treatise 4, chapters 3 through 6.) While ibn Daud gives the impression that there are no differences between what he and Saadia say (208b10-11), a careful study of both works will show that this is not the case. However, again in the interest of confining the length of this paper, this issue will not be discussed here.

The Ordering of the Universe

Ibn Daud's discussion presupposes the neo-Platonic theory of divine overflow that he stated in Part 2, introduction and Principle 4, chapter 3. On this view all kinds of entities can be catalogued into a hierarchy in which the kinds of things that are above other kinds of things are judged to be in some sense morally superior. In this hierarchy God occupies the highest place, and matter, which is identical with potency (201b1-2) and is designated by the term, *"hyle"* (202a2), occupies the lowest place. The more inferior a thing is, i.e., the lower its place in the hierarchy, the less knowable it is to God. In ibn Daub's words "He conceives of (everything whose existence is remote from Him in order) WITH DEFICIENCY (italics are mine) that is proportional to the remoteness (of the thing known)" (201b10-11). Ibn Daud does argue that this lack of knowledge does not constitute an imperfection in God, because the deficiency is inherent in the object of knowledge and not in God as the knowing subject. In other words, God knows these things as well as they can be known and in this sense His knowledge of them is perfect. Ibn Daud does not discuss directly whether *hyle* is in any sense knowable to God. He does say that *hyle* is inconceivable. (201b16) But that does not mean that God cannot know *hyle*, since God also is said to be inconceivable (201b6) and there would be no doubt that God knows Himself. Furthermore, even though God is inconceivable, human beings can achieve some knowledge of God (2:3 and 2:6:1). Hence, this statement does not rule out in principle that there can be some form of human knowledge of *hyle*. Let me suggest that as ibn Daud conceived of the matter, while neither God nor *hyle* can be directly apprehended, as those things that are intermediate between these two extremes can be apprehended, God and *hyle* both can be known as ultimate principles through which all that is intermediate can be understood. Everything in the universe is ordered hierarchically on the basis of what moves it and what it moves, so that if a moves b which moves c and this order of causation is not reversible, then we may say that a is superior to b which is superior to c. In principle this hierarchy presupposes something that moves but itself is not moved, viz., God, and something that is moved but itself does not move anything, viz., *hyle*. To this extent, viz., as causal principles through which the universe is comprehended, human beings can be said to know God and *hyle*.

Presupposing the above general picture of the universe, ibn Daud states two arguments in support of the claim that God is not the source of evil. The first argument (202a6-11) reads that if both good and evil come from God, then God must be composite; God cannot be composite and He is the source of all good; therefore, God cannot be the source of evil. The principles that link the antecedent and consequent parts of the major premise of the argument are that no single thing can be the cause of contrary effects, and that what contains multiple things is not simple. As this argument must be understood, entities, parts of entities, predicates of entities and principles all are indiscriminately called "things". For this reason the notion of "simple" as it applies to God is radical and very dissimilar from an ordinary use of the term.

The second argument (202a11-203a2) is based on ibn Daud's account of attributes that express deficiency. Ibn Daud argues that evil is due to a deficiency in something; all deficiencies are privations, and nothing makes a privation; hence, God cannot make or cause any evil. Ibn Daud notes that some deficiencies seem to be affirmative, namely, darkness, poverty and vice, but he argues that darkness is only lack of light, poverty is only lack of wealth, and vice is only lack of virtue. His prime examples of deficiency are human ignorance and the absence of an elephant in Spain (202b4-9). While someone must cause an elephant to be in Spain, nothing causes an elephant not to be there. Similarly, while someone must cause a human being to have knowledge, nothing causes a human being not to have knowledge.

Ibn Daud notes the following objection to his second argument :(203a2-7). Some deficiencies are accidental and some are essential. That there are no elephants in Spain is accidental, since given what Spain is there need not be any elephants in it. Furthermore, since the presence or absence of elephants has nothing to do with the nature and therefore the end of Spain, the presence or absence of elephants there is neither a defect nor an excellence in Spain. However, this is not the case with human ignorance. To know is part of the nature of man. Therefore, lack of knowledge in man is a deficiency. Furthermore, what is natural to a thing needs no external cause, but what is true of something by force, i.e., unnaturally, must have an external cause (Cf. Aristotle: 8,4,254b7-33). Therefore, since it is unnatural for a human being not to have knowledge, this deficiency must have a cause.

Ibn Daud offers no direct reponse to this objection. Rather, in the form of a response he introduces a third argument (203a7-204b16) which in effect grants that his second argument is invalid. The central claim in this third argument is that there is very little evil in the world compared to the amount of good. *Prima facie* this argument is irrelevant to the claim that God is not the source of evil, since it does not deny that there is evil and that God is the source of everything that exists. The implicit contention underlying this argument is that while there is evil, if there were any less evil there could not be a world. In other words, while this world is not perfect, it is the best of all possible worlds. As in the case of divine knowledge, while divine creation is not perfect in absolute terms, God's handiwork is as perfect as is possible and in this sense God as creator is perfect.

More specifically, ibn Daud argues as follows:

1) Things are what they are either because of their matter or because of their form.

2) Since some material things are good and others are evil, the *hyle* that is common to the elements of all material things, and itself cannot move anything, cannot be the cause of anything being evil. Hence, insofar as evil is a consequence of matter, the source lies in the nature of the mixture of simple elements into compounds and the dispositional properties that arise or do not arise as a consequence of that mixture. Hence, some seeds will grow well because they are mixed with one kind of soil while other seeds will grow poorly because of the kind of soil in which they are placed, but a seed in itself and soil in itself have no deficiency, i.e., a given seed may be deficient for a given soil and a given soil may be deficient for a given seed, but neither in itself is deficient (Cf. 203a10-203b2). But God did not directly create these mixtures. Rather these mixtures are determined by the forms that God created.

3) But all things have the best possible form. If God gave to everything the form that is absolutely best, then there would exist only one thing, viz., God, and there would not be a universe. Insofar as a plant is not an animal it is imperfect; insofar as an animal is not a human it is imperfect; insofar as humans are not like Moses, they are imperfect; and insofar as Moses is not an angel, he is imperfect (203b6-16). Consequently, since divine mercy intended there to be a universe, that same mercy led God to give to different things different forms. Therefore, the sources of deficiency in things is their form, but without such deficiency the world would be worse than it is, since there would be no world at all. Thus, when put in its proper context no deficiency is really a deficiency (203b16-204b16). With respect to the functioning of the whole, the various levels of

deficiencies in things are essential to the interrelationship of things through which the universe exists. These seeming inferiorities are only deficiencies when they are seen in isolation from the interests of the universe as such. Consequently, travelers from their isolated perspective consider rain bad whereas without rain there could be no food (204a10-12), human beings consider ignorant people to be bad but without ignorance no man would do the kind of physical labor needed for civilization as a whole to survive (204a12-204b6), and while the wind sometimes causes ships at sea to sink, the blowing of the wind also is essential to life on this planet (204b13-16).

In the case of human beings an individual sins because he has a weak character. Weak character is either a consequence of poor training or of a bad nature. To the extent that it is the result of a bad nature, the cause of that individual's vice is his particular material mixture. In Part 1, chapter 2 ibn Daud describes the genesis of mixtures from form and matter as follows: The initial mixture of the matter that is common to all physical things with a form that ibn Daud calls "the form of absolute body" (24b3) yields a cohesive, tri-dimensional mass (24b4-6). This mass serves as the matter that is mixed with four different forms to yield the elements fire, air, water and earth (24b11-13). In subsequent mixtures these different elements serve as matter to be combined with other forms through which arise different species of entities as well as entities within a given species that differ in their natural disposition to become perfected, i.e., to achieve their appropriate excellences or virtues. In Part 1, chapter 6 ibn Daud matches each of the four elements with what he designates as primary qualities. Water is associated with cold, earth with dry, air with moist and fire with heat (60b17ff). Any material entity, including a human being, in physical terms is a composite of each of these four elements. To the extent that the element water dominates his mixture he will tend to be cold; to the extent that earth dominates he will tend to be dry; to the extent that air dominates he will tend to be moist, and to the extent that fire dominates he will tend to be hot. Based on this earlier summary of his interpretation of Organic Chemistry, ibn Daud now explains that people who tend to have the vice of intemperance are people in whom heat is excessive (204b16-205a9) and people who tend to have the vice of stupidity are people in whom cold is excessive (205a10-14). Again, while intemperance and stupidity are bad from the perspective of the people who lack the appropriate human virtues, from the perspective of civilization as a whole such people are needed and therefore good in this best of all possible worlds. For God to have caused such people to be better disposed than they are would mean that God is not as good as He is.

Human Choice and Providence

While natural endowment inclines some human beings to be better than others, natural endowment in itself is insufficient to account for human virtue and vice. Human beings can choose either to realize or to suppress their natural tendencies. Hence, someone naturally inclined to have a virtue may never become virtuous in that respect while someone naturally inclined to have a vice may choose to and succeed at overcoming that deficiency. If there were no choices, ibn Daud argues, the prophets would not have been sent to teach the ignorant the difference between good and evil and God would not have revealed His commandments (205a16-205b6). In other words, that there is choice is necessary presupposition of Rabbinic Judaism without which there could be no system of *mitzvot*. Consequently that there is choice is a given. The issue that remains is what it is and how it is possible.

Ibn Daud divides attributes into the categories of the necessary, the impossible and the possible. While he states that these modal properties modify attributes, in fact his usage suggests that they modify states of affairs. For example, he tells us that rationality in man is a necessary attribute and rationality in a stone is an impossible attribute (205b6-9). Then he distinguishes two kinds of possible states of affairs. Some states are possible with respect to ignorance (205b11-12) and other states are possible because God endowed them with possibility (206b5-8).

Ibn Daud gives two examples of states that are possible with respect to ignorance. One is that the King of Babylonia just died or is alive. The other is that there will or will not be a lunar eclipse this month. Both sets of alternatives are only possible to us because we do not know which alternative in either set is the case. In fact, however, there is no option. The life or the death of the King of Babylonia is necessarily the case because it is a past event. The absence or presence of a lunar eclipse in the course of the next four or five weeks also is necessarily the case because such events are completely determined by natural laws that do not admit variation. Hence, the first kind of possibility is in fact no possibility. Rather, it consists of states of affairs that only seem to be possible. Only the second kind of possible event properly can be called "possible." In this case possibility consists of a set of mutually exclusive future events that God has determined to be indefinite at the present moment. "The second kind of possibility is that which is possible because God gave it possibility. He created it as a thing that can bear one or the other of two contrary attributes. How a possibility like this occurs or does not occur is not remote from God's knowledge. (In both cases) He created that possibility" (206a5-8).

At this point ibn Daud curtly notes the following objection that he scornfully labels as sophistical. His so-called Sophist asks, "Is God ignorant of the end of the matter?" (206a8-9) In fact the objection is critical. On ibn Daud's analysis there is a category of future events such that while God may know that they may or may not happen, He does not know that they will or will not happen. To this extent at least divine knowledge would be deficient in that there is something that is in principle knowable but for some reason God does not in fact know it.

Ibn Daud's response to the objection is that if God knew all future events, then all events would be necessary, but if everything is necessary, then two disastrous consequences would follow. No one would work because "what will happen already is decreed" (206a14). And no one would worship God, because "prosperity or its opposite already is decreed" (206a15). Presumably ibn Daud thinks that this response constitutes one more instance of his general thesis that while God's handiwork is not absolutely perfect, it is the best of all possible alternatives and in this respect it is perfect. God chooses not to know everything, because if He did know everything, there could be neither human labor nor human religion, which is worse than God having limited knowledge. But his position in this case is far more precarious than ibn Daud seemed to recognize. Even if we grant the assumption that people will labor and pray only if they believe that their efforts can change something—an assumption that is far from being self-evident—God could choose a world in which He knows everything, but does not allow human beings to know that He knows everything. In other words, if the only objection to denying possibility is its consequences for human productivity, then there need be only one kind of possibility, viz., what is possible with respect to ignorance, which is on ibn Daud's terms not really possibility at all. In fact ibn Daud's sophist has raised a critical issue that will haunt the discussion of divine knowledge and divine providence for at least the next two hundred years (Cf. Gersonides: III).

Based on the above classification of what he calls attributes, ibn Daud distinguishes between contingent and necessary events in terms of their causes. Concerning contingent events "all of their causes are not from God by a primary intention" (206b1), whereas concerning necessary events they are. Note that on these terms it is not the case that a contingent event is not determined by causes. It only is the case that God is not the direct cause of the event and the determination of the event is not a primary intention by God. Logically it may be the case that a so-called contingent event is caused by God and that God is aware of His causal activity. All that need be the case on these terms for an event to be contingent is that divine causal activity must not be directed primarily at the event in question. It is doubtful that ibn Daud would have accepted this consequence of his definition. His earlier distinction between kinds of possibilities suggests that he intended possibility to be more than a formal category. In some sense an event that is contingent is in fact and not just in principle optional. But it is no less clear that a contingent event is neither causeless nor indeterminate. Both necessary and contingent events are determinate. The difference lies solely in what it is that determines an event.

As ibn Daud describes contingents, some of them have natural causes (207a16-207b2), some of them are accidents (206b9), and/or some of them are voluntary. An event is voluntary when the immediate cause of the event is an act of some agent's volition or choice. Note that as ibn Daud discusses the matter it can be claimed that if a given agent wills an act and what he willed was determined by natural causes, that act is contingent.

The main purpose for which God gave choice to human beings is to enable them to avoid what ibn Daud calls "evil accidents". Consider the following example: Through the divine laws of Meteorology it is determined that there will be a storm today on the Mediterranean Sea and through the divine laws of Physics it is determined that any ship at sea today will sink and the people on board that ship will drown. The storm is a necessary event, but the drowning of the people is not. If they are at sea necessarily they will drown, but their drowning was in no sense the intention of the state of affairs ultimately determined by God. For this reason the drowning is contingent, and since no one on board the ship intentionally drowned, their death is an evil accident. However, if they had known the divine laws of Meteorology and Physics they would have realized that a sea voyage today would be fatal. Then through the exercise of choice they could have avoided this mishap. In other words, it is contingent whether these people will live or die. If they die their death is an accident, and if they live their life is due to choice. Now it may be argued that since none of these people would choose to die, in fact what happened was not contingent. Those who died died necessarily because of their ignorance, and those who lived lived necessarily because of their knowledge. To this objection we may infer that ibn Daud's defense would be that there is nothing in this objection so stated that would conflict with ibn Daud's claim that the life or death of these people is contingent. On his terms a contingent event is as much determined by causes as is a necessary event. The only difference is what causes determine the event and the context in which those causes operate.

Although all events are determined ibn Daud has no doubt that there also is choice and as he uses this term there is no conflict between these two claims. An event is chosen when an immediate cause of the principal action involved is an act of volition by the principal agent of the event. God gave human beings choice so that they may avoid evil accidents, but human choice can in no way interfere with the primary intentions of divine activity as revealed in the Torah and disclosed through science. Some people naturally are inclined to choose well. Others are not so fortunate, but through warnings and/or punishment they may learn to overcome their natures and choose well in spite of themselves. It is for this latter reason that God gave to Israel the commandments embodied in the Torah. Furthermore, every choice that an individual makes alters his nature. As an intemperate person continuously chooses to be temperate he gradually becomes temperate; as an ignorant person continuously through great effort achieves knowledge he becomes wise (207b12-208a14). In other words, while nature determines how a person chooses, choice determines nature. Consequently, a person may do what he cannot do, and in the course of doing it, it may happen that he will become able to do it in the future. The paradox of the statement only is apparent. Rather, what the statement shows is the subtlety and complexity of ibn Daud's understanding of the relationship between causation and choice.

WORKS CONSULTED

Aristotle
1928 *Physics*. Translated from the Greek by W. David Ross. London: Oxford University Press.

Ibn Daud, Abraham
1160 *AL-'AQIDA AL-RAFI'A* (The Exalted Faith). (No existing manuscripts of the original.) Hebrew translation in 1392 by Semuel Motot entitled *'EMUNAH HA-NISSA'AH*. Mantua, Ms. 81. Hebrew translation at the end of the fourteenth century by Šelomo ben Labi entitled *'EMUNAH RAMAH*. Vatican ms. 259, Vatican ms. 341, British Museum ms. 1069, Montefiore ms. 274, Munich Hebrew ms. 201, Bodleian Mich. 57, Jewish Theological Seminary of America (J.T.S.) ms. 2238, J.T.S. ms. 2239, J.T.S. ms. 2243. (All page and line references given in the body of the article refer to Bodleian Mich. 57.)

1852 *EMUNAH RAMAH*. A reproduction of Montefiore ms. 274 with a German translation based exclusively on this one manuscript, by Simson Weil. Frankfort a.M.

Gersonides (Levi ben Gershom)
1866 *MILḤAMOT HA-ṢEM*. Leipzig.

Saadia ben Joseph Al-Fayyumi
1880 *KITAB AL-AMANAT WA'L-I'TTQADAT*. Edited by S. Landauer. Leyden.

1948 *The Book of Beliefs and Opinions*. Translated from the original Arabic and the Hebrew translation of Judah ibn Tibbon by Samuel Rosenblatt. New Haven: Yale University Press.

Samuelson, Norbert
1970 "The Problem of Free Will in Maimonides, Gersonides and Aquinas". *Central Conference of American Rabbis Journal* 17, 1.

THE SELF AS HELMSMAN

LISTON O. MILLS

VANDERBILT DIVINITY SCHOOL, NASHVILLE, TN 37240

F OR almost 1900 years confidence in the Divine Helmsman enabled persons to deal with both the grandeur and misery of their lives. Their faith persuaded them of their origin as his creation and their destiny as his people. Within the context of covenant, the community was assured of God's steadfast love and faithfulness. Around this assurance they organized themselves; they had a center. Persons knew that God required them to love mercy, do justice and walk in humility. The prospect of God's presence made the requirement, even to the point of renunciation and sacrifice, acceptable. Despite injustice and in the midst of devastation, persons comprehended their misery as part of the purpose. The partial meanings of their lives and the myriad questions they encountered were caught up in a grand and transcendent and partly unknown plan whose future was secure.

Lamentations, or satisfaction, over the demise of this world view and the culture which supported it, or was its product, have furnished a litany for the scholarly community for well over a century. Western culture has undergone an extended period of what Philip Rieff calls "deconversion" and "reconversion."[1] The deconversion is the dissolution of the unitary system of common belief and symbols of the Judeo-Christian tradition. The reconversion *to the symbols of science* expresses an anti-creedal analytic attitude which promises to lift our repressions and to teach us reality about ourselves and our world.

It seems unnecessary and is beyond my ability to describe this transition in detail. It is important to point out, however, that loss of confidence in the Helmsman has been accompanied by a certain disorganization of personality. Bereft of the protective cultural myths, the collective ideologies and the communal affirmations of faith, persons have searched anxiously for some alternative source of meaning, some center that would hold. Finally we seem to have concluded that we cannot look beyond ourselves for meaning. Rank and Rieff's "Psychological Man" must

235

justify himself to himself and regards the psychologist as the logical and reasonable successor to the theologian and philosopher.

It would be simpler if the new guides spoke with one voice, showing us clearly who we are and what our lives mean, but they do not. Working out of differing understandings of science and with conflicting assumptions about persons, the psychologists compete for the right to describe the self who will replace the Helmsman. Sigmund Freud and psychoanalytic theory form the headwaters of one stream. Pavlov and John Watson are the progenitors of another. Yet another, the "Third Force," count Otto Rank and Alfred Adler as their forebears and Carl Rogers, Gordon Allport, and Abraham Maslow as recent champions. Of the three, Americans seem attracted to the "Third Force" or the Humanistic Psychologies. Freud and the Freudians are too pessimistic about our possibility, root us too firmly in our histories, and deny our freedom to decide and be. The Behaviorists, as represented by B. F. Skinner, have captured university psychology departments and continue to gain ground as an approach to therapy, but their elitism and tendency to control makes them suspect by the populace at large.

Humanistic psychology alone seems to have captured our culture's imagination. It is, notes Russell Jacoby, "deeply entangled in the social reality."[2] As a movement it is difficult to characterize. During the 1960's, Abraham Maslow called attention to a loose collection of thinkers, describing them as a "Third Force," an alternative to the dominant traditions of Behaviorism and Psychoanalysis. Since then the movement has accumulated representatives as diverse as Carl Rogers and Bioenergetics, EST and Encounter, Gestalt and Transactional Analysis. The roots of this fresh approach lie everywhere: in personal counseling, existentialism, neo-Freudian analysis, Jung, Organismic Psychology, etc. Joel Kovel suggests that it is best described as an amalgamation of the existentialist attitude—emphasis on direct experience and the present— with a traditional humanistic confidence in the perfectability of persons.[3] Thus people are encouraged to elevate themselves through new forms of experience which serve to heighten and cleanse consciousness. There is a decided shift away from the pathological to more ordinary forms of unhappiness and alienation. And the angst of European existentialism has disappeared, as has the skepticism and ambiguity of Freud. In their place are joy, fulfillment, energy, flow, acceptance.

Because Humanistic Psychology has become a cultural force of major dimensions, and because it is an American and contemporary trend, I intend in this essay, first, to present the point of view of one of its representatives, and, second, to comment on the viability of the under-standing of the self he describes as the center of our lives. I have chosen Carl Rogers as the representative of Humanistic Psychology. Actually he more than represents the approach; one writer suggests that "it would be better to call the approach representative of him."[4] No one has contrib-uted more substantially to American psychology and psychotherapy and no one has spread their influence more widely than he. I will present a summary statement of my understanding of Rogers' view of the self and then comment on it.

Carl Rogers and the Human Potential

Carl Rogers enbodies in his career and intellectual pilgrimage the disenchantment with the Judeo-Christian heritage and the search for an alternative in psychology. Born in 1902, Rogers was reared in a family "where hard work and a highly conservative (almost fundamentalist) Protestant Christianity were about equally revered."[5] He left for the University of Wisconsin with interests in agriculture but soon changed to ministry as a result of his involvement with the YMCA. In 1922 he visited China as a representative of the World Student Christian Federation and returned with a vision of "Christianizing industrial, political, social and international relationships."[6] Shortly thereafter he enrolled at Union Theological Seminary in New York. Although his study there was satis-fying, he found that he "could not work in a field where I would be required to believe in some specified religious doctrine." He "wanted to find a field in which I could be sure my freedom of thought would not be limited."[7]

Rogers found this field in the Psychology Department of Teachers College, Columbia University. His view of the self began to take shape amidst the ideas of Dewey and Thorndike. His commitment to science and pragmatism found support with the capable, academically oriented clinicians. In addition he had opportunity to examine psychoanalysis as reflected by the psychiatric staff in a clinic in which he trained. In 1931 he took his first position in the Child Study Department of a Rochester, N. Y. Social Agency. Thus began a vocation as psychotherapist which has consistently focused attention on the fact of change in personality and behavior. His approach to therapy and his view of persons emerge from his experience with clients.

The Theory of Therapy

Rogers' commitment to behavior and personality change caused him to attend closely the factors and circumstances which seemed to encourage altered behavior. His central learning from this work may be stated succinctly: "If I can provide a certain type of relationship, the other person will discover within himself the capacity for growth, and change and personal development will occur."[8] Therapeutic help results neither from the therapist's superior knowledge or skill nor from intensive training. "Change appears to come about through experience in a relationship."[9]

The ingredients of this hypothesis form the core of Rogers' approach to therapy and his expansion of and comment on them make up the substance of most of his work. The "certain type relationship" requires that the therapist possess three characteristics. First, the therapist must be genuine or transparent. This involves being what one appears, with no facade and no pretense, so that the therapist's reality beckons to that of the client. Second, the therapist should manifest "unconditional positive regard" for the client, i.e. "a warm regard for him as a person of self-worth—of value no matter what his condition, his behavior, or his feelings."[10] Finally, the therapist must demonstrate "empathic understanding," i.e. a continuing desire to understand the client's thoughts and feelings as these seem at the moment. This freedom constitutes an implicit permission for clients to explore all aspects of their experience without censor by the therapist. Rogers concluded that evaluation in any form is threatening to persons and therefore decided to suspend all moral and diagnostic judgments in his effort to understand and enter the client's world.

If the therapist is successful in establishing this relationship, the client will discover an innate capacity to use it as a basis for growth. Rogers' experience "forced (him) to conclude that the individual has within himself the capacity and the tendency, latent if not evident, to move forward toward maturity."[11] This tendency to self-actualization, i.e. to expand, extend, become autonomous, develop, mature, is evident in all organic and human life in that the organism seeks to express and activate all its capacities and enhance itself. It may be buried, "but it is my belief that it exists in every individual and awaits only the proper conditions to be released or expressed."[12]

To Rogers, then, the therapist is not so much an expert or guide as a companion. The willingness to accompany the client means the latter is emboldened "in his frightening search for himself."[13] No guarantees for a successful journey are given. But when the client can, to however slight a degree, respond to and participate in this relationship, "then I believe that change and constructive personal development will invariably occur—and I include the word invariably only after long and careful consideration."[14]

The change which is the culmination of this process is a reorganized self dealing more constructively with life and enjoying more satisfactory relations with others. Even a brief time in such relations, research shows, manifests itself in "profound and significant changes in personality, attitudes, and behavior, changes that do not occur in matched control groups."[15] Persons are more integrated, effective, show fewer neurotic or psychotic symptoms, are more realistic, more self-confident and self-directing, more open to their experience, more accepting of others, deny and repress less, etc. They become more like the person they wish to be.

The Theory of the Self

I have mentioned that Rogers' view of the self grows directly out of his experience as a psychotherapist. His clinical study revealed a certain pattern and orderliness in the client's quest to discern a goal and purpose in life. When given the psychological freedom to move in any direction, the "organismically chosen direction" demonstrated general qualities common among a variety of individuals.[16]

What Rogers discovered, first, was that the core of the person is positive. Experiencing one's feelings, discovering the unknown elements of the self, experiencing "the feelings which at an organic level he is," fosters the learning that hostile, contradictory and anti-social feelings are neither the deepest nor the strongest in persons. The organism which is their inner core is both "self-preserving and social."[17] This real self "is something which is comfortably discovered in one's experience, not something imposed on it."[18] Persons become themselves—"not a facade of conformity to others, not a cynical denial of all feelings, not a front of intellectual rationality, but a living, breathing, fluctuating process—in short he becomes a person."[19]

The discovery of this positive core means that the organism may be trusted. Human nature is not to be feared as we have been taught by Freud and the Puritans. Indeed, "When a Freudian such as Karl Menninger tells me . . . that he perceives man as . . . 'innately destructive,' I can only shake my head in wonderment."[20] When persons are functioning freely, their behavior is "exquisitely rational." Rogers continues:

When we are able to free the individual from defensiveness, so that he is open to the wide range of his own needs, as well as the wide range of environmental and social demands, his reactions may be trusted to be positive, forward-moving, constructive. We do not need to ask who will socialize him, for one of his own deepest needs is for affiliation and communication with others. As he becomes more fully himself, he will become more realistically socialized. We do not need to ask who will control his aggressive impulses; for as he becomes more open to all of his impulses; his need to be liked by others and his tendency to give affection will be as strong as his impulses to strike out or to seize for himself. His total behavior . . . will be more balanced and realistic, behavior which is appropriate to the survival and enhancement of a highly social animal.[21]

Rogers professes little patience, then, with those who understand persons to be basically irrational and destructive. Given freedom the individual will move "with subtle and ordered complexity toward the goals his organism is endeavoring to achieve."[22] The human tragedy is not that persons are evil and destructive. The basic tragedy is that persons do not allow themselves to experience themselves fully and thereby unlease their potential for growth and maturity. The source of this rift, this gulf between experience and awareness, is conditional love. Others have taught them that it is dangerous to be open to the experience of themselves and their environment. This disparity between feeling and awareness is reinforced by rigid constructs in society. Neurotic behavior and human misery are the inevitable outcome of the refusal to trust oneself.

Maturity for Rogers is to be one's organism, one's experience.[23] And to be one's organism is to be in process. It is not a state, not even one of virtue, contentment, or happiness. It is not a condition to which one adjusts or at which one arrives. It is instead a direction emerging out of the unity and harmony which exists in our feelings and reactions. One accepts oneself "as a stream of becoming," "a flowing river of change," "a fluid process," "a continually changing constellation of potentialities." The process is not always consistent; it is in flux. It is not simple but complex. It is to be

continually engaged in discovering that to be all of himself in this fluid sense is not synonymous with being evil or uncontrolled. It is instead to feel a growing pride in being a sensitive, open, realistic, inner-directed member of the human species, adapting with courage and imagination to the complexities of the changing situation. It means taking continual steps toward being, in awareness and in expression, that which is congruent with one's total organismic reactions. To use Kierkegaard's more aesthetically satisfying terms, it means "to be that self which one truly is."[24]

This, says Rogers, is the good life from the point of view of the therapist. These persons have moved away from facades and away from "oughts." They have moved from meeting the expectations of others and from trying to please others. To such persons "the only question which matters is: 'Am I living in a way which is deeply satisfying to me, and which truly expresses me?' "[25] This openness to inner and outer experience offers a richness of life that is not for the faint-hearted. Those willing to launch "fully into the stream of life," who are willing to stretch and grow and to become more and more of their potentialities, will find this prospect enriching, rewarding, challenging and meaningful.[26]

The Politics of the Self

In Rogers' later writings his reflections on the socio-cultural significance of his work come clear. At the same time, however, he has demonstrated a genuine awareness of his times and has commented frequently to the effect that his work was applicable on a wider scale than one-to-one and group psychotherapy. American society with its materialism, competitiveness, and commitments to technology and positivism tends to control and distort rather than to enhance and encourage human growth. As a result, from his earliest days he has encouraged industrial, political, educational, and church leaders to test the value of his hypotheses for their work. He has lamented our society's lack of faith in and recognition of the social sciences, an apostasy which precludes utilization of their findings on a variety of social, political, economic and international issues.

I say that such concerns have always been evident in Rogers. However, in the past decade they have become primary for him; the balance between therapy and involvement in the larger ramifications and applications of Client-Centered Therapy shifted. Social events and encouragement from his friends caused Rogers to see the radical and revolutionary nature of his ideas and their political influence in the culture. He was indeed radical, he concluded, in that he had gone to the root of many cultural concepts and values; his revolutionary standing was confirmed by the "altered thinking about power and control in relationships between persons."[27] He saw the results in groups as diverse as marriage and racial strife, as education and international relations. A quiet revolution, he noted, had already begun, pointing "to a future of a very different nature, built around a new type of self-empowered person who is emerging."[28]

From his work in therapy Rogers extrapolates the concepts to undergird his political proposals. It is revolutionary in itself, he argues, to trust the directional tendencies of the organism since society's institutions give only lip service to democracy while actually seeking to control and direct.

If institutions would renounce and avoid all control of and decision-making for individuals, if they would provide a context of trust and mutual understanding, then the political base for a new society would be established. The actualizing tendency of trustworthy organisms would tend to its own fulfillment; its selective and directional tendencies would prove constructive. Results show "that the choices made and the directions pursued and the actions taken are increasingly constructive personally and tend to social harmony."[29]

Rogers fully expects his views to be disputed. Just as professional therapists have proven reluctant to relinquish control of the healing process, so the established social authorities and institutional leaders resist affirming that persons possess the innate and organismic wisdom to order and pursue their own lives. It is just this reluctance which fosters the rift in individual and corporate life and leads to distress, perversity, oppression and injustice. It is a rift engendered and confirmed by conditional love, for to be loved conditionally, to be controlled by such love, whether its origin be personal or cultural, insures a perverse channeling of the actualizing tendency into destructive behaviors. Rogers perceives his approach as an alternative to those which foster the rift and lead to pollution, overpopulation, hunger and racial strife. He acknowledges the inherent difficulty of transforming individual approaches to large groups and social problems, but he argues that these problems are largely "technological."[30] Thus science provides us an alternative; there is no reason to despair. "When the world is ready, we can say tentatively and with humility that we are ready to begin."[31]

The basis for Rogers' hope lies in what he discerns as the emerging "new political figure." Despite a culture in which violence spreads, the family is in disarray, institutions are decaying, and the economic future uncertain, Rogers finds persons who "are choosing a new kind of democracy."[32] These persons, from all walks of life, "present a new face to the world, a pattern which has not, in my judgment, ever been seen before, except in rare individuals."[33] They are concerned for authenticity and are tired of the climate of hypocrisy and deceit in which they were reared. They are open about sexual relationships, straightforward in their dealings, and impatient with inflexible, bureaucratic institutions.

Rogers suspects that such persons may replace institutions with "small, informal, nonhierarchical groups . . . bound by a sense of community with no lasting lines of authority and no desire to expand, but carrying on diverse and creative activities."[34] They may seek "to humanize institutions from the inside, simply disregarding meaningless rules."[35] These persons appear indifferent to material rewards; they are neither power hungry nor achievement hungry. "When they seek power, it is for other than selfish purposes."[36] They are caring persons, giving freely and nonmoralistically, seeking always new forms of community, of intimacy and closeness. They are aware that personal life is filled with temporary relationships, that they will move about and be apart from family and relatives, and so they establish intimate bonds quickly, leaving them behind without undue conflict and mourning. Rogers continues:

These new persons have a trust in their own experience and a profound distrust of all external authority. Neither pope nor judge nor scholar can convince these individuals of anything that is not borne out by personal experience. So they often decide to obey those laws that are personally regarded as sound and just, and to disobey those that seem unsound and unjust, taking the consequences of their actions. On a minor issue, they smoke marijuana in defiance of laws regarded as unreasonable and unfair, and risk being busted. On major issues they refuse to be drafted when they regard a war as reprehensible; they give out secret government documents when convinced the people should know what has been going on; they refuse to reveal the sources of news reports for the same reason. This is a new phenomenon. We have had a few Thoreaus, but we have never had hundreds and thousands of people, young and old alike, willing to obey some laws and disobey others on the basis of their own personal moral judgment, and living with the consequences of their choice. These persons have a high regard for self, and for their competence to discriminate in issues involving authority.[37]

Such persons are in the minority to be sure. Yet their impact is entirely out of proportion to their numbers, "and this has, I believe, significance for the future."[38] Their presence may indicate our culture "to be on the verge of a great evolutionary-revolutionary leap."[39]

Comments

It is clear that in Rogers the self has replaced the Helmsman. It is also clear that Rogers thinks his work offers an alternative basis for understanding persons and their lives in society. Although he speaks with tentativeness, he is convinced that he knows something about persons our predecessors did not. Our question is, does he? Does the light he sheds on the self justify elevating it to the status of guide and stay, to the position of helmsman even if not Divine? Is his view of the self comprehensive enough to include all the facets and dimensions of human life and ennoble them and give them meaning? One does not need to quarrel with Rogers notion that we have been deceived and have deceived ourselves in confusing our institutions and cultural values with the eternal. And one can also allow that many of our renunciations do not strengthen but impoverish life. Moreover, it is unnecessary to question Rogers' substantial contribution to our understanding of psychotherapy and the ways people are helped. It is necessary to ask whether the self he describes is able to bear the burden he places on it.

In effect Rogers replaces the broken center of faith in a Divine Helmsman by calling us to trust ourselves. His confidence is in a trustworthy organism which needs only proper conditions to flourish. The constant use of the term "organism" is itself revealing and a clue to his orientation. Basically a biological term, it usually refers to the preprogrammed workings of members of the vegetable and animal kingdom.[40] Left to itself and unhindered by the intrusions of family and culture, the organism unfolds, becomes fully-functioning, the self one truly is. One does not need guidance, authority, rules; these are obstacles which when removed allow the authentic, truthful and social self to emerge. Rieff notes this new model for persons when he says: "No longer the Saint, but the instinctual Everyman, twisting his neck uncomfortably inside the starched collar of culture, is the communal ideal . . ."[41] In creating his Rousseau-like image in which persons are born free and enslaved by parents and culture, Rogers wishes to remove the collar altogether.

The great tragedy for this view of the organism is that persons have not learned to trust themselves. Yet the tragedy is not of their making; they are victims who have not participated in their undoing. The rift is imposed from without. It stems from the conditional love of parents, the restrictions of institutions, the requirements of society. In such context, the Divine Helmsman, insofar as he makes demands, becomes simply another obstacle whose removal hastens fulfillment. Such sentiments bring to mind Yeats' lines, his prayer for his daughter.

> I have walked and prayed for this young child an hour
> . . .
> Considering that, all hatred driven hence,
> The soul recovers radical innocence
> And learns at last that it is self-delighting,
> Self-appeasing, self-affrighting,
> And that its own sweet will is Heaven's will . . .[42]

One cannot but wonder whether Rogers' fully-functioning person has an underside that he ignores. His persons appear one-dimensional. The dialectic posed by the arrow that flies by day and the terror that stalks by night is missing. Discussions about human life cannot finally revolve around the question as to whether persons are basically good or evil with either freedom or control as the prize. Yet Rogers seems to pose the problem just this way. Having discovered nobility, courage, yearning for love in persons, he concludes that their only problem is one of tyrannical expectations. His fully-functioning person seems an abstraction, a form from which the life force emerges without boundaries.

It is just this question of the boundaries of life that Rogers does not seem to take seriously enough. To experience oneself fully is not simply to experience possibility and potential. "Full humanness," says Ernest Becker, "means full fear and trembling, at least some of the waking day."[43] Fully-functioning persons seem abstract because they do not tremble under the weight of their lives. As they shed their layers of protective defenses, they discover a good core, but they are not painfully introduced to finitude, dread of death, and despair over the real nature of the world. To quote Becker again:

What does it mean "to be born again" for man? It means *for the first time to be subjected* to the terrifying paradox of the human condition, since one must be born not as a god, but as a man . . . Only this time without the neurotic shield that hides the full ambiguity of one's life . . .
. . . .
When you get a person to emerge into life, away from his dependencies, his automatic safety in the cloak of someone else's power, what joy can you promise him with the burden of his aloneness? When you get a person to look at the sun as it bakes down on the daily carnage taking place on earth, the ridiculous accidents, the utter fragility of life, the powerlessness of those he thought most powerful— what comfort can you give him from a psychotherapeutic point of view?[44]

Such comments heighten the lack of a dialectic in Rogers. They underscore our question as to the adequacy of this view of the self to serve as helmsman. Rogers' trustworthy organism and fully-functioning person are only half the truth about persons. He offers possibility at the expense of historical existence. To be sure Rogers frequently affirms the limitations, mistakes, and errors of judgment; he laments distortions as well as the injustices and horrors of life; and he often refers to the individual's responsibility for decisions as the key to his approach. But such facts are not constitutive of the human core. That remains trustworthy and our best hope. To affirm that a truly human condition requires finitude is to turn Rogers around. Neurosis then is only partly the fruit of personal history; its deeper significance offers a solution to the real dimensions of human life. Repression then is not falsification but truth.

Each is an attempt to come to terms with both possibility and finitude. The neurotic construction of rigid psychological boundaries is an effort to deal with reality. In a sense the neurotic condition is a confession that one has seen too much, too much of human vulnerability and too much truth, to be able to utilize the illusions and cultural fictions that would make possible the enjoyment of partial and modest victories, some fulfillment in home and work, and the enduring of defeats. In this sense neurosis has a historical dimension. It is not a problem when communal ideologies are embracing and convincing, when they make it easy for persons to be confident and secure in "their personal heroism."[45] But modern life has seen the failure of these ideologies, and Rogers' contact with the victims is the root of his concern and the occasion for his solution. My point here is to suggest that one cannot resolve the dilemma by becoming the self one truly is, for this self, with its possibilities and limitations, its nobility and fear, is a problem in and to itself.

This discussion of the historical embeddedness of the person leads to a second question concerning Rogers' view of the self. His emphasis on the present as the only relevant time frame and on the self as process would seem to undercut the possibility of individual identity and particularity. Moreover, his commitment to self-actualization as the goal of life makes it problematic whether his ideal person could sustain the communities he envisions as emerging.

I have already mentioned that the loss of faith in the Helmsman and of the communal affirmations and cohesion it implied led to a certain disorganization of personality. Our culture's preoccupation with the "identity crisis" is a footnote to this fact. Roger's response to the dilemma has been his view of what one writer calls the "fluid self."[46] Thus the ideal person is "a flowing river of change," "a fluid process," "a continually changing constellation of potentialities." To such persons in flux, the past is irrelevant and the future unknowable. Their watchwords are "immediacy," "spontaneity," "the here and now." To find oneself, then, does not seem to mean the discovery of a person with a history in a time and place. It is instead always to be on the move.

This understanding of the self makes personal identity seem difficult at best. This is true because the very concept of "identity" is a historical one; it implies sameness and continuity over time. Thus an individual's identity is rooted in a history of association with persons and places to which this person has responded and who have confirmed and responded to him/her. To be sure, some notion of dynamic is required; persons must reorganize themselves and consolidate this sense of self. But such reorganization requires a sense of past and a prospect of future. It cannot flourish simply in the "here and now." My colleague, Professor Peggy Way, suggests in this regard that Rogers has sacrificed the developmental for the growth metaphor. Certainly he does not reflect the developmental views of a Freud or Erikson. Their persons grow through sequential crises the negotiation of which leaves a residue that forms elements of the person's identity. In Rogers the residue is gone. He finds that a person's history does not help him understand that person, gives little attention to development, and discourages his graduate students from reading the case histories of their clients since it might interfere with their focus on the present. In a culture characterized by rootless autonomy, an emphasis on the present is understandable. But identity means that though a person is open to change, something essential remains and that "something" is rooted in a history.

Just as Rogers seems to lose personal identity in his preoccupation with the present, so his neglect of choice and decision appears to cause the loss of individuality. In reading Rogers one is struck at how all the persons in his cases are alike. Little distinguishes one from another. This lack of definition seems to me to stem from his view of the self as an automatically unfolding process. The person is not formed by decisions made over time and in relation to other people, by the ways one comes to terms with inner and outer necessities. It is experienced and possesses its own "wisdom" in the form of self-regulating "thermostatic controls." Thus Rogers can define volition as "simply the subjective following of a harmonious balance of organismic direction."[47] Contrast this rather passive flowing with the stream with Kierkegaard's insistence that it was in the either/or of choice that one came to terms with onself: "It is the point at which a man gives up what he could be and chooses what he will be." Kilpatrick goes on to comment on this either/or requirement in Kierkegaard:

Every choice requires a renunciation: to choose one thing is to lose something else. But a man must choose, must commit himself; otherwise he remains only possibilities. By his choices, painful as they must be, a man defines himself.[48]

Individual identity requires decisions and renunciations. But if one lives in the light of one's potential, one is reluctant to choose and to foreclose the future.

Persons reluctant to foreclose their futures for fear of inhibiting their growth are unlikely to establish sustaining communities. Yet to come to oneself requires deep ties to other people. Not only do I come from some place, have a history, not only am I fashioned by decisions and choices which limit me, I do this in the midst of a people. Thus terms such as fidelity, loyalty, commitment, purpose and direction come to have significance. We need a different set of terms to describe Rogers' ideal community. Indeed his view of the self as never fixed and open to all experience means that a premium is placed on non-binding commitments. Persons are hungry for intimacy, but they fear present institutions, e.g. marriage, because the promises and expectations foreclose their flow. One never knows whether one will be the same tomorrow as today, whether one will have the same values, live in the same place, need the same persons. Thus one should be capable of instant intimacy and openness, but one should not lock one's future to persons and causes. Rogers removes the risk from relations but he also negates the possibility of depth in community. Persons who do not grieve the loss of friends and associates in whose presence they found life and hope are not open and in touch with themselves. Their openness is a pose, a defense against vulnerability and risk. Part of being mortal is the risk required in making commitments to persons and ideals. The outcome can never be clear, but the leap must be ventured if one is to have a fully human life. Rogers' person does not find life with others; life is only in the self. The community which arises from such persons cannot sustain life in depth for it is a way of using all relations and groups with loyalty to none.

Rather than Rogers' view of the self encouraging persons to a new organization of personality, he seems to have encouraged an endless moratorium as a way of life. His persons are committed only to testing, experimenting, experiencing. Meaning comes only in relation to a self without limits or definition. There is a time in life when it is no doubt proper to be enamored with one's potential, to look for oneself. And it is true that the quest of some is hampered and distorted by partial truths about and experiences of themselves and their world. It is true that society and its institutions often are coercive of persons and reinforce pathologies. But it is also true that one cannot live forever on one's potential. There are points at which one must decide among potentials, all of which may not be the same or of equal importance, and one's values determine the choice. Persons become not simply by experiencing themselves but by deciding about themselves and assuming responsibility for themselves. One finds meaning and a sense of identity, one finds a center for the organization of the personality, only by going outside the self. "To the extent to which he commits himself to something beyond himself, to a cause greater than himself," to that extent one finds oneself.[49] Self-actualization as a goal easily becomes self-indulgence, but as a by-product of commitment it is to be treasured.

Before concluding it is important to raise a question about the path that Rogers has taken to his view of the self, i.e. whether it is able to provide the truth we need. He understands his theory to be a move away from the determinism of Freud and Skinner with its emphasis on control and towards freedom and veneration of the person. In a classic debate and in subsequent writing, he has accused Skinner of attempting to "use our growing knowledge to enslave people in ways never dreamed of before, depersonalizing them, controlling them by means so carefully selected that they will perhaps never be aware of their personhood."[50] He rejects Skinner's vision of a totally planned and administered society and replaces it with his own view of the new society described above. At this point, Rogers own commitment to science and its method comes through. Christopher Lasch says:

Characteristically, he (Rogers) thought the questions could be decided only by further research. If "sound research" supported Skinner's view of human dependence, "then a social philosophy of expert control is clearly implied." If it is indicated that men and women have at least a "latent capacity" for understanding and self-reliance, "then a psychological basis for democracy would have been demonstrated."[51]

I include this quote from Lasch to demonstrate how complete is Rogers' faith in his scientific method. The fate of democratic institutions will be determined by a retreat to the clinic or the laboratory. The cumulative wisdom of the race is not a factor; he does not argue, for example, that the capacity for self-mastery and understanding, his very endeavor, could flourish only under democratic institutions. He understands history simply as the generator of tradition and repression. It is not a repository of options which one can neither evaluate nor dismiss unless one comes to terms with it. As a result the sole standard by which he judges the value and results of present practice and thought is science and its method.

Thus Rogers leads us to confidence in science and ourselves. But can this method lead us to the truth we need to know? Our confidence and his has been that since science shows us how things work, it can also show us how we work, with the hope that, knowing the cause of all things, we would control all things. Psychology and psychotherapy, in this instance Rogers, wanted to show us why we felt bad, unhappy, inadequate and inferior, on the assumption that if we knew the reasons, knew after all that this is the way we are in the evolutionary scheme of things and what we must do about it, we would quit scolding ourselves, accept ourselves and find peace and fulfillment. But as Becker reminds us, science as represented by psychology could only find part of the reason for our experience, "the part caused by the objects—trying to be good for them, fearing them, fearing leaving them, and the like."[52] We should not minimize the importance of this partial discovery. Persons freed from neurotic guilt, the unnecessary conflicts of their past, the ways in which they are chained and blocked from development do indeed become more honest with themselves, more sure of themselves, and enjoy more freedom and spontaneity in their lives and relations.

But Rogers has erred in that he has identified the guilt and unhappiness growing out of past relations with persons and institutions as *the* human problem. Actually it is only *part* of the problem. When the distraught emerge from the consulting room or the encounter group there looms before them still the problem of why they are alive, have problems, experience terror, are mortal. Becker again aids us when he says:

Psychology narrows the cause for personal unhappiness down to the person himself, and then he is stuck with himself. But we know that the universal and general cause for personal badness, guilt, and inferiority is the natural world and the person's relationship to it. All the analysis in the world doesn't allow the person to find out *who he is* and why he is here on earth, why he has to die and how he can make his life a triumph. It is when psychology pretends to do this, when it offers itself as a full explanation of human unhappiness, that it becomes a fraud that makes the situation of modern man an impasse from which he cannot escape. Or, put another way, psychology has limited its understanding of human unhappiness to the personal life-history of the individual and has not understood how much individual unhappiness is itself a historical problem in the larger sense, a problem of the eclipse of secure communal ideologies of redemption.[53]

A view of the self based on part of the truth about persons is no solution. Rogers cannot finally respond to Becker without resorting to the very theological questions he seeks in the name of science to flee.

Conclusion

We have come full circle. Modern persons may have difficulty affirming the Divine Helmsman, but Rogers' alternative, that we trust ourselves, is inadequate. We cannot change the world simply "by legislating the grotesque out of it."[54] Finally psychology must give way to theology. It need not give way to theologians, but it must ask the theological questions. It must do so because the human condition is such that persons cannot endure unless they are able to translate their possibility and peril, their heroism and cowardice, their omnipotence and their terror of death into meaningful affirmations on the largest possible scale. Rogers' problem is not that he takes life seriously; it is that he does not take it seriously enough. The abiding attraction of the Divine Helmsman is that he promises to deal with all of life and summons men and women to the highest and most difficult endeavor. Persons are rightly suspicious when they are called only to joy.

NOTES

[1] Philip Rieff, *The Triumph of the Therapeutic: Uses of Faith After Freud* (New York: Harper & Row, 1966) 7.

[2] Russell Jacoby, *Social Amnesia: A Critique of Contemporary Psychology from Adler to Laing* (Boston: Beacon Press, 1975) xvii.

[3] Joel Kovel, *A Complete Guide to Therapy: From Psychoanalysis to Behavior Modification* (New York: Pantheon Books, 1976) 108-110.

[4] *Ibid.*, 111.

[5] T. L. Holdstock and C. R. Rogers, "Person-Centered Therapy" in *Current Personality Theories,* ed. by Raymond J. Corsini (Itasca, Illinois: F. E. Peacock, 1977) 128.

[6] Christopher Lasch, Review of *On Becoming Carl Rogers* by Howard Kirschenbaum, *The New Republic* (March 31, 1979) 30.

[7] Carl R. Rogers, *On Becoming a Person* (Boston: Houghton Mifflin Company, 1961). I have attempted to use as much of Rogers' language as possible in this section.

[8] *Ibid.*, 33

[9] *Ibid.*

[10] *Ibid.*, 34.

[11] *Ibid.*, 35.

[12] *Ibid.*

[13] *Ibid.*

[14] *Ibid.*

[15] *Ibid.*, 36.

[16] *Ibid.*, 186f.

[17] *Ibid.*, 92.

[18] *Ibid.*, 114.

[19] *Ibid.*

[20] Carl R. Rogers, "The Nature of Man," in *The Nature of Man in Theological and Psychological Perspective,* ed. by Simon Doniger (New York: Harper, 1962) 93.

[21] Rogers, *Becoming a Person,* 194.

[22] *Ibid.*, 195.

[23] *Ibid.*, 103.

[24] *Ibid.*, 181.

[25] *Ibid.*, 119.

[26] *Ibid.*, 194.

[27] Carl Rogers, *Carl Rogers on Personal Power: Inner Strength and Its Revolutionary Impact* (New York: Delacorte Press, 1977) xii.

[28] *Ibid.*, xiii.

[29] *Ibid.*, 15.

[30] *Ibid.*, 118.

[31] *Ibid.*, 138.

[32]*Ibid.*, 261.

[33]*Ibid.*, 265.

[34]*Ibid.*, 268.

[35]*Ibid.*

[36]*Ibid.*, 269.

[37]*Ibid.*, 274.

[38]*Ibid.*

[39]*Ibid.*, 282.

[40]William Kilpatrick, *Identity & Intimacy* (Delta Books, New York: Dell Publishing Co., Inc., 1975) 49.

[41]Rieff, 8.

[42]William Butler Yeats, "A Prayer for My Daughter," in *Selected Poems and Two Plays of William Butler Yeats*, Edited and Introduction by M. L. Rosenthal (Collier Books, New York: The Macmillan Co., 1962) 92, 93.

[43]Ernest Becker, *The Denial of Death* (New York: The Free Press, 1973) 58. I should confess my indebtedness to Becker and his superb study. His influence will be seen throughout this section of the paper.

[44]*Ibid.*, 58, 59.

[45]*Ibid.*, see Chapter Nine, "The Present Outcome of Psychoanalysis," for a discussion of the various dimensions of neurosis.

[46]Kilpatrick, 3. Also see 3-7 for his discussion of the ingredients of identity.

[47]*Becoming a Person*, 158.

[48]Kilpatrick, 42f.

[49]Kilpatrick, 53

[50]*Becoming a Person*, 399f.

[51]Lasch, 31.

[52]Becker, 192. Becker's discussion of psychology's failure and the necessity for raising the theological question is unusally fine.

[53]*Ibid.*, 193.

[54]*Ibid.* This is Becker's phrase although I cannot locate the precise source.

INDEX

BRUCE D. NAIDOFF

INDEX OF BIBLICAL REFERENCES

OTHER ANCIENT LITERATURE

INDEX OF AUTHORS

INDEX OF HEBREW AND GREEK EXPRESSIONS